I0105033

John Earl Russell

An Essay on the History of the English Goverment and

Constitution

John Earl Russell

An Essay on the History of the English Goverment and Constitution

ISBN/EAN: 9783741173073

Manufactured in Europe, USA, Canada, Australia, Japa

Cover: Foto ©ninafisch / pixelio.de

Manufactured and distributed by brebook publishing software
(www.brebook.com)

John Earl Russell

An Essay on the History of the English Goverment and Constitution

AN ESSAY ON THE HISTORY

OF

THE ENGLISH GOVERNMENT

AND

CONSTITUTION

FROM THE REIGN OF HENRY VII. TO THE PRESENT TIME.

BY

JOHN, EARL RUSSELL.

'Methinks I see in my mind a noble and puissant nation rousing herself like a strong man after sleep, and shaking her invincible locks; methinks I see her as an eagle renewing her mighty youth, and kindling her undazzled eyes at the full midday beam, purging and unscaling her long-abused sight at the fountain itself of heavenly radiance, while the whole noise of timorous and flocking birds, with those also that love the twilight, flutter about, amazed at what she means, and in their envious gabble would prognosticate a year of sects and schisms.'

MILTON.

NEW EDITION.

LONDON:

LONGMANS, GREEN, AND CO.

1872.

TO

THE MEMORY

OF

CHARLES, EARL GREY,

THE CONSTANT FRIEND OF MR. FOX

IN PUBLIC AND IN PRIVATE LIFE;

THE UNDAUNTED CHAMPION OF CIVIL AND RELIGIOUS FREEDOM

IN ALL TIMES AND IN ALL CIRCUMSTANCES;

THE ENLIGHTENED LOVER OF HIS COUNTRY IN ALL HER

PERILS AND PERPLEXITIES,

THIS BOOK

IS DEDICATED

AS A TOKEN OF AFFECTION AND ADMIRATION,

BY

THE AUTHOR.

PREFACE

THE EDITION OF 1865.

I HAVE ATTEMPTED in the present edition to perform the task which I had till now abandoned as hopeless—namely, to amalgamate the recent with the earlier work; and instead of giving the retrospect from 1820 to 1864 in the shape of an Introduction, I have placed it at the end as a concluding chapter.

Besides this leading difference, some additions and many omissions distinguish the present from the last edition.

R.

MEMORANDUM.

In the edition of 1866 I made some further alterations. They were few in number, but not unimportant.

R

CONTENTS.

CHAPTER I.

FIRST PRINCIPLES OF THE ENGLISH GOVERNMENT AND

CONSTITUTION 1

CHAPTER II.

HENRY THE SEVENTH 12

CHAPTER III.

HENRY THE EIGHTH 16

CHAPTER IV.

THE REFORMATION 21

CHAPTER V.

QUEEN ELIZABETH 26

CHAPTER VI.

JAMES THE FIRST 31

CHAPTER VII.

CHARLES THE FIRST 38

CHAPTER VIII.

CAUSES OF THE DISSOLUTION OF THE ENGLISH FORM OF

GOVERNMENT UNDER CHARLES THE FIRST . . 56

CHAPTER IX.

PAGE

CROMWELL, CHARLES THE SECOND, AND JAMES THE
    SECOND   59

CHAPTER X.

THE REVOLUTION   64

CHAPTER XI.

DEFINITIONS OF LIBERTY   68

CHAPTER XII.

CIVIL LIBERTY   69

CHAPTER XIII.

PERSONAL LIBERTY   77

CHAPTER XIV.

POLITICAL LIBERTY   87

CHAPTER XV.

LAWYERS   98

CHAPTER XVI.

RISE OF PUBLIC CREDIT UPON THE BASIS OF A FREE
    CONSTITUTION   100

CHAPTER XVII.

PARTY   104

CHAPTER XVIII.

WILLIAM AND MARY.—ANNE   112

CHAPTER XIX.

IMPEACHMENT.—BILLS OF PAINS AND PENALTIES. .   117

CHAPTER XX.

GEORGE THE FIRST AND GEORGE THE SECOND . .   124

CHAPTER XXI.

PAGE

GEORGE THE THIRD.—BEGINNING OF HIS REIGN.—
AMERICAN WAR 132

CHAPTER XXII.

THE SENSE OF JUSTICE 135

CHAPTER XXIII.

OF AN EXTREME REMEDY AGAINST THE ABUSES OF
POWER; AND OF MODERATION IN THE USE OF
THE REMEDY 137

CHAPTER XXIV.

CRIMINAL LAW 140

CHAPTER XXV.

PUBLIC SCHOOLS 145

CHAPTER XXVI.

POOR-LAWS 150

CHAPTER XXVII.

WAR WITH THE FRENCH REPUBLIC . . . 153

CHAPTER XXVIII.

LIBERTY, THE GREAT SOURCE OF THE WEALTH OF NA-
TIONS, AND ESPECIALLY OF THAT OF ENGLAND . 155

CHAPTER XXIX.

NATIONAL DEBT 161

CHAPTER XXX.

THAT A FREE GOVERNMENT REQUIRES PERPETUAL JEA-
LOUSY AND FREQUENT RENOVATION . . . 168

CHAPTER XXXI.

CONSTITUTION OF THE HOUSE OF COMMONS . . 172

CHAPTER XXXII.

PAGE

STANDING ARMY 189

CHAPTER XXXIII.

OF THE INFLUENCE OF JURIES IN INTERPRETING AND
MODIFYING THE LAWS 194

CHAPTER XXXIV.

INFLUENCE OF THE CROWN 200

CHAPTER XXXV.

LIBERTY OF THE PRESS.—PROBABLE FATE OF THE ENG-
LISH CONSTITUTION 204

CONCLUDING CHAPTER . . 210

NOTES 279

THE ENGLISH GOVERNMENT

AND

CONSTITUTION.

CHAPTER I.

FIRST PRINCIPLES OF THE ENGLISH GOVERNMENT AND CONSTITUTION.

' It is now the generally received opinion, and I think a probable opinion, that to the provisions of that reign (viz. of Henry the Seventh) we are to refer the origin, both of the unlimited power of the Tudors, and of the liberties wrested by our ancestors from the Stuarts; that tyranny was their immediate, and liberty their remote consequence; but he must have great confidence in his own sagacity, who can satisfy himself that, unaided by subsequent events, he could from a consideration of the causes have foreseen the succession of effects so different.'—*Fox's History of James II.*

IT would undoubtedly have required a sagacity of no ordinary kind to have predicted, at the commencement of the arbitrary sway of the House of Tudor, the course of weak misrule and daring opposition,—of fierce contention, and not less cruel victory, which, marking with a line of blood the history of the Stuart dynasty, at length ended in a peaceable revolution, and the establishment of regular liberty. But those who have seen the harvest can have no doubt that the seed was in the ground; and at this day it ought to be within our power to point out what were the elements of freedom in the state of England, during the reign of the Tudors, which have been since developed in her matchless

B

constitution.   Among them, we may, without hesitation, enumerate the following circumstances.

In the first place, the sovereignty of England did
not reside in the King solely.   All matters of great
state importance were made subjects of deliberation
in the King's high court of Parliament, which was
called together expressly for that purpose.   In case
of war, it was the business of that assembly to consider of means for carrying it on: if the succession
was disputed, or a regency required, an appeal was
made to their judgment; and all laws intended to
be permanently binding on the people received the
sanction of their authority.   Nor did the princes
of the House of Tudor attempt by any means to
diminish or undervalue the importance of Parliament.
The crown of Henry the Seventh rested on a Parliamentary Act.   Henry the Eighth repeatedly
employed the name, and acknowledged the power
of Parliament to change the succession.   In the
reign of Elizabeth, the offence of saying that the
Queen by the authority of Parliament had not power
to dispose of the succession to the crown was made
high treason during her life, and a misdemeanour
with forfeiture of goods and chattels after her decease.
Thus, however arbitrary the acts of these sovereigns,
nothing was taken from the reverence due to the
Parliament, the great council of the King, the grand
inquest of the nation, and the highest court in the
kingdom.   The power given to Henry the Eighth,
to issue proclamations equal in validity to laws, was
indeed a direct blow to parliamentary government.
But this Act was in force only eight years, and contained a proviso that these proclamations should not
be contrary to the established laws of the realm.
During the reigns of Mary and Elizabeth, the Parliament, however subservient, was yet a principal
instrument in carrying on the government.   Hence
arose a necessity, not indeed that a King of England

should relinquish all hope of exercising tyrannical power, but that, if successful, he must have his Lords and Commons accomplices in his tyranny.   If these bodies therefore should ever claim practically that share in the state which the laws virtually allowed them, or if they should refuse their support to the measures of the Crown, the King must either submit to their claims, or by discontinuing parliaments, give fair warning to the people that the form of government was changed.

Secondly.   The nobility were not separated from the people by odious distinctions, like the other feudal nobility of Europe.   Various causes have been assigned for this difference ; without discussing them, I shall content myself with stating the fact. It would not be correct to suppose, however, that the feudal system has not existed in England in a very odious shape.   After the Conquest, the feudal tenure seems to have been adopted by all the principal landholders of England, in a great council held in the year 1086.* Wardships, liveries, primer seisins, and ouster-lemains, values and forfeitures of marriage, fines for alienation, tenures by homage, knight-service and escuage, as well as aids for marrying the King's daughter, and knighting his son, all ligaments of the feudal system, are enumerated as part of the law of England, by the Act of Charles II., which abolishes them.   Happily, however, the system was not allowed to throw its roots very deep into the soil.   A practice, which was growing general, of sub-infeudations, or granting inferior feuds by the mesne lords, with the same conditions as the chief, was restrained by the Act of *Quia emptores* (18 Edw. I.), which directs that upon all sales, or grants of land in fee, the subtenant shall hold, not of the immediate, but of the

* Blackstone, b. ii. c. 4.

B 2

4 FIRST PRINCIPLES OF THE CH. I.

superior lord. A corrective to the tyranny of the
feudal system was also to be found in the constitution of our county courts, the cradle of our liberties,
in which are to be found the origin of our juries,
and the model of our parliaments. Here the free
tenants met to do justice between man and man;
and here, it is probable, they deliberated on the
means of affording the assistance they were bound
to give, to defend their country against an enemy.

Thus much with respect to the free tenants.
The state of the villeins is, perhaps, a subject of
still more importance. The main difference between
the two classes was this. The free tenant held his
land, on condition of performing certain fixed services; the villein also frequently held land, but was
bound to perform services, base in their nature, and
generally undefined in their extent. Here was real
servitude. How soon it began to be abrogated we
know not, but we are told by Sir Thomas Smith,
who was secretary to Edward VI. and Queen Elizabeth, that in all his time he never knew any instance
of a villein in gross, that is, of a villein transferable
by sale, and not attached to the soil, in the kingdom; and that the few villeins attached to the soil
who remained, were such only as had belonged to
bishops, monasteries, and other ecclesiastical corporations. The last claim of villenage recorded in our
courts, was in the fifteenth year of James I. This
great change, which had been silently operating
in the condition of the people of England, is probably
to be attributed to various causes,—the absence of
foreign armies,—the necessity of conciliating the
people during the civil wars,—and above all, the
inherent justice and piety of the nation.

There were several ways in which a villein attached to the soil could obtain his freedom. He
might be manumitted. Or if his lord brought an
action against him, the lord was supposed to allow

his freedom. Or if he went into a town and settled
there, he, in a certain time, enjoyed its immunities,
and became free. Or, lastly, if he could show that,
for time out of mind, he and his ancestors had been
registered in the roll of the lord's court, as having
possession of the land he held, he obtained a pre-
scriptive right against his lord. This was done by
producing a copy of the court roll, and hence the
term copyholder. It has been supposed by some
that copyhold was known before the conquest. At
whatever time it originated, the early prevalence of
freedom is nobly characteristic of the English nation. Villenage was known in France till near the
end of the eighteenth century; in Spain it was only
abolished in the nineteenth; in Germany it is hardly
extinct; in Russia it was abolished by the present
Emperor, to his immortal honour, in 1864. But the
spirit of the English people, and the equality of the
common-law, have always been a just corrective of
the degrading institutions and customs imported
from other countries. Magna Charta itself is a
noble and singular proof of the sympathy then
existing between the barons and the people of England. Philippe de Comines speaks of the humanity
with which the nobility treated the people in the
civil wars. It would seem that Englishmen have
always felt that, if the order of civil society required
the relations of superior and inferior ranks, nature
conferred feelings and capacities with impartial
justice upon all.

Intimately connected with this spirit, is the absence of any distinction between gentleman and
roturier. Sir Thomas Smith is perhaps the first
author who takes notice of the difference of the
title of gentleman in England and on the Continent.
I subjoin an extract from his work:—' Ordinarily
the King doth only make knights and create barons,
or higher degrees; for as for gentlemen, they be

made good cheap in England. For whosoever
studieth the laws of the realm, who studieth in the
universities, who professes liberal sciences, and, to
be short, who can live idly and without manual
labour, and will bear the port, charge, and counte-
ance of a gentleman, he shall be called Master, for
that is the title which men give to esquires and other
gentlemen, and shall be taken for a gentleman : for
true it is with us as is said, *Tanti eris aliis quanti
tibi feceris;* and, if need be, a king of heralds shall
also give him, for money, arms newly made and invented, the title whereof shall pretend to have been
found by the said herald in perusing and viewing of
old registers, where his ancestors, in times past, had
been recorded to bear the same. . . . A man may
make doubt and question whether this manner of
making gentlemen is to be allowed or no; and for
my part I am of that opinion, that it is not amiss.
For, first, the prince loseth nothing by it, as he
should do, if it were as in France: for the yeoman
or husbandman is no more subject to taile or tax in
England than the gentleman: no, in every payment
to the King, the gentleman is more charged, which
he beareth the gladlier, and dareth not gainsay for
to save and keep his honour and reputation.'[*]—' The
law,' says Mr. Hallam, ' has never taken notice of
gentlemen.[†] From the reign of Henry III., at
least, the legal equality of all ranks below the peerage was, to every essential purpose, as complete as
at present. Compare two writers nearly contem-
porary,—Bracton with Beaumanoir, and mark how
the customs of England and France are distinguish-
able in this respect. The Frenchman ranges the

[*] ' De Republicâ Anglorum,'
lib. i. c. 20, 21

[†] The Statute of Merton cer
tainly affords an exception to this
remark, when it speaks of the
wards of noblemen being dispa-

raged by marrying *villeins, or
others as burgesses.* But the
same Act allows that such marriages, if made by the ward's consent after fourteen years of age,
are legal.—*J. R.*

people under three divisions,—the noble, the free,
and the servile; our countryman has no generic
class but freedom and villenage.   No restraint seems
ever to have lain upon marriage.   The purchase of
land held by knight-service was always open to all
freemen.   From the beginning our law has been no
respecter of persons.   It screens not the gentleman
of ancient lineage from the judgment of an ordinary
jury, nor from ignominious punishment.   It confers
not, nor ever did confer, those unjust immunities
from public burthens which the superior orders ar-
rogated to themselves upon the Continent.   Thus,
while the privileges of our Peers, as hereditary
legislators of a free people, are incomparably more
valuable and dignified, they are far less invidious in
their exercise than those of any other nobility in
Europe.   It is, I am firmly persuaded, to this peculiarly democratical character of the English monarchy
that we are indebted for its long permanence, its
regular improvement, and its present vigour.   It is
a singular, a providential circumstance, that, in an
age when the gradual march of civilization and commerce was so little foreseen, our ancestors, deviating
from the usages of neighbouring countries, should,
as if deliberately, have guarded against that expan-
sive force, which, in bursting through obstacles
improvidently opposed, has scattered havoc over
Europe.' *
Thus we see that the nobility of England formed no
separate caste.   Their sons, not excepting the eldest,
were, in all respects, *part and parcel* of the commons
of the land.   It was decided, by votes of Parliament, both in the reign of Henry VIII. and in that
of Elizabeth, that the eldest son of the Earl of Bedford was entitled to sit in the House of Commons.
No decision could well be more auspicious.   The

* Middle Ages, vol. ii. p. 19.

heirs to a peerage, instead of feeling that petty pride, and indulging that insolent ignorance, which high rank has so great a tendency to breed, were members of an assembly in which they deliberated with the knights, citizens, and burgesses of the land: they thus imbibed the feelings, and became acquainted with the wants of the people. When a struggle was to be made for freedom, many of them sympathised in the cause; scarcely any quitted their country; thus their importance survived even the democratic revolution of 1649.

Thirdly. The last and the greatest element of freedom which existed in England was the constitution of her House of Commons. Some persons, indeed, have considered that all virtue was taken away from that body by a law of Henry VI., which limits the right of voting in counties to forty-shilling freeholders; and have dated the fall of the liberties of England from the period when villenage was gradually giving way to freedom. To such an opinion I certainly do not subscribe. Nor is it my intention to enter here into any controversy respecting the origin of our representation; a discussion belonging properly to an earlier period than that we are now speaking of. The points to which I shall now confine my remarks are the Principle of Representation, and the Nature of our own Representation generally.

It has been observed, that in the ancient commonwealths, the people, who decided on public affairs, were all of a higher order than those of the poorer class, who in England read newspapers and take an interest in political questions. But this is a complete mistake. Slaves, it is true, had nothing to do with political functions, but the poorest artisans, who were free, had a voice in the public councils. The manner in which their votes were to be given formed a difficulty which the ancient states did not altogether successfully vanquish. If the

promiscuous multitude were admitted, with equal
suffrages, into the public assemblies, as at Athens,
the decisions were hasty, passionate, unjust, and ca-
pricious. If a method was adopted, as that of centuries at Rome, of giving a weight to property against
numbers, it was difficult to avoid putting the scale
entirely in the hands of the rich, enabling them
to outvote the poor, and thus making an odious distinction between the richer and poorer, higher and
lower classes of the community.   This evil was
greatly felt at Rome, and the expedient of setting
up another and independent assembly, which decided
by numbers only, was a very rude and a very imperfect remedy.*

The principle of representation nearly, if not entirely, overcomes these obstacles.   A certain number
of persons are chosen by the people at large, whose
commission it is to watch over the interests of the
community.   Consisting naturally and inevitably of
persons of some fortune and education, they are not
so likely to be borne away by the torrent of passion
as the general, unsifted mass of the nation.   Depending upon the people ultimately for their power,
they are not so liable to act from personal interest,
or a corporation spirit, as a body of men whose
power is attached for ever to their rank in the State.
If the representative assembly is entrusted for no
very short period with the concerns of the people,
and if the members of it are always capable of being
re-elected, it will evidently become enlightened on
all the interests, and capable of discussing, with ability, all the great movements of the State.   The
most powerful minds in the nation will be brought

---

* See Hume's Essays.   Essay on some Remarkable Customs.

——— My soul aches
To know, when two authorities are up,
Neither supreme, how soon confusion
May enter 'twixt the gap of both.
                              Coriolanus, act iii.

to bear on any important measure of policy or justice; and, at the same time, the humblest individual
in the country is sure, through some channel or
other, to find a hearing for his injuries in the presence of the representatives of the whole people.

It is essential to remark, that in the English
House of Commons the knights sate in the same
assembly with the citizens and burgesses. There
are few things in our early Constitution of more importance than this. Cities and towns, however necessary their assistance for granting aids and taxes,
are not likely to obtain, in a feudal country, that
kind of respect from the other bodies in the State
which would enable them to claim a large share of
political power. The separation of the mercantile
class from the rest of the community was perhaps
one of the chief causes of the failure of the Spanish,
and other early constitutions similar to our own. It
is at the present day (1865) the greatest defect in
the constitution of Prussia, depriving the Senate of
all popular character, and the House of Representatives of their proper weight, and the moderating influence of men of landed property. But in England,
the knights, who represented the landed property of
the country, gave a stability and compactness to the
frame of the House of Commons, and placed it on a
broad foundation, not easily shaken by any king who
should attempt its overthrow.

The sitting of the knights, citizens, and burgesses
in one assembly, was perhaps partly owing to that
equality of civil rights, which has before been mentioned; no imaginary distinction separated the country knight of ancient lineage from the city merchant
of recent fortune. It was not, however, always the
rule, and has rather been established by one of those
happy unions of fortune and counsel to which the
English Constitution owes so much;—I know not,
indeed, if I ought to call it fortune. It was a part

of the practical wisdom of our ancestors to alter and
vary the form of our institutions as they went on;
to suit them to the circumstances of the time, and
reform them according to the dictates of experience.
They never ceased to work upon our frame of government, as a sculptor fashions the model of a
favourite statue.   It is an art that till of late years
had fallen into disuse, and the disuse was attended
with evils of the most alarming magnitude.

CHAPTER II.

HENRY THE SEVENTH.

' The King, to speak of him in terms equal to his deserving, was
one of the best sort of wonders, a wonder for wise men. He had
parts, both in his virtues and his fortune, not so fit for a common-
place as for observation.'—*Lord Bacon, Life and Reign of Henry VII.*

THE battle of Bosworth Field put an end to the
long and destructive contest which had wasted the
blood, and disfigured the fair face of England, in
the quarrel between the Houses of York and Lancaster. Such a contention is little less disgraceful
to mankind than it would have been to have made
the white and red roses the subject, instead of the
symbols, of hostility, and affords but too much
ground for the assertion of a democratic writer, that
hereditary right has caused as long and as sanguinary
wars as elective monarchy.

Henry, who was crowned in the field of battle,
lost no time in proving he was as well able to keep,
as to acquire a throne. He immediately summoned
a parliament, and obtained from them the passing of
a statute, not declaring that he was lawful heir to
the crown; not asserting the right of conquest, or
of election; but enacting 'that the inheritance of
the crown should rest, remain, and abide in the
king.' He procured this statute to be confirmed by
the Pope's bull. In the same spirit of peace and
moderation he caused many exceptions to be inserted
in the Acts for attainting the adherents of King
Richard. A few years afterwards he procured a
law to be passed, declaring that no one should be
called in question for obeying a king *de facto.* He

thus quieted the minds of his subjects, and added
more to the stability of his government than he
could possibly have done by displaying what Bacon
calls the wreath of fire,—to wit, his own descent,
and that of his queen, the claim of conquest, and
the authorities, parliamentary and papal.   Among
these titles, that of the House of York seems to have
given him little satisfaction, and he took care not to
crown his queen for a considerable time after his
marriage.   Indeed, it is certain that, whether from
prejudice or policy, his Lancastrian partialities influenced his conduct during the whole of his reign.

One of Henry's first endeavours was to procure a
law to prevent conspiracies among the great, and
riots among the people.   In a parliament assembled
in the third year of his reign, Morton, Archbishop
of Canterbury and Chancellor of the kingdom, spoke
the following words:—' His Grace (*i. e.* the King)
saith, that it is not the blood spilt in the field that
will save the blood in the city; nor the marshal's
sword that will set this kingdom in perfect peace;
but that the true way is to stop the seeds of sedition
and rebellion at the beginnings, and for that purpose
to devise, confirm, and quicken good and wholesome
laws against riots and unlawful assemblies of people,
and all combinations and confederacies of them by
liveries, tokens, and other badges of factious dependence; that the peace of the land may by these
ordinances, as by bars of iron, be soundly bound in
and strengthened, and all force, both in court,
country, and private houses, be suppressed.'

The chief law passed by Parliament with the
view here explained, was an Act confirming the
authority of the Star Chamber in certain cases.
The Star Chamber, composed of prelates, peers,
counsellors, and judges, had an undefined jurisdiction without the intervention of a jury over many
offences not capital, and over actions proving a

design to commit offences not actually committed.
'But that which was principally aimed at by this
Act,' says Lord Bacon, 'was force and the two
chief supports of force, combination of multitudes,
and maintenance or headship of great persons.' The
danger to liberty, of entrusting power so large and
arbitrary to persons named by the Crown, does not
appear to have struck any one at this time; and
Lord Bacon is lavish in his praises of the Star
Chamber, calling it one of the sagest and noblest
institutions of this kingdom. But long civil war
induces a people to surrender liberty for peace, as
long peace induces them to encounter even civil
war for liberty.   One of the next Acts of the Parliament was the sanction of an arbitrary tax.   This
species of tax, known by the name of Benevolence,
had been raised by Edward IV., without the consent of Parliament, and abolished by Richard III.
in a very remarkable statute.   It was now revived
by Act of Parliament on the occasion of a war with
France.   But the real object was to amass money;
for Henry had scarcely landed in France when he
concluded a peace by which he was to receive
745,000 ducats (about £186,000 sterling) and a
tribute of 25 crowns yearly.

This reign was much disturbed by rebellion.   Attachment to the House of York, and the burthen of
taxes, seem to have been the chief causes of discontent.   Bacon attributes an insurrection in the North
to respect for the memory of Richard III.,—a proof
that his government, in that part of the kingdom at
least, had not been very oppressive.

The chief end of Henry's administration was to
restrain the inordinate power of the great barons.
Two laws enacted for this purpose, the one facili-
tating the sale of entailed lands by what is called
breaking an entail, and another suppressing retainers,
were, with other statutes, and the extensive authority

given to the Star Chamber, eminently conducive to
the object for which they were framed.   In thus
directing his policy, Henry adopted views prompted
indeed by his own jealous temper, but which ultimately were beneficial to his country.   The course
of justice became steady, disorders were suppressed,
the tranquillity of the whole country was secured
and the Commons, being no longer oppressed by
feudal power, or distracted by domestic war, were
enabled to acquire, first wealth, then importance,
and lastly freedom.   Bacon, it is true, attributes
many of the disturbances which still afflicted the
country during this reign to the neglect and distrust
of the nobility shown by the King.   But the fault,
if it were one, was on the right side.   Had not
Henry governed his nobles with a strong hand, a
powerful oligarchy might have perpetuated in this
country the barbarous licence of Poland.   The arts,
the letters, and the strength of the kingdom, under
the sway of Elizabeth, are in great part to be attributed to the policy of her grandfather.

The last years of Henry were disgraced by the
cruel and arbitrary exactions of which Empson and
Dudley were the vile and execrated instruments.
His successor, with a generous magnanimity not un-
common in the world, gave up the offenders, and
profited by the offence ; sent the collectors to the
scaffold, and kept the money in his treasury.

CHAPTER III.

HENRY THE EIGHTH.

' When love could teach a monarch to be wise,
And gospel light first dawn'd from Bullen's eyes.'—*Gray*.

THE reign of Henry the Eighth is justly esteemed the most arbitrary in our annals. Yet it affords many curious precedents of the authority of Parliament. One of the first of these is the Act granting tonnage and poundage. The King had levied these duties for some time by his own prerogative. But in the sixth year of his reign he met with resistance, and was obliged to apply to Parliament for their sanction. The Act that was passed is curious. It condemns those who had resisted, but at the same time grants to the King, *de novo*, the duties of tonnage and poundage. Upon the whole, this precedent, though inconsistent with itself, makes against the power assumed by the Crown. For if the King had the right to raise those duties, the Act would have been merely declaratory. The making a new enactment proves, with whatever terms it might be qualified, that the King was not previously entitled by his prerogative to levy tonnage and poundage, and that his orders on this subject might be resisted with impunity. So, indeed, the Act seems to have been understood; for at the commencement of the four following reigns, we find the duties in question regularly granted by Parliament, in the first year of the reign*.

* Statutes 1 Edw. VI. c.13, 1 Mary, st. 2, c. 18, 1 Eliz. c. 20, 1 James, c. 33. By all these Acts, tonnage and poundage are granted for life. They are all amongst the last Acts of the

Another remarkable precedent is afforded by an indiscreet step of Wolsey.   Wishing to impose a very heavy tax, he determined to go himself into the House of Commons, for the purpose of silencing, by his presence, all opposition.   Many were disposed to resist his admission into the House ; but when that point had been conceded, the Speaker, Sir Thomas More, opposed the opinion of the majority, that he should be admitted with a few followers only.   The Speaker was of opinion that they should receive him ' with all his pomp, with his maces, his pillars, his pole-axes, his cross, his hat, and the great seal too.'   The Cardinal being thus admitted, made a long and eloquent oration against the King of France, declared that the King could not do otherwise than join with the Emperor against him, and demanded of the Commons the sum of £800,000 as the estimated charge of the war.   'At this request,' as we are told by the great-grandson and biographer of Sir Thomas More, ' the House was silent; and when the minister demanded some reasonable answer, every member held his peace. At last, the Speaker, falling on his knees, with much reverence, excused the silence of the House, abashed, as he said, at the sight of so noble a personage, who

session. Notwithstanding these statutes, Mr. Hume asserts, that Henry's ' successors, for more than a century, persevered in the like irregular practice, if a practice may deserve that epithet, in which the whole nation acquiesced, and which gave no offence. But when Charles I. attempted to continue in the same course, which had now received the sanction of so many generations, so much were the opinions of men altered, that a furious tempest was excited by it, and historians, partial or ignorant, still represent this measure as a most

violent and unprecedented enormity in this unhappy prince.' And with reason. These duties were not granted to Charles as they had been to his predecessors, and he attempted to revive the practice which was not permitted to Henry VIII.   Whether Mr. Hume is right in supposing that Edward, Mary, Elizabeth, and James levied these duties, during the few months they were not in force, or whether he has not fallen into an error, in supposing they were levied before they were granted by Parliament, I will not presume to determine.

C

was able to amaze the wisest and most learned men
in the realm; but with many probable arguments
he endeavoured to show the Cardinal that his coming thither was neither expedient nor agreeable to
the ancient liberties of that House;' and, in conclusion,
told him, 'that except all the members could put
their several thoughts into his head, he alone was
unable, in so weighty a matter, to give his grace a
sufficient answer. Whereupon the Cardinal, dis-
pleased with the Speaker, suddenly rose up in a rage
and departed.' The result was, that a subsidy was
granted, but much less than the Cardinal had asked.

In 1526, Wolsey sent commissioners by his own
authority to levy a sixth part of the goods of the
laity, and a tenth part of the goods of the clergy;
but the commissioners were resisted, and Henry
was obliged to disavow his minister, and annul the
commission.

Yet in the same reign in which so much spirit
was shown, a magistrate of London was sent to the
wars in Scotland, where he was soon after killed,
because he had refused to contribute to a benevolence.* What a confusion of law and custom!
how uncertain the bounds of right and prerogative!

The arbitrary nature of the government of Henry,
on every subject but that of taxes, is well known.
In all his violations of law and justice he was strenu-
ously supported by his Parliament. When he wished
to rid himself of his wives, Parliament assisted him;
when he desired to put to death his ministers, Parliament condemned them without a trial; when at
length he chose to make laws by his own will only,
Parliament gave him authority to do so. It is no
wonder, therefore, to find him holding high the
privileges of Parliament. A curious instance of this
occurs in the case of a Mr. Ferrers, a member of the

* Henry's History of England.

House of Commons, who was arrested for debt. The House immediately released him, and imprisoned those who had arrested him.   Henry upon this occasion made the following speech to the House on the question of privilege :—' He first commended their wisdom in maintaining the privileges of their House ; which he would not have infringed in any point.   He alleged that he, being at the head of the Parliament, and attending in his own person in the business thereof, ought in reason to have privilege for himself and all his servants in attendance on him. So that, if Ferrers had been no burgess, but only his servant, in respect of that he ought to have privilege as well as any other.   For I understand,' says he, ' that you enjoy the same privilege, not only for yourselves, but even for your cooks and horse-keepers.   My Lord Chancellor here present hath informed me, that when he was Speaker of the Lower House, the cook of the Temple was arrested in London, on an execution upon the statute of staple. And, because the said cook served the Speaker in that office, he was taken out of execution by the privilege of Parliament.   Likewise, the judges have informed us, that we at no time stand so high in our estate royal as in the time of Parliament ; when we, as head, and you as members, are conjoined and knit together into one body politic; so that whatsoever is done or offered during that time against the meanest member of the House is judged as done against our own person and whole court of Parliament.   The prerogative of which court is so great, that, as our learned in the laws inform us, all acts and processes, coming out of any other inferior courts, must for that time cease and give place to the highest.'

Thus did Henry exalt the power of the Parliament, which had so vigorously supported him.   But it does not appear that in so doing they had gone

beyond the wishes of their constituents. Henry
seems upon the whole to have been a popular
tyrant; and there is some truth in the remark of
Mr. Hume, that the English of this age, like Eastern
slaves, were inclined to admire those acts of violence
and tyranny which were exercised over themselves
and at their own expense.

CHAPTER IV.

THE REFORMATION.

' He that would do right to religion cannot take a more effectual course than by reconciling it with the happiness of mankind.'— *Tillotson.*

THE Reformation in England was by no means similar in its history to the great revolution of men's minds which took place in Switzerland, Scotland, and Germany. It was begun by the King, in consequence of his desire to put away his wife and marry another; and this quarrel was not only unconnected with the doctrine of Luther, but that doctrine was at the same time condemned, and its supporters capitally punished. Had the Pope been as complying as he had often been before, Henry VIII. would have been, if not one of the most pure and holy saints, one of the most faithful and zealous servants that the Church of Rome could boast of possessing. Even after the breach seemed irreparable, propositions were made from Rome, and were accepted by Henry; * but as his messenger did not arrive on the day fixed, the Emperor's party in the Consistory took advantage of the failure of punctuality to obtain a vote closing the door upon reconciliation for ever. The messenger of the King of England arrived only two days too late to reconcile his master with the Pope, and arrest the progress of religious light in this country.

The breach with the Church of Rome would still not have led immediately to the Reformation, had not Cranmer, holding the high station of Archbishop

* Burnet's Hist. of Ref., vol. i. p. 136.

of Canterbury, with Cromwell, many of the Peers, and a large number of the educated class, endeavoured to conduct the nation, step by step, to abjure the errors and superstitions of the Roman Catholic worship. At the same time, they were obliged, even for the sake of the cause they favoured, to retain many ceremonies to which the people were attached, and which the English reformers copied from the Roman Church, as the Roman Church had originally copied some of their ceremonies from the heathen worship.

The first step which Henry took against the Church of Rome after the divorce was the dissolution of the monasteries. The motive which induced him to adopt this measure was probably a spirit of rapacity; for with all his power he found it a very difficult matter to squeeze money from his subjects. With the sum to be derived from the sale of the monasteries, he proposed to make harbours all round the coast of England; a plausible pretext, rather than a *bond fide* reason, for his confiscations. Those of the nobility who had adopted the opinions of the reformers, gave willingly in to the measure, and no doubt their zeal was quickened by the share they got of the spoil. The abuses which prevailed in the monasteries were not, however, a groundless pretext. The relations of the visitors who were appointed by the King to reform the monasteries, and report their state, display grounds for believing that they were anything rather than seminaries of piety and morality.[*]

The next steps taken in the road of reformation were some directions respecting the worship of

* Burnet, Hist. of Ref., book i. p. 196. Dr. Lingard, indeed, refuses credit to those charges: he observes with truth that they were *ex parte* statements, to which the accused had no opportunity of replying. It would be difficult, on the other hand, to suppose all the facts alleged to be fabrications. Monks and nuns are not infallible or impeccable beings.

images and praying to saints, and, what was much
more important, a permission to the people to read
a translation of the Bible, in St. Paul's Church.
The people flocked to the place, and one person was
generally chosen to read aloud to the rest, till the
bishop, alarmed at the concourse, forbade the practice, as a disturbance to the service of the church.
The destruction of some of the images exposed to
the public several scandalous cheats.*

The outset of the Reformation in England was
marked by a more cruel and insupportable religious
tyranny than had ever subsisted under the Papal
dominion. In the times of Popery, the articles of
faith were placed in the custody of the priest; and
the people received from him some knowledge of
the doctrines of Christianity, some notion of the
duties of morality, and an unbounded reverence for
the authority and magnificence of the Church. But
Henry VIII., after partly removing the veil of
ignorance from the eyes of his people, required
them not to go a single step further than he himself
did; and commanded the nation by Act of Parliament to believe six articles of faith therein laid
down, and whatever else the King might choose to
ordain.

To punish men for their opinions on speculative
articles of belief, is one of the luxuries which tyranny
has invented in modern times. Dionysius and Do-
mitian knew nothing of it. It was enjoyed by
Henry to its full extent. He was not, like Philip II.
or Charles IX., merely the minister of bigotry of
which he was himself the disciple. He taught from
his own mouth the opinions which were to regulate his
subjects; he contained in his own breast the rule of
orthodoxy; and he had the triumph of confuting the
heretic whom he afterwards had the gratification to
burn.

* Note (A) at the end of the volume.

The religion established by Henry VIII. was so
far from being the reformed church of Luther or of
Calvin, that he prided himself on maintaining the
Roman Catholic faith after he had shaken off the
supremacy of the Pope. His ordinances indeed
vibrated for a short time between the old and the
new religion, as he listened more to Cranmer or to
Gardiner; but the law of the Six Articles, which
contains the creed he finally imposed on his people,
maintains and confirms all the leading articles of the
Roman belief. They were as follows:—

First, That, in the sacrament of the altar, after
the consecration, there remained no substance of
bread and wine, but under these forms the natural
body and blood of Christ were present. *Secondly*,
That communion in both kinds was not necessary
to salvation to all persons by the law of God.
Thirdly, That priests after the order of priesthood
might not marry by the law of God. *Fourthly*,
That vows of chastity ought to be observed by the
law of God. *Fifthly*, That the use of private masses
ought to be continued; which, as it was agreeable
to God's law, so men received great benefit by
them. *Sixthly*, That auricular confession was expedient and necessary, and ought to be retained in
the Church.

The actual Reformation in England was the work
of the Duke of Somerset, Protector, in the early
part of the reign of Edward VI. In the first year
of that reign, he sent visitors to persuade the people
not to pray to saints, to procure that images should
be broken; and to exhort the nation generally, to
leave off the use of the mass, dirges, and prayers in
a foreign language. By Act of Parliament in the
same year he prohibited speaking against giving the
sacrament in both kinds; in that and the two following years he established the liturgy of the Church
of England. The law of the six articles was re-

pealed.   The Reformation in England was thus
made by the Crown and the aristocracy.   The
people, though agitated by religious disputes, seem
to have been hardly ripe for so great a revolution.
Insurrections of a serious nature took place in
Devonshire, Norfolk, and elsewhere.   The preaching of the Roman Catholic priesthood produced so
strong an impression, that all the means of authority
were put in motion to counteract it.   The clergy
were first ordered not to preach out of their parishes
without a licence, which of course was granted only
to the favoured sect; and this not proving sufficient,
preaching was altogether prohibited,*—a singular
step in the history of the Reformation !

On the other hand, Mary, on succeeding to the
throne, found it an easy matter to revive the ancient
worship.   Nor did she hesitate to call frequent new
Parliaments, who each went beyond the former in
the road of reconciliation.   The first refused to re-
establish the law of the six articles ; but only one
year afterwards, the nation was formally reconciled
to the Church of Rome, and the Parliament thanked
the Pope for pardoning their long heresy.   He said,
with equal candour and truth, that he ought to
thank them for putting a rich country again under
his dominion.

* Burnet, Hist. Ref.

CHAPTER V.

QUEEN ELIZABETH

'Sur ce sanglant théâtre, où cent héros périrent,
Sur ce trône glissant, dont cent rois descendirent,
Une femme, à ses pieds enchaînant les destins,
De l'éclat de son règne étonnait les humains.
C'était Elisabeth; elle dont la prudence,
De l'Europe à son choix fit pencher la balance,
Et fit aimer son joug à l'Anglois indompté,
Qui ne peut ni servir, ni vivre en liberté.
Ses peuples sous son règne ont oublié leurs pertes;
De leurs troupeaux féconds leurs plaines sont couvertes,
Les guérets de leurs blés, les mers de leurs vaisseaux,
Ils sont craints sur la terre, ils sont rois sur les eaux.
Leur flotte impérieuse, asservissant Neptune,
Des bouts de l'univers appelle la Fortune;
Londres jadis barbare est le centre des arts,
Le magasin du monde, et le temple de Mars.'
La Henriade, chant 1.

QUEEN ELIZABETH is the greatest of English, perhaps of all modern sovereigns. In a period remarkable for long and sanguinary wars, she made her name respected abroad, without a waste of blood or treasure; and, in a time of great political ferment, she maintained the most absolute authority at home, without any loss of the affections of her people. She obtained glory without conquest, and unlimited power without odium.

The means by which results so extraordinary were obtained, comprise all the springs of her foreign and domestic policy. Three principal sources of her fame and success, however, may be discerned.

First.—She made herself the head of the Protestant interest in Europe. To do this, it was not

necessary to place herself in the front of a con-
federacy of belligerent powers.   It was sufficient to
give the sanction of the name of England, a rich
and united kingdom, to the cause which she supported.   The spirit and enterprise of her subjects,
with some assistance from her, did the rest.   By
this policy, also, she pleased the popular feeling of
her kingdom, and opened a channel in which all
the restless action of her nobility and gentry might
be borne out and find a current.   The national fame
was likewise a gainer by the reputation acquired
by English knights and soldiers, in fighting against
the League in France, and Philip II. in the Netherlands.   The country assumed her proper station in
the van of the defenders of liberty; the blood of
Sir Philip Sidney was shed in the cause of the
freedom of the world; and tyrants trembled at
the name of Elizabeth and of England.

Secondly.—She took care not to ask too much
money of the people.   Her treaties with Henry IV.
and with the Netherland States resemble more the
hard bargain of a Swiss Canton than the generous
alliance of a powerful and friendly sovereign.   She
well knew that Parliament held the purse, and must,
therefore, become absolute master of a distressed or
expensive sovereign.   In her situation economy was
power.   Happy would it have been for Leo X., for
Charles I., for Louis XVI., if they and their immediate predecessors had been aware of this keystone of their fate!   The Reformation, the civil
wars of England, and the revolution in France, had
their rise in disordered finances.   Men may perhaps
submit to be oppressed, but will not easily consent
to pay a dear price for the oppression.

Thirdly.—She yielded to the popular voice, and
cultivated popular favour, whenever it could be done
with dignity and safety.   She could be severe and
kind by turns.   Thus, having at one time excited

great murmurs among the House of Commons by
forbidding liberty of speech, she soon thought proper to revoke her commands. But nothing shows
her policy better than her conduct respecting monopolies. There was hardly any article of which
a monopoly was not granted by the Crown. The
evil grew so grievous that even Elizabeth's House
of Commons echoed with angry speeches and
universal complaint. The Queen instantly yielded.
She did not acknowledge that the debates of the
House of Commons had any weight with her, but
she informed them, through her Secretary of State,
that she consented to quash those monopolies that
were illegal, and to submit to an inquiry with respect to the rest. Secretary Cecil made an apology
to the House for having compared them to a school,
and said, he by no means intended to deny the
freedom of speech.*

In her manners also the Queen took care to show
the greatest confidence in the people. No one
knew better how to buy the nation's heart with
a phrase, to declare, on occasion, that her treasure
was better in her subjects' purses than in her own
coffers, and that her best guards were the affections
of her people. She was well aware that nothing is
so pleasing as the condescension of supreme power.
She therefore displayed her greatness by the pomp
of her state, and her goodness by the affability of
her language.

By such means Queen Elizabeth was enabled to
maintain a stable authority over an unquiet people
in a restless age. France was distracted by civil
war; the King of Spain was employed in a bootless
and bloody quarrel with his insurgent subjects in
the Netherlands; Germany was shaken in every
limb by the Reformation; but the Queen of Eng-

* Note (D) at the end of the volume.

land reaped the reward of prudence and courage
in the tranquillity and affectionate obedience of her
kingdom and people.   Her power was enormous.
When the Commons remonstrated, she speedily dissolved them.   At one time she told them not to
meddle in affairs of state.   Still less did she permit
any proposal of alteration in the Church; and she
repeatedly imprisoned, or procured to be imprisoned,
those who gainsayed her high pleasure in these matters.*   She dispensed with those laws which were
unpalatable to her, and regulated the behaviour of
her people by ordinance and arbitrary mandate.   She
forbade the cultivation of woad, as offensive to her
royal nostrils.   The Court of Star Chamber and the
Court of High Commission not being sufficiently
arbitrary, it was ordered that every person who imported forbidden books, or committed other offences
specified, should be punished by martial law.   Those
who employed the press as an organ of discussion
were speedily condemned.   Mr. John Udall, a Puritan minister, charged with having written ' a slanderous and infamous libel against the Queen's Majesty,'
was tried for a felony, and convicted.   The sentence
was never executed, but the poor man, after several
years' confinement, died in prison.   The judge told
the jury to find him only author of the book, for the
offence of writing it had been already determined to
be felony by the judges.   A gentleman who had
written a book to dissuade the Queen from marrying
a French prince, was sentenced by a law of Queen
Mary to lose his hand.   A Puritan of the name of
Penry was condemned and executed for seditious
papers found in his pocket.   Struck by these arbitrary proceedings, Mr. Hume has compared the
government of Elizabeth to the modern government
of Turkey, and remarking that, in both cases, the

* Note (C) at the end of the volume.

sovereign was deprived of the power of levying money on his subjects, he asserts 'that in both countries this limitation, unsupported by other privileges, appears rather prejudicial to the people.' It is needless to say much on this fanciful analogy, so unworthy of a great historian. Did it ever happen that a Turkish house of commons prevailed on the Sultan to correct the extortion of his pashas, as the English House of Commons induced Elizabeth to surrender the odious monopolies? Did Queen Elizabeth ever put to death the holders of those monopolies without trial, in order to seize their ill-gotten wealth? In fact, the authority of the House of Commons made some advances during the reign of Elizabeth. The very weight of the power that was used to crush their remonstrances shows the strength of their resistance. The debates of the House of Commons during this reign fill a volume and a half of the old parliamentary history. An attentive observer of this country, at that period, would scarcely have failed to remark, that the force of free institutions was suspended, but not destroyed, by the personal influence of Elizabeth; and while he acknowledged that no sovereign ever carried the art of reigning further, he would perceive that the nation had granted her a lease for life of arbitrary power, but had not alienated for ever the inheritance of freedom.

It was happy for the country that Queen Elizabeth found it her interest to embrace the Protestant religion, and that, by the foolish as well as atrocious plots of the Roman Catholics, she was forced to cultivate still more strongly the affections of the Protestant party. Boast as we may of our Constitution, had Queen Elizabeth been a Roman Catholic, or James II. a Protestant, there would have been no liberty in England.

CHAPTER VI.

JAMES THE FIRST.

'Every one pointed to her (Queen Elizabeth's) white hairs, and said with that peaceable Leontius, "When this snow melteth, there will be a flood."' — *Hall's Sermons.*

DURING the latter years of Elizabeth, all classes of people were impatient for the accession of her successor. There is nothing so irksome to mankind as continued demands for a long series of years from the same person upon their admiration and their gratitude. In proportion as the novelty wears out, weariness succeeds to wonder, and envy to weariness; the many, like fastidious critics, begin to find faults where they saw nothing but beauties before, and some are angry that there are so few faults to find. The young love to censure what the old extravagantly praised, and the giddy are disgusted with the monotony of excellence. There might perhaps, however, be other causes why the English nation should desire the reign of James. A new spirit had arisen during the latter years of Elizabeth, both in religion and politics. A large party, known by the name of Puritans, had been formed, or rather, increased and united, who aimed at a further reformation in the Church. The Romish ceremonies, which had been preserved in our form of worship, found no indulgence in the minds of this stern sect; and, had the Puritans been able to execute their wishes, the power and revenues of the bishops would have been submitted to their crucible. Their bold and uncompromising principles led them also to free principles

of government; their understandings quickly stripped
a king of his divinity, and their hearts raised the
subject to a level with the sovereign.   Besides
the progress of these opinions, a new standard of
political right had been introduced by the general
study of Greek and Roman authors.   Not only had
the glories of the ancient republics kindled a flame
in the breasts of generous men, but the diffusion of
classical knowledge had prepared the upper classes
of society to require more enlightened methods of
proceeding, and a more regular distribution of
powers and privileges than had ever before been
found necessary.   The community was advanced in
wealth, in arts, in literature, and in morals.   Above
all, the Reformation was a perpetual source of inquiry and discussion; the minds of men had taken a
start towards improvement, and nothing could stop
their course.

The reforms which this new world manifestly demanded, were naturally postponed till after the
death of Elizabeth.   Her age and her reputation
merited, her vigour and experience enjoined, forbearance.   But James, a foreign king, without reputation of glory or of firmness, did not enforce by
his character the same submission.   A resolution
seems to have been taken to insist upon all the
ancient privileges of Parliament, together with all
the legal liberties of the subject; and if these should
be found incompatible with the old prerogatives of
the Crown, or the new pretensions of the Tudor
dynasty, to make the King yield to his people, and
not the people to the King.

James soon had ample occasion to remark the
disposition of his subjects.   Not all the rejoicings
which attended his march, nor the new honours
which he so lavishly threw away, could disguise the
truth.   A petition from upwards of a thousand
clergymen of the Puritan persuasion was presented
to the King on his road to London, praying for ' a

reformation in the church service, ministry, livings, and discipline.' He issued writs for the calling of a Parliament, accompanied with instructions to the people what kind of persons they should elect, commanding them not to choose outlaws, and bidding them send the returns to his Court of Chancery, there to be examined and judged. In pursuance of these instructions, the election of a Sir Francis Goodwin, chosen for the county of Buckingham, an outlaw, was declared to be void; a new writ was issued from the Chancery, and Sir John Fortescue was returned in his room. The Commons declared the election of Sir Francis Goodwin to be valid, and that all matters concerning the election of Members of Parliament were cognizable in the House of Commons only. This had been an old subject of dispute with Queen Elizabeth; the precedents were assertions on both sides, and no decisive conclusion. The Commons had voted that the 'discussing and adjudging of such like differences belonged only to the House;' and had passed a resolution that outlaws might be elected: the Judges had declared that they could not, and Queen Elizabeth had complained to her last House of Commons that outlaws were admitted. James, after contesting the point, proposed that both Goodwin and Fortescue should be set aside, and a new writ should be issued *by the warrant of the House.* The right of the Commons to decide in all matters of election was thus admitted.

In the same Parliament, a warden of the Fleet was arrested by the House for having imprisoned a member; a compensation for wardship and purveyance was proposed; and a conference with the Lords was desired on the subject of religion. The instructions given by the Commons to those who were to conduct the conference are remarkable. A relaxation is desired for such as were unable to reconcile themselves to the cross in baptism, the ring in mar-.

riage, and the surplice; but on the subjects of faith,
and the sacraments, every person in the kingdom is
to be required by Parliament to conform to the law
of uniformity. So far were the ideas of these reformers from real toleration! James was alarmed
at each and all of the pretensions of the Commons,
and there remains a draft of a very able address
reported from a Select Committee of that House
(though never adopted by the House itself), complaining of the misinformation he had received, and
entering at large into every subject which had been
discussed. They mention the ill-treatment they had
received on the subject of their privileges during the
latter years of Queen Elizabeth; attribute their
acquiescence to respect for her sex and age; and
express their surprise and sorrow that in this first
Parliament of King James, their rights should have
been more invaded than ever.* The session ended
without any decisive result: except tonnage and
poundage, the King obtained no supply; and except
on the question of new writs, the Commons got no
redress.

The alarm of the Gunpowder Plot produced plen-
tiful grants to the King. At the end of December,
1609, James dissolved his Parliament, and with the
exception of a session of two months in 1614, more
than ten years passed over without any sitting of
Parliament. Forced loans, arbitrary taxes from
private persons, and new monopolies, supplied the
wants of his treasury in the interval. At length, in
the year 1620, a Parliament met, to which every
Englishman ought to look back with reverence.
Having first voted the King two subsidies, and
having discouraged all recurrence to past complaints,
they set themselves vigorously to examine the pre-

* Mr. Hume has laboured, but without success, to weaken the authority of this document, which, it seems, makes against his theory.

sent grievances of the subject. James adjourned
them, and imprisoned Sir Edwin Sandys, one of
their most useful members.   Undismayed by this
step, they petitioned the King, on his next meeting,
to defend his son-in-law the Elector Palatine against
the Catholic interest of Europe, to break off the
match of his son with Spain, and to turn his sword
against that formidable power.   James threatened
the Commons with punishment: they maintained
their privileges: he told them they were derived
' from the grace and permission of our ancestors and
us.'   To this pretension they returned the following
memorable answer :—

'The Commons, now assembled in Parliament,
being justly occasioned thereunto, concerning sun-
dry liberties, franchises, privileges, and jurisdictions
of Parliament, do make this protestation following:—
That the liberties, franchises, privileges, and jurisdictions of Parliament are the ancient and undoubted
birthright and inheritance of the subjects of England;
and the arduous and urgent affairs concerning the
King, State, and the defence of the realm, and of
the Church of England, and the making and maintenance of laws, and redress of mischiefs and grievances, which daily happen within this realm, are
proper subjects and matter of counsel and debate in
Parliament; and that in the handling and proceeding of those businesses, every member of the House
hath, and of right ought to have, freedom of speech,
to propound, treat, reason, and bring to conclusion
the same; that the Commons in Parliament have
like liberty and freedom to treat of those matters in
such order as in their judgments shall seem fittest;
and that every such member of the said House hath
like freedom from all impeachment, imprisonment,
and molestation (other than by the censure of the
House itself) for or concerning any bill, speaking,
reasoning, or declaring of any matter or matters,

touching the Parliament, or Parliament business;
and that if any of the said members be complained
of and questioned for anything said or done in Parliament, the same is to be showed to the King, by
the advice and assent of all the Commons assembled
in Parliament, before the King give credence to any
private information.'

James, greatly wroth at this proceeding, sent for
the Journal of the House of Commons to his council,
and tore out the protestation with his own hand.
He dissolved the Parliament; he imprisoned Coke,
Selden, Pym, Phillips, and Mallory,* all members
of the dissolved House of Commons. He was not
aware that the force of the protestation he tore out
was not in the parchment or the letters of a book,
but in the hearts and minds of his subjects; and he
little expected that, by confining the persons of a
few commoners, he was preparing the imprisonment
and death of his son.

If we look at the position of the adverse parties
at this time, we shall see that James was attempting, most unseasonably, a new mode of government.
The nature of the Gothic monarchies was generally
the same. The king, who had first ruled together
with his people in rude harmony, came, in time, to
exercise certain powers of government which he
called prerogative; and the people who, in early
times, assembled on every occasion to discuss grievances, and laws, and treaties, became in the progress
of civilization divided into cities, and had their privileges set down in general and particular charters
which they called their liberties. Both prerogative
and privilege were liable to misconstruction, and
sometimes overflowed their banks; but the King
always spoke with respect of the liberties of his
subjects, even when he illegally imprisoned their

* The people should have these   John Hampden, the founders of
names by heart. They were, with   the liberties of England.

persons; and the people professed their veneration
for monarchy, even when they deposed their king.
Queen Elizabeth, acting in this spirit, abjured the
notion of infringing the rights of her subjects, at
the same time that she occasionally encroached
upon, and always narrowly confined, the rights she
professed to maintain.   She acknowledged the *liberties* of the people without doubt or hesitation, but
made use of her own dictionary for the definition
of the term.   James attempted a new system: he
denied the existence of privileges altogether, except
by sufferance; and without possessing the wisdom of
an ordinary man, he claimed, in an inquiring age,
the infallibility of the Deity.   ' As it is atheism
and blasphemy,' he said, ' in a creature to dispute
what the Deity may do, so it is presumption and
sedition in a subject to dispute what a king may do
in the height of his power.   Good Christians will
be content with God's will, revealed in His word;
and good subjects will rest in the King's will, revealed in his law.'   Such was the impious folly
of James!   His sayings do him credit as a wit;
his learning was not unbecoming a scholar; but
his conduct made him contemptible as a king.
How vain then to pretend that all the ancient
privileges of the English nation were to depend
upon his nod!

CHAPTER VII.

CHARLES THE FIRST.

'There was ambition, there was sedition, there was violence; but no man shall persuade me that it was not the cause of liberty on one side, and of tyranny on the other.'—*Lord Chatham, quoted by Grattan* (*Letter to the Citizens of Dublin*, 1797).

THE accession of Charles I. found the nation engaged in hostilities with Spain, which was then esteemed the most powerful monarchy in Europe.

An attempt has been made to throw upon the first Parliament of Charles the charge of bad faith and want of generosity, because they did not, previously to all inquiry into grievances, grant to their young King a sufficient sum to enable him to prosecute with due vigour the war which they had brought on by their advice and encouragement. Now, even if it were true that the Commons were the authors of the war, still it would not follow that they did wrong in considering the abuses of the executive government, before they supplied it with fresh means of setting law and economy at defiance. A rigid inquiry into the public means and the public expenses was at all events justly due to the nation, of which they were the representatives. In point of fact, however, the war was not theirs, but Buckingham's; it had been refused to the parliamentary address of the people, and granted to the private pique of the favourite.*

* 'Instead of judiciously mollifying the misunderstandings betwixt the two Houses and the King, he (Buckingham) unadvisedly (for in Spain he had received some affronts upon some arrears he had made) runs the King into a war with that nation.' —*Warwick's Memoirs*, p. 13. (Sir Philip Warwick was a courtier.)

In considering the requests of the House of Commons from the commencement of the reign, we must never lose sight, as they never lost sight, of the ancient statutes of the realm. By Magna Charta it is established, that no freeman is to be imprisoned, or otherwise injured, but by the judgment of his peers, or the law of the land: therefore the judgments of the Star Chamber, and the commitments by the Sovereign's pleasure, were anomalous innovations. By a law of Edward I. no taxes were to be raised except by the authority of Parliament; therefore forced loans, benevolences, and monopolies were illegal. By two laws of Edward III. Parliaments were ordained to be held once a year or oftener; therefore an attempt to govern without the regular advice and continual authority of Parliament, amounted to a subversion of the established constitution of the State. Nor is it to any purpose, even as an *argumentum ad hominem*, to say that frequent violations of all these laws took place under the reign of particular sovereigns, especially the Tudors. The uninterrupted practice of trial by jury, the solemn usage of granting supplies in Parliament, and the frequent meetings of that high court, prove that none of these rights had become obsolete, and that the exertions of prerogative incompatible with them were irregularities to be amended, and not examples to be followed.

The great stand made by Hampden and his associates, against the payment of ship-money, was the immediate cause which prevented the establishment of arbitrary monarchy in England, as in France and Spain. He refused to pay to the King the sum of twenty shillings: the Judges in Westminster Hall decided against him. but the country was roused, and overbalanced by their sympathy the judgment of a court of law. Let us hear the testimony of Lord Clarendon on this subject; his reasoning is so

pregnant, that I make no apology for inserting it at
length. 'Lastly, for a spring and magazine that
should have no bottom, and for an everlasting supply of all occasions, a writ was framed in a form of
law, and directed to the sheriff of every county of
England, "to provide a ship of war for the king's
service, and to send it, amply provided and fitted,
by such a day, to such a place;" and with that writ
were sent to each sheriff instructions, that, "instead
of a ship, he should levy upon his county such a sum
of money, and return the same to the Treasurer of
the Navy for his Majesty's use," with direction in
what manner he should proceed against such as refused : and from hence that tax had the denomination
of *ship-money*, a word of a lasting sound in the
memory of this kingdom, by which for some years
really accrued the yearly sum of £200,000 to the
king's coffers : and it was in truth the only project
that was accounted to his own service. And, after
the continued receipt of it for about four years together, it was at last (upon the refusal of a private
gentleman to pay twenty or thirty shillings as his
share), with great solemnity, publicly argued before
all the judges of England in the Exchequer Chamber, and by much the major part of them the King's
right to impose asserted, and the tax adjudged lawful ; which judgment proved of more advantage and
credit to the gentleman condemned (Mr. Hampden)
than to the King's service.

'For the better support of these extraordinary
ways, and to protect the agents and instruments who
must be employed in them, and to discountenance
and suppress all bold inquirers and opposers, the
Council Table and Star Chamber enlarge their jurisdictions to a vast extent, "holding" (as Thucydides
said of the Athenians) "for honourable that which
pleased, and for just that which profited;" and being
the same persons in several rooms, grew both courts

of law to determine right, and courts of revenue to
bring money into the treasury; the Council Table
by proclamations enjoining to the people what was
not enjoined by the law, and prohibiting that which
was not prohibited, and the Star Chamber censuring
the breach and disobedience to those proclamations
by very great fines and imprisonment, so that any
disrespect to any acts of state, or to the persons of
statesmen, was in no time more penal, and those
foundations of right by which men valued their security, to the apprehension and understanding of wise
men, never more in danger to be destroyed.   •

   ‘ And here I cannot but again take the liberty to
say, that the circumstances and proceedings in those
new extraordinary cases, stratagems, and impositions,
were very unpolitic, and even destructive to the services intended.   And if the business of ship-money,
being an imposition by the State, under the notion
of necessity, upon a prospect of danger, which private
persons could not modestly think themselves qualified
to discern, had been managed in the same extraordinary way as the royal loan (which was the imposing
the five subsidies after the second Parliament spoken
of before) was, men would much easier have submitted to it, as it is notoriously known that pressure
was borne with much more cheerfulness before the
judgment for the King than ever it was after; men
before pleasing themselves with doing somewhat for
the King’s service, as a testimony of their affection,
which they were not bound to do, many really believing the necessity, and therefore thinking the
burthen reasonable; others observing that the advantage to the King was of importance, when the damage
to them was not considerable, and all assuring themselves that when they should be weary, or unwilling
to continue the payment, they might resort to the
law for relief, and find it.   But when they heard this
demanded in a court of law, as a right, and found it,

by sworn judges of the law, adjudged so, upon such
grounds and reasons as every stander-by was able to
swear was not law, and so had lost the pleasure and
delight of being kind and dutiful to the King, and
instead of giving, were required to pay, and by a
logic that left no man anything which he might call
his own; they no more looked upon it as the case of
one man, but the case of the kingdom, nor as an imposition laid upon them by the King, but by the
judges, which they thought themselves bound in
conscience to the public justice not to submit to. It
was an observation long ago by Thucydides, " that
men are more passionate for much injustice than for
violence, because," says he, " the one coming as from
an equal seems rapine, when the other, proceeding
from one stronger, is but the effect of necessity." So,
when ship-money was transacted at the Council Board,
they looked upon it as a work of that power they were
all obliged to trust, and an effect of that foresight
they were naturally to rely upon. Imminent necessity and public safety were convincing persuasions;
and it might not seem of apparent ill consequence
to them, that upon an emergent occasion the regal
power should fill up an *hiatus*, or supply an impo-
tency in the law. But when they saw in a court of
law (that law that gave them title to, and possession of, all that they had) reason of state urged as
elements of law, judges as sharp-sighted as secretaries
of state, and in the mysteries of state; judgment of
law grounded upon matter of fact, of which there
was neither inquiry nor proof, and no reason given
for the payment of the thirty shillings in question,
but what included the estates of all the standers-by;
they had no reason to hope that doctrine, or the pro-
moters of it, would be contained within any bounds,
and it was no wonder that they, who had so little
reason to be pleased with their own condition, were
no less solicitous for, or apprehensive of, the inconveniences that might attend any alteration.

'And here the damage and mischief cannot be expressed that the Crown and State sustained by the deserved reproach and infamy that attended the judges, by being made use of in this and like acts of power, there being no possibility to preserve the dignity, reverence, and estimation of the laws themselves, but by the integrity and innocency of the judges. And no question, as the exorbitancy of the House of Commons, in the next Parliament, proceeded principally from their contempt of the laws, and that contempt from the scandal of that judgment: so the concurrence of the House of Peers in that fury, can be imputed to no one thing more than to the irreverence and scorn the judges were justly in, who had been always before looked upon there as the oracles of the law, and the best guides to assist that House in their opinions and actions. And the Lords now thought themselves excused for swerving from the rules and customs of their predecessors (who, in altering and making of laws, in judging of things and persons, had always observed the advice and judgment of those sages) in not asking questions of those whom they knew nobody would believe, thinking it a just reproach upon them (who out of their courtship had submitted the difficulties and mysteries of the law, to be measured by the standard of what they called general reason, and explained by the wisdom of State) that they themselves should make use of the licence, which the others had taught them, and determine that to be law, which they thought to be reasonable or found to be convenient. If these men had preserved the simplicity of their ancestors, in severely and strictly defending the laws, other men had observed the modesty of theirs, in humbly and dutifully obeying them.

'Upon this consideration, it is very observable that, in the wisdom of former times, when the pre-

rogative went highest (as very often it hath been
swollen above any pitch we have seen it at in our
times), never any court of law, very seldom any
judge, or lawyer of reputation, was called upon to
assist in an act of power; the Crown well knowing
the moment of keeping those the objects of reverence and veneration with the people; and that
though it might sometimes make sallies upon them
by the prerogative, yet the law would keep the
people from any invasion of it, and that the king
could never suffer, whilst the law and the judges
were looked upon by the subject, as the asylum for
their liberties and security. And therefore you
shall find the policy of many princes hath endured
as sharp animadversions and reprehensions from the
judges of the law, as their piety hath from the
bishops of the church; as having no less influence
upon the people, under the reputation of justice, by
the one, than under the ties of conscience and religion, by the other. To extend this consideration
of the form and circumstances of proceeding in
cases of an unusual nature a little further; as it
may be most behoveful for princes, in matters of
grace and honour, and in conferring of favours upon
their people, to transact the same as publicly as
may be, and, by themselves or their ministers, to
dilate upon it, and improve the lustre by any addition, or eloquence of speech (where, it may be,
every kind word, especially from the prince himself,
is looked upon as a new bounty); so it is as requisite in matters of judgment, punishment, and
censure upon things or persons (especially when
the case, in the nature of it, is unusual, and the
rules in judging as extraordinary) that the same be
transacted as privately, and with as little noise and
pomp of words, as may be. For (as damage is much
easier borne, and submitted to by generous minds,
than disgrace) in the business of ship-money, and

many other cases in the Star Chamber and at the
Council Board, there were many impertinences,
incongruities, and insolencies, in the speeches and
orations of the judges, much more offensive, and
much more scandalous, than the judgments and
sentences themselves. Besides that, men's minds
and understandings were more instructed to discern
the consequence of things, which before they considered not. And undoubtedly my Lord Finch's
speech in the Exchequer Chamber made ship-
money much more abhorred and formidable than
all the commitments by the Council Table, and all
the distresses taken by the sheriffs in England : the
major part of men (besides the common uncon-
cernedness in other men's sufferings) looking upon
those proceedings with a kind of applause to themselves, to see other men punished for not doing as
they had done; which delight was quickly determined, when they found their own interest, by the
unnecessary logic of that argument, no less concluded
than Mr. Hampden's.

' He hath been but an ill observer of the passages
of those times we speak of, who hath not seen many
sober men, who have been clearly satisfied with
the conveniency, necessity, and justice of many sentences, depart notwithstanding extremely offended
and scandalized with the grounds, reasons, and
expressions of those who inflicted those censures;
when they found themselves, thinking to be only
spectators of other men's sufferings, by some unnecessary inference or declaration, in probable danger
to become the next delinquents.'

In this able summary we have a clear statement
of the causes of disagreement between the King and
his people, a demonstration of the tyranny as well
as the folly of the King, and a satisfactory explanation of the distrust of the people.

Lord Strafford, most unfortunately for himself,

for his King, and his country, fell out of the ranks
of the friends of liberty, and encouraged Charles to
persist in a resistance, which, perhaps, he might
otherwise have abandoned.   Devoid of all public
principle, and the slave of his malignant passions,
even the patriotism of Strafford is to be attributed
to his animosity to the Duke of Buckingham. With
a mixture of baseness and boldness seldom equalled,
he made himself the tool of his personal enemy, for
the purpose of breaking down all the safeguards of
the subject, contained in that petition of right,
which he had been among the foremost to ask for
and obtain.   He had not the excuse of saying that
he opposed new pretensions of the Commons. or
that he had left his friends when they went beyond
the bounds of legality and loyalty.   The measures
in which he assisted were violations of those laws
which it was his glory to have recognised and established.   He had himself said, ' We must vindicate :
—what ? new things ? no :—our ancient, legal, and
vital liberties, by reinforcing the laws enacted by
our ancestors ; by setting such a stamp upon them,
THAT NO LICENTIOUS SPIRIT SHALL DARE HENCE-
FORTH TO INVADE THEM.' When Deputy in Ireland, he made large promises to the Roman Catholics
to serve the King's present convenience, without
any intention of keeping them.   He solicited an
earldom, as the reward of his services, with an importunity that shows his ambition to have been of
the meanest kind. When in the north, he persecuted
with the utmost cruelty a Sir David Foulis, who had
omitted to pay him some trifling mark of respect.*
His conduct to Lord Mountnorris in Ireland was of
the same kind.   Upon the whole, he was a violent,
unprincipled man, destitute of any elevation of soul ;
for his request to the King to let him die can

---

* Macdiarmid's Lives, vol. ii. p. 121.

hardly be thought sincere; and there can be little
doubt that, till the end of his career, he expected
to rise to supreme power by pressing his foot upon
the necks of the people.   The intrepidity of his
character, his powers of eloquence, the virtues of
his private life, and, above all, the unjust manner
in which he was condemned to death, have rescued
his name from that abhorrence with which every
lover of his country would otherwise have regarded
it. The execution of Strafford casts a stain upon all
parties in the State.   The House of Commons were
instigated by passion; the House of Lords acted
from fear; and Charles, from some motive or other,
which, at all events, was not the right one. The
admission of the mob to overawe the deliberation of
Parliament was a sure sign that law was about to be
subverted.

In a contest between a king who refuses any limitation of his prerogative and a people who require it,
there can be no equitable agreement.   The ordinary
authority of a limited king, the power of calling out
an armed force, of proroguing and dissolving Parliament, cannot be entrusted to a sovereign whose main
object it is to destroy, by means of a party, all limitation.   William III., Anne, and the first sovereigns
of the House of Brunswick, might be safely entrusted with the prerogative, because no party in the
nation wished to see arbitrary power in their hands;
but Charles I. could not, because the Cavaliers would
have been unanimous in repealing the restrictions
imposed by Parliament.   Hence, when the popular
party had provided sufficient checks for the people
against a king, they were obliged to devise fresh
ones against King Charles.   After the plot of the
royalists in the army, and still more when war had
actually commenced, they were forced to ask for securities unnecessary and improper in ordinary times.
This forms the only justification of the law respect-

ing the militia, the bill for continuing the Parliament,
and the articles of Uxbridge. It was too much to
expect that the victorious party should lay down
their arms, quietly permitting the liberties they had
wrested from the Crown to be again surrendered by
a packed Parliament; and their own lives to be at
the mercy of a king to whom the power of the sword
had been again entrusted. The difficulty was in-
separable from the case. The king's prerogative is
so great, that nothing but the established opinion of
the whole nation can prevent his absorbing every
other authority in the State.

The events of the reign of Charles, if we apply the
principle I have laid down, are not difficult to account
for. The King commenced by quarrelling with Parliaments, and by an attempt to raise money without their
authority, punishing at the same time in an arbitrary
manner all who ventured to speak or write in behalf
of the ancient liberties of their country. In this
career he found, in high stations, and even on the
bench of judges, willing and unprincipled instruments.
At length he was obliged to call a Parliament. They
reformed abuses, punished the tools of tyranny, and
insisted upon keeping in their own hands the armed
force of the country, lest the King should use the
first moment after the dissolution of Parliament to
re-establish his illegal power. Charles preferred trying the chance of war to agreeing to these conditions.
In the course of the war, his papers, taken at the
battle of Naseby, convinced the Parliamentary party
that any concessions he might make would be, in his
mind, concessions to power and not to right, and
that he would think himself entitled, if he should
ever have the means, to repossess himself of his former
authority. It there came to light, that, at the time
when he treated with the two Houses, he entered a
protest in the council book declaring that they were
not a Parliament, in the face of his own designation

of them as such. Hence it appeared clear, that he
thought himself at liberty to use any means to re-
acquire that absolute power which he considered his
birthright. And here, in my mind, was the error
of Lord Clarendon and the constitutional Royalists.
Literally their proclamations and proposals were
more conformable to the Constitution than those of
their adversaries; it is evident that the Parliament
went, in their proposed terms of peace, beyond the
limits of the ancient laws of the kingdom, and
that they proposed to bind the prerogative of
Charles more closely than precedent, and example,
and legal rule would justify. But if we pass from the
letter to the spirit of the controversy, we shall see
that the Parliament were endeavouring, by new restrictions on royal power, to obtain a necessary security for the performance of the old, and that the
King was attempting, by the offer of plausible terms,
to get into his hands the power of destroying all opponents, and breaking down every barrier to his will.
The very conscience of Charles ordered him to deceive his enemies and make himself absolute.

In the course of the contest the period arrived
when, in the opinion of Hyde and Falkland, the King
had conceded enough, and the Parliament could not
without danger to the monarchy insist upon more.
Their views and their conduct have received the
high sanction of Mr. Hallam. After quoting the
words of Lord Chatham, ascribed to him by Mr.
Grattan and recorded in the motto of this chapter,
Mr. Hallam says, 'But as I know (and the history
of eighteen years is my witness), how little there
was on one side of such liberty as a wise man would
hold dear, so I am not yet convinced that the great
body of the Royalists, the peers and gentry of England, were combating for the cause of tyranny.'*

* Hallam's Const. Hist. of England, vol. ii. p. 146, ed. 1854.

E

The question, however, was not whether the peers
and gentry of England who followed Charles I. were
combating for the cause of tyranny. The question for
Hampden and Pym to consider was, whether, if they
trusted to Charles I., they had any security against
tyranny?   Charles V. of Germany had in the preceding century put down liberty and established
tyranny in Castile, Aragon, and Tuscany; Charles
VIII. of France had put down the representative
States of France, by which act, says De Comines,
he laid a heavy burthen on his soul.   Let us admit
to the great historical sagacity of Mr. Hallam that
the Grand Remonstrance 'was hardly capable of
answering any other purpose than that of reani-
mating discontents almost appeased, and guarding
the people against the confidence they were beginning to place in the King's sincerity.'*   Still the
question for Hampden and Pym to consider was,
whether they could advise or allow the people to
place confidence in the King's sincerity; and whether,
if they did so, the English Government would not be
reduced to the form which the French Government
had assumed under Louis XIII., and the Spanish
under Philip II.   There can be no doubt, I think,
that, in the Grand Remonstrance, the majority of
the Commons went beyond the limits which constitutional statesmen in ordinary times are bound to
respect.   But the King, it is clear, never intended to
observe the promises he made, or to keep within the
boundaries of any law which he swore to observe.
In his opinion breach of faith was wise policy,
arbitrary government just prerogative, and the punishment of any of his subjects who resisted his will
a rightful exercise of sovereignty.   The popular party
had to defend not only their liberties but their lives;
to wrestle with the violence and treachery of Charles
in order to preserve their own heads from the block

and their country from the slavery of France and Spain.*

Let us for a few moments, by way of illustration, contemplate the King's conduct in the attempt to arrest the Five Members.

He had recently made Falkland his secretary of state. That excellent man had been most reluctant to accept the office, and had only yielded to the urgent solicitations of his friend Mr. Hyde. He thus became the person chiefly responsible in the King's Council. Lord Clarendon, in a passage which has been omitted in the earlier editions of the History, and which has been placed in an Appendix by later editors, says, in reference to the plan for seizing the Five Members: ' In this restraint, the King, considering rather what was just than what was expedient, *without communicating it to any of his Council, and so not sufficiently weighing the circumstances and way of doing it, as well as the matter itself, resolved,*' &c. . . . 'and so on the third day of January, about two of the clock in the afternoon, he sent for Sir Edward Herbert, his attorney-general, and delivered a paper to him in writing, which contained a charge against those he meant to accuse; and commanded him forthwith to go to the House, and in his name to accuse those persons to the House of Peers of high treason. The attorney accordingly went, and standing up told their lordships, that he did in his Majesty's name and by his especial command, accuse the Lord Kimbolton, a member of that House, Mr. Pym, Mr. Denzicl Hollis, Mr. John Hampden, Mr. William Strode, and Sir Arthur Haslerig, of high treason and other misdemeanours,' &c.† This is very explicit. But Lord Clarendon goes further, and after saying who did not counsel the King, mentions ex-

* See especially Forster's 'Essays on the Grand Remonstrance' and on the 'Arrest of the Five Members,' who, by the way, never were arrested.

† Hist. App. vol. ii. p. 604.

E 2

pressly who did.   For after saying that Lord Digby
pretended to Lord Kimbolton that he did not know
from whom that counsel proceeded, Lord Clarendon
adds, ' Whereas he (Lord Digby) was the only person
who gave the counsel, named the persons, and particularly the Lord Kimbolton,' &c. *

Although both Mr. Hallam and Mr. Forster distrust Lord Clarendon's account, it is very difficult to
get rid of this explicit testimony.   If true, which I
cannot but believe, it shows Charles to have been utterly incapable of acting as the King of a constitutional
monarchy; it shows that, after inducing Lord Falkland, Sir John Culpepper, and Mr. Hyde to be his
advisers, he accused of high treason a peer and five
members of the House of Commons without their
previous knowledge.   There can be no doubt, I think,
that if by violence he had been able to procure the
condemnation of Pym and Hampden, he would
have beheaded them, as his son afterwards executed
Russell and Sydney.   Thenceforward the question
could be decided by arms alone; and while we may
find it difficult to pronounce that the cause of the
Commons was the cause of liberty, it is clear, I think,
that the cause of Charles was the cause of tyranny.
Charles was, in fact, incapable of keeping faith with
those who resisted his will.

When the civil war was at an end, and the King
was defeated by his subjects, a new party had arisen,
who went a step beyond the Presbyterians, both in
religion and politics.   The toleration which the
Presbyterians had originally asked, in matters of
dress and ceremonial, the Independents wished to
extend to faith and doctrine, and were thus the
earliest advocates of religious liberty.   The political
freedom which the Presbyterians hoped to enjoy under the ancient kingly government of England, the

* Hist. vol. ii. p. 129.

Independents thought would best be secured by a republican constitution. Their views with respect to the King were tinged by the most erroneous notions, drawn from Scripture. They imagined the Sovereign ought to die, that the sins of the war might be expiated by him, and not by them. Ludlow, in vindication of the King's execution, quotes, with self-applause, a passage from the Book of Numbers :—' That blood defileth the land, and the land cannot be cleansed of the blood that is shed therein, but by the blood of him that shed it.' He continues, ' And, therefore, I could not consent to the counsels of those who were contented to leave the guilt of so much blood upon the nation, and thereby to draw down the just vengeance of God upon all; when it was most evident that the war had been occasioned by the invasion of our rights, and open breach of our laws and constitution on the King's part.'* This reason, if good for any thing, makes it not only the right but the duty of a party victorious in civil war, to put to death their adversaries in cold blood. Strange infatuation!

Charles fell a sacrifice at last, because Cromwell had lost his popularity by negotiating with him, and wished to regain his credit with the army. He had found reason to suspect, in the course of the negotiation, that Charles, always insincere, had no real intention of being reconciled with him, and that the democratic troops whom he commanded were ready to break out into mutiny in consequence of his supposed apostasy. In his anger he said, ' I will cut off his head, with the crown upon it.' Cromwell's reconciliation was written in the King's blood. The deed, unjust and unwise as it must be esteemed, was, as Mr. Fox has said, not done in a corner. Elizabeth had not brought Mary to a public

* Ludlow's Memoirs, i. 267.

trial. Machiavel, in a chapter in which he shows,
' that a people accustomed to live under a prince,
if by any accident it becomes free, with difficulty preserves its liberty,' says that, ' for the difficulties and evils which must be encountered, there
is no more powerful, or more effectual, or more salutary, or more necessary remedy than to put to death
the sons of Brutus,' that is to say, to give a striking
example of severity against those who would be the
chiefs of a counter-revolution.[*] Such, no doubt, was
the manner in which Cromwell viewed the death of
Charles. It put an end to all hesitation, broke the
spirit of the Royalists, and pledged him for ever to
the enemies of the Stuarts.

By the nation at large the capital punishment of
the King was not demanded, and was very soon
lamented. When living, he was a baffled tyrant;
when dead, a royal martyr.

In fact, Charles was an obstinate, prejudiced, and
foolish man, possessed of considerable talents, exempt
from most vices, and possessing but few virtues.

The fate of the Parliament was much more important to the State than that of the King. From the
moment they were obliged to raise an army, their independence was in danger. The exclusion of the eleven
members was an act of force, destructive of legal
government. The diminution of their numbers, till
at last they consisted of not more than one hundred
members, and often less; their subordination to military members, and their taking refuge with the army,
were the preludes to their final exclusion and dissolution. The minds of men, which had been led into
the war by reverence and attachment to legal forms
and established precedents, were now left without
star or compass to guide them. Many, no doubt,
had supposed that a war against Charles I. was, like

* See Note (D) at the end of the volume.

a war against Henry III., a proper method of seek-
ing a redress of grievances.   They imagined that,
after some contest, the King would yield to his subjects in arms, and consent to resettle the nation.
But when they found all established authority subverted, all government made a matter of question
and conjecture, they knew not where to look for
liberty or for law.   In their utter inability to remedy
this confusion, they turned their eyes to the strongest, and sought · protection for their property and
their lives.

CHAPTER VIII.

CAUSES OF THE DISSOLUTION OF THE ENGLISH FORM OF GOVERNMENT UNDER CHARLES THE FIRST.

' Cunctas nationes et urbes, populus, aut primores, aut singuli regunt; delecta ex his et constituta reipublicæ forma laudari facilius quam evenire, vel, si evenit, haud diuturna esse potest.'—*Tacitus.*

Such was the deliberate judgment of Tacitus; a judgment, indeed, contradicted by the event, but which nevertheless is marked with the utmost perfection of thought, to which speculative reasoning could reach. Indeed, the history of the English Government, whilst it finally disproves, affords, in its course, ample justification for the opinion of Tacitus. Let us first consider what, in his profound mind, must have struck him as an obstacle to the success of a constitution made up of monarchy, aristocracy, and democracy. Was it the difficulty of forming a balance between the three powers? Surely not. Any schemer may lay out the plan of a constitution, in which the three powers shall each possess the authority, which in theory it ought to have. Indeed, there is scarcely any constitution which a man of sense can draw up that will not appear more plausible in this respect than the English. What more absurd, *à priori*, than that the King should have the sole power of making peace and war, whilst the Commons have the sole power of granting money?

It is not then the difficulty of balancing powers which has been overcome by the successful refutation which our history affords to the dictum of Tacitus. The grand problem which has been solved is, how the three powers shall come into action without dis-

turbance or convulsion. Many a workman can make
an automaton; few indeed can make him play at
chess. More than one sculptor can form a beautiful
statue; none but Prometheus could give it life.
The first disturbance which is likely to occur in
such a constitution as ours, is a collision between the
King, as sovereign, and Parliament formed of Lords
and Commons, considered as his advisers.   The
King, by the Constitution, has, and must have, the
power of naming his own servants, who are to carry
on the business of the executive government.   But
if these servants violate the laws, betray the cause,
mistake the interests, or squander the blood of their
country, it is as certain that the great council of
the nation must have the power of demanding and
enforcing their dismissal.   Two such opposite pretensions have naturally given rise to contest and
calamity.

In the reigns of Henry III., Edward II., and
Richard II., the misrule of the King's servants led
to the total subversion of his authority; and on more
than one occasion, commissioners were appointed
by Parliament, who exercised all the prerogatives
which the law has placed in the King.   Such provisions amount to a revolution in the State for the time
being.

After the accession of the House of Tudor,
another kind of revolution took place; and the
King, in his turn, swallowed up the powers of Parliament.

When Charles I. and his people began their dissensions, the great chasm, which separated one part
of the Constitution from another, again opened, and
threatened destruction to the State itself.   The first
opposition party, afterwards called the Presbyterians,
perceived the difficulty, and they imagined the
method of solving it since so successfully adopted.
Their expedient for ensuring a peaceable and long

duration to our limited monarchy was, that the
friends of the people should become the ministers
of the Crown.   Charles accepted the proposal, and
named the persons to be promoted; but was soon
disgusted with their advice, which ill accorded with
his own arbitrary notions.   He plunged rashly into
a civil war, and it quickly became too late to expect
accommodation.   New politicians naturally arose,
who maintained that it was folly to expend so much
blood for the uncertain hope of the King's sanction
to popular men and popular measures, when equal
benefits might be secured by abolishing the kingly
office altogether.   Thus the prophecy of Tacitus was
again accomplished; the nobles had overwhelmed
the King and the people; the King had domineered
over the nobles and the people; and now the people
extinguished the King and the nobles.   The three
powers of the realm, although each had a legal right
to its portion of authority, were still confounded,
trampling upon, and triumphing over one another.
The Constitution was still in its chaos.   The hour,
in which the elements were to be parted; in which
variety and contrast were to subsist without disorder;
when the King and the Commons were to separate
from, and yet support each other, was not yet
arrived.

At length, however, George I. and his successors
understood that harmony could only be obtained by
giving the confidence of the Sovereign, to men who
had already obtained the confidence of the House of
Commons.   The House of Stuart refused this essential condition, and lost the crown; the House of
Hanover complied with it, and may they long occupy
the throne !

CHAPTER IX.

CROMWELL, CHARLES THE SECOND, AND JAMES THE SECOND.

'But certainly it can never be worth the scratch of a finger to remove a single person, acting by an arbitrary power, in order to set up another with the same unlimited authority.'—*Ludlow.*

CROMWELL did much for his country. He augmented her naval glory, and made her name formidable to all the legitimate sovereigns, to whom his birth was a subject of derision : the smile on their faces was checked by the terror in their hearts. He made use of this wholesome intimidation to secure the liberty of foreign Protestants, and before he died he perceived the danger to Europe from the growth of the French power, which he thenceforth determined to restrain. At home he held the balance, upon the whole, evenly and steadily ; he gave to no sect the preponderance of State favour; and were it not that the questionable nature of his claim provoked rebellion, and made severity necessary to him, he would not have been a harsh ruler. Many would admire his character had he been born a sovereign, and some would praise him with more cordiality had he never become one.

The quarrels between the army and the Parliament, and the generals of the army among themselves, resemble more nearly the dissensions between the Senate and the soldiery of Rome on the choice of an Emperor, than anything else in modern history. They were the obvious preludes of a restoration. The Restoration was in its turn the presage of cruel executions, of violated faith, of gratuitous confidence,

of transient joy, and bitter disappointment. The
execution of Sir Harry Vane disgraced both Clarendon and Charles, and is one of the most cruel
and perfidious acts in English story. Nor in the
course of a long reign did the King perform anything to atone for the vengeance of the exile. He
trampled on the rights, and shed the best blood
of the nation, from which he had received the
crown: he crouched at the feet of France, at a
time when, of all others, England ought to have
resisted French ambition; and thus made himself
odious as a tyrant, only to become contemptible as
a slave. Yet the Restoration once determined upon,
there is much to be said for those who have been
constantly the objects of censure for bringing in
the King without conditions. The best security for
liberty was, that the King could have no revenue
without the consent of Parliament: if that power
were wisely reserved, no condition was necessary;
if it were improvidently parted with, none could be
effectual. Clarendon saw this, and did his duty to
his country. James also saw it, and hated Clarendon
for his conduct. Nor is the subsequent despotism of
Charles any proof of the improvidence of those who
restored him. The pension from Louis XIV. was
a resource which set at defiance all limitations on
kingly power : had William III. accepted pay from
the French king, he might have laughed at the
remonstrances of his Parliament.

The characters of Charles II. and Shaftesbury,
the one indolent and careless, the other violent and
rash, both inconsistent and unprincipled, gave a
variegated colour to the whole reign. A profligate
king, a religious people; excess of tyranny, excess
of faction; the worst of governments, the best of
laws; the triumph of party, the victory of despotism,
are all to be found in this short period. It is difficult to say for what reason Charles, a witty and
heartless man of pleasure, embarked in the vast

undertaking of making himself absolute. Perhaps his easy temper made him yield to the suggestions of his brother; perhaps he merely consented to the advice of his courtiers. The ready way of accomplishing this design, once adopted, was, as he conceived, to obtain money and troops from France. And as his father's throne had been overturned by religious fanaticism, he proposed to lay the foundation of his own upon a religion of blind obedience. The scheme not running on smoothly, however, he gave it up, partly from laziness, and partly from prudence,—contenting himself with charitable donations from France, from time to time. The virulent opposition of Shaftesbury, and the attempt to exclude his brother from the throne, again roused him to exertion; and when he had got rid of the Oxford Parliament, he seems to have determined never to call another.

This open suspension of all constitutional liberties, Parliament disused, the Press in the chains of a censorship, the Habeas Corpus Act little regarded, juries mere tools of tyranny, seems to have induced the friends of liberty to consider whether the time for resistance was not arrived.

Barillon relates, in his correspondence with his court, that the opposition were at this time divided into two parties, one led by Shaftesbury which preached rebellion, and the other, called the Southampton House Party, led by Lord Russell, which dissuaded all recurrence to force. Lord Russell, however, though he perceived that the people were disposed to be quiet; and though he knew, as he said on his trial, that a rebellion could not be made then, as formerly, by a few great men, seems to have been persuaded to attend a meeting at the house of Shepherd a wine-merchant, where the means of resistance were discussed. Lord Russell, as Lord Howard, was obliged to confess, said but little, and his offence was, as Lord Russell himself said, misprision of treason at most. For Lord Russell never seems to have changed the opinion he had formed against the proposed rising. But the evidence obtained was quite sufficient for the Court. By means of perjured witnesses, unjust constructions of law, and a servile jury, he was convicted and executed. Sydney, with even less evidence against him, followed Russell to the scaffold. Charles revelled in their blood, and went on in his riotous and vicious course. Thus, without activity or anxiety, by merely taking advantage of events as they arose, he procured for himself an authority which those of his family who made kingcraft their occupation, never possessed. He subdued the liberties of England, because it gave him less trouble than to maintain them, but still, the men who, though unsuccessful, could propose and carry through the House of Commons a bill for the exclusion of the next heir from the throne, evinced a spirit of honesty and freedom which no hazard could quell. The Bill of Exclusion was the legal warning of the Revolution.

The reign of Charles II., as has been observed, was an era of bad government, but of good laws. The Act of Habeas Corpus was the greatest of these laws. It is the best security for liberty ever devised; but it must not be supposed that it was invented during this reign. The writ itself is old, and various laws mention and confirm it, but it never was made capable of certain application till the time of Charles II.; and even after that time, the island of St. Nicholas, in Plymouth harbour, continued to be used as a state prison, beyond the reach of law.

James formed his designs on a very different mould from those of his brother. Rash, obstinate, and bigoted, he settled in his own mind that he would make himself an arbitrary king, and the Roman Catholic religion the religion of the state. Which of these projects he intended to finish first,

I own, does not seem to me to be worth very anxious
dispute, since it is very clear that both objects were
in his view.   He pursued them with that stupid
obstinacy which is so frequently fatal to a man
without talent. His want of sense was accompanied,
as it often is, with a want of heart; and as he could
not himself reason, he felt no pity for those who
could. ' It is in my power to pardon,' he said to
one of his victims. ' I know it is in your power,
but it is not in your nature to pardon,' was the
reply.   His opinions appeared to his own mind infallible truths, and he knew no mode of convincing
those who doubted, but by executions.

The faults of the House of Stuart may all be
traced to the scholastic pedantry of James I. Generally speaking, these sovereigns were not tainted
with the spontaneous cruelty, the unjust caprice, or
the sordid fear, which go to the formation of a tyrant.
But they were intimately persuaded that they were
destined to inherit arbitrary power ; and they went
on inflicting taxes and fines, and confiscation, and
death, from a bigoted persuasion of their own divine
right to govern as they pleased.   James I. drew
this notion from the old civil lawyers, and their
imitators in Italy and Germany.   He bequeathed it
to his son, who lost his head in consequence of his
perseverance in maintaining it. His grandson James,
in trying to carry it fully into execution, fell unpitied from the throne. The whole family have since
been exiles, and the last male descendant of James II.
died a cardinal at Rome.   This was paying dear for
the failure of an erroneous theory ; but England
would have paid a still dearer price had it succeeded.
The House of Tudor had made Parliaments their
organs, and had succeeded.   The House of Stuart
had endeavoured to govern in defiance of Parliament,
and failed.   Charles I. died on the scaffold, and
James II. in exile in the cause of unsuccessful
tyranny.

CHAPTER X.

THE REVOLUTION.

'He who wishes to reform an ancient state, and constitute it into a free country, ought to retain at least the shadow of the old forms.' —*Machiavel.*

THERE are few examples of revolutions which have led to immediate good. This consideration ought to induce men who have any influence over their countrymen to be very cautious how they engage in projects which may put to hazard all that exists, unless they have a very sure prospect of obtaining what is proposed.

The Revolution of 1688 appears to my mind the perfection of boldness, and of prudence.

The Tory party in general were not so much alarmed at the subversion of liberty, as at the innovations introduced in religion. 'Church and King,' in the order in which those words are used, was their motto and their faith. In their anxiety to preserve the Church, they appealed to the Prince of Orange; but they never intended he should supplant the legitimate King. The Earl of Nottingham proposed in the House of Lords that the Prince of Orange should be regent; the Duchess of Marlborough bears testimony to her husband's surprise upon finding that the crown was to be transferred to William; and the Earl of Danby avowed, upon Sacheverell's trial, that it had never been his wish or expectation that James should be dethroned.

Had those who invited the Prince of Orange to England satisfied themselves with obliging James to call a Parliament, the rest of his reign must have passed in continual jealousy. It would have been still more absurd to have given William the power, and James the title of king. That title, which is not the private patrimony of an individual, can only belong properly to the person who is qualified to exercise the office. The Princess of Orange being the nearest of blood (except the infant son of James), and a Protestant, the Prince of Orange (himself the nephew of James) was the fit person to be king. He had, besides, this merit in the eyes of the Whigs, that his right to the crown, and the right of the people to their liberties, were thenceforth to be placed on the same foundation, and opposed to the same Pretender.*

The more violent of the Whigs were not satisfied with changing the dynasty. They looked to extensive reforms both in Church and State: they wished to change our ecclesiastical laws, and remodel the House of Commons. Others desired to abolish the monarchy, and constitute a republic. But the leaders of the Revolution knew, with Machiavel, that nothing so much tends to give stability to a change of government, as an adherence to old forms and venerated institutions. They knew that, to enter upon a discussion of new projects, however plausible, at such a moment, and in the face of a large adverse party, would expose their work to be presently overthrown, and could only lead to endless conflicts and unsatisfactory decisions. For these reasons, the leaders of the Revolution contented themselves with confirming, by solemn statute, all the ancient liberties of England, and protesting against those particular violations of them which had taken place in the late reign. Whether the securities they took were sufficient to form the basis

---

* Had the crown continued in the House of Stuart, it would have been, I believe, at the present day (1865), on the head of the ex-Duke of Modena.

of a good government, or whether they were but
half-measures, satisfying the eye, but not the appetite, we shall see in the following chapters.

It is curious to read the conferences between the
Houses on the meaning of the words ' deserted ' and
' abdicated ; ' and the debate in the Lords, whether
or not there is an original contract between king and
people.   The notion of a tacit contract, by which
the king and his subjects are to be guided in their
relations with each other, is certainly not correct.
The king, without any contract whatever, is bound
to carry into execution the laws which are entrusted
to his care.   This is the simple duty of his office.
But if at any time the people should require of him
new liberties, he is bound to give them the species
of government which the state of the nation, and
the knowledge of the age, may demand.   The foundation of every durable government is the common
consent of the realm.

The notion of an original contract, however, was
the theory of the friends of liberty in every part of
Europe.   The Spaniards had asserted it in the
beginning of their contest with Charles V.; and,
indeed, it had a foundation in the origin of all the
feudal governments.   The only debate in the House
of Lords was between those who asserted the original contract and those who maintained the divine
right of kings.   In short, the question was, whether
or not kings derived their power from the people.
It was decided that they did ; and the next resolution
was, in substance, that James had abused that
power, and had thereby become amenable to the
nation.   For such is the clear meaning of the vote
of the two Houses, declaring that James, having
broken the original contract between king and
people, having violated the fundamental laws, and
having withdrawn himself out of the kingdom, had
abdicated the throne, and that the throne was thereby

vacant. Nothing could be more creditable to the temper and justice of the English people than the calm discussion of this question—nothing more decisive of their wisdom and love of freedom than the judgment which they pronounced.

CHAPTER XL

DEFINITIONS OF LIBERTY.

'The liberties of nations are from God and nature, not from kings.'—*Algernon Sidney*.

MANY definitions have been given of liberty. But none of these are comprehensive enough, and indeed liberty is not all of one kind. A nation may have one kind, and be quite deprived of another. The greatest advantages, however, which a community can procure to itself, by uniting under one government, may, perhaps, be contained under the titles of Civil Liberty, Personal Liberty, and Political Liberty.

By civil liberty, I mean the power of doing that, and that only, which is not forbidden by the laws. This definition comprehends the security of person and of property.

By personal liberty, I mean the power of doing that which in itself is harmless, as speaking or writing, and of which the abuse only is criminal. Religious freedom and eligibility to office may also be comprehended under this head.

By political liberty, I mean the acknowledged and legal right of the people to control their government, or to take a share in it.

Each of these kinds of liberty should be allowed to exist in as great a proportion as possible. They were all comprehended by Cromwell's Representative under the names of 'the peace and security, the rights and privileges of the people.'

CHAPTER XII.

CIVIL LIBERTY.

'The laws of England are the birthright of the people thereof; and all the Kings and Queens who shall ascend the throne of this realm, ought to administer the government of the same, according to the said laws; and all their officers and ministers ought to serve them respectively according to the same.'—*Statute* 12 & 13 *Will. III.* c. 2.

CIVIL liberty comprehends the security of person and property. For if a man is only allowed to do that which the law permits, he is liable to punishment should he raise his hand against his neighbour in violation of law; and if he is free to do all that the law does not forbid, he cannot be called in question for a legal exercise of his rights.

'In walking over a large field with about thirty attendants and slaves, Hassan told the owner that he had done wrong in sowing the field with barley, as water-melons would have grown better. He then took some melon-seed out of his pocket, and giving it to the man, said, "You had better tear up the barley, and sow this." As the barley was nearly ripe, the man, of course, excused himself from complying with the Kashef's command. "Then I will sow them for you," said the latter; and ordered his people immediately to tear up the crop, and lay out the field for the reception of the melon-seed. The boat was then loaded with the barley, and a family thus reduced to misery, in order that the governor might feed his horses and camels for three days on the barley-stalks.' * Every one must feel that, in a

* Burckhardt's Travels in Nubia, vol. i. p. 94.

country where this could happen, there can be no
security for property.

Tavernier tells us of a king of Persia, who ordered
the heads of all the beasts he had killed in one day's
chase to be set up in the form of a pyramid. When
it was done, the architect came and told him that
the pyramid was complete, with the exception of one
large head for the summit. 'I think yours will do
very well for that,' said the king; and to this brutal
joke sacrificed an innocent man. In such a country
there can be no security for life.

When Athens was in its splendour, there arose
that detestable class of men, who gained their liveli-
hood by informing against the best and worthiest of
their fellow-citizens, and holding out to the rapacity
of a sovereign mob the temptation of a rich forfeiture. It should never be forgotten by those who
are disposed to admire a democratic government,
that the word *sycophant* had its origin in the most
popular of all democracies.

Nicophemus and Aristophanes, public function-
aries, were accused of malversation. On some
change in the government, they were imprisoned,
and secretly made away with without a trial. Their
property was confiscated. The amount disappoint-
ing the greedy accusers, a prosecution was instituted
against the brother of the widow of Aristophanes
for embezzling the sum that was deficient. What is
the language of his advocate upon his trial? An
appeal to feelings of justice and generosity? No:
he plainly intimates the rapacity of the judges. 'I
know how difficult it will be,' he says, 'to refute
the received opinion of the great riches of Nicophemus. The present scarcity of money in the city,
and the wants of the treasury which the forfeiture
has been calculated upon to supply, will operate
against me.' *

* Mitford's History of Greece, vol. v. p. 96.

During the reign of terror in France, men were put to death for relationship to suspected persons, for acquaintance with the condemned, for having wept at the death of the King, and a thousand vague and trivial offences.

Thus unlimited despotism and uncontrolled democracy are found to be equally unfavourable to the existence of civil liberty. The examples I have adduced are extreme cases; but in every state, where either the monarch, the aristocracy, or the multitude is allowed to have exorbitant power, civil liberty is incomplete; that is to say, a subject of such a government cannot be sure that, even when he obeys all the laws, he may not be taxed or imprisoned by arbitrary mandate. Witness the gabelle and the Bastille of the French monarchy, the prisons of Venice, and the banishments of Florence. All these states were professedly under the government of laws, but to some of their citizens these laws were but a shield of paper. It may, however, generally be observed, that the violations of justice in a monarchy are more frequent; in a democracy, more striking. It seems more natural and tolerable that a king, revered as a kind of superior being, should oppress a slave, than that an assembly of freemen should maltreat an equal.

Let us now see how civil liberty is provided for in England. It is declared by the King, in *Magna Charta*, the earliest and the best law upon our statute-book, that no freeman shall be any way destroyed, unless by the judgment of his peers, or the law of the land: '*Nullus liber homo aliquo modo destruatur, nisi per legale judicium parium suorum, aut per legem terræ.*' This admirable law, however, was frequently violated in times of disorder. It was renewed very frequently; but notwithstanding these renewals, and the claims of the Petition of Right, the subject had no effectual remedy against

wrong, till a law of Charles II. provided means for
an easy execution of the ancient writ of *Habeas
Corpus*. This Act, well known by the name of the
Habeas Corpus Act, commands, that upon written
complaint from or on behalf of any person confined
in prison, except on a charge of high treason or
felony, the Lord Chancellor and the Judges shall,
upon pain of forfeiting the sum of £500, deliver a
writ, ordering him to be brought into court.   The
writ is to be delivered, and the prisoner is to be
brought into court within twenty days; and if his
offence is bailable, he is to be discharged upon offer-
ing bail, and entering into a recognizance to appear
at his trial.   If his offence is charged as treason or
felony, and if the prosecution is not followed up
within the second term after his commitment, he is
to be discharged.   If no offence is specified in the
warrant of commitment, his imprisonment is illegal,
and he must be instantly discharged.   Besides this
protection, the Judges go into the country twice
every year, with a commission of gaol-delivery for
clearing all the prisons.   These securities, however,
availed not against James II., who employed the
island of St. Nicholas, in Plymouth harbour, for a
State prison, in the same manner as Cromwell had
before made use of the isle of Jersey.   Since the
Revolution, however, the Act of *Habeas Corpus*,
when in operation, has always been found of power
to protect the subject. Of the suspensions of that law,
I shall speak hereafter ; I would now remark only,
that the suspensions prove the practical efficacy of
the *Habeas Corpus* Act, as much as the renewals of
Magna Charta prove the practical inefficacy of that
great compact.   All the precautions taken to prevent
arbitrary imprisonment, however, would be worth
nothing if the trial when it took place could be un-
fairly and oppressively conducted.   To prevent so
dreadful an evil, we have the institution of trial by

jury. The sheriff, a man of substance in the county, returns from twelve to twenty-three freeholders (usually men of property), to serve as a Grand Jury. To them a bill of indictment, or accusation, is preferred; they examine witnesses in support of it; and unless they find probable grounds to proceed upon, the bill of indictment is thrown out, and the prosecution cannot be persisted in. To form the second, or Petty Jury, who are to try the cause, the sheriff returns the names of freeholders, or persons otherwise qualified according to law, to the number of not less than forty-eight, nor more that seventy-two. The names are put into a glass, and the twelve first drawn form the jury. At this period, the prisoner may challenge any whom he can reasonably accuse of partiality, or whose characters have been degraded by the sentence of a court of justice. In treason, he may challenge peremptorily thirty-five. When the trial is over, the twelve jurymen remain enclosed together without separating or conferring with others, till they can deliver a unanimous verdict.

Nothing can appear less perfect in theory than the institution of trial by jury. What can be more liable to abuse, it may be said, than the choice given to the sheriff, an officer appointed by the Crown? What more prejudicial to an accused person than the previous decision of twenty-three men of wealth and figure, formed upon hearing one side of the question only? What more likely to create confusion of right and wrong, than to require a unanimous verdict, and thus make the guilt or innocence of a prisoner depend on the mental incapacity, the moral obstinacy, or even the physical strength of a single juror? These objections I shall not attempt to answer; the veneration which the English have for trial by jury, like the admiration they entertain for Shakspeare, must be taken as a practical proof of its excellence; and it would be as absurd to at-

tempt to demonstrate that a people long free attribute
their freedom to a slavish institution, as to endeavour, like Voltaire, to prove that a people long civilised admire barbarous and ridiculous poetry.   It
must be admitted, however, with respect to trial by
jury, that it is liable to be perverted in bad times,
and that the condemnation of Sydney was an act
which equalled, if it did not surpass in violence, the
attainder of Strafford.   This institution, therefore, is
rather an instrument of liberty in her prosperity,
than a protector in her adversity; it is to be trusted
as the companion, but not to be relied upon as the
survivor of free parliaments, and a free press.   During
the reigns of Henry VIII. and Charles II. juries
were effectually perverted, and became the submis-
sive organs of tyranny.   But, since the Revolution,
the general respect that has prevailed for right and
justice, has prevented abuse, and, upon the whole,
juries have kept the balance even between the safety
of government and the liberty of the subject.

Trial by jury leaves, properly speaking, but little
power to the judge.   When the trial is over, the
judge recapitulates the evidence, and explains the
law upon the subject.   The decision upon the facts
is left entirely to the jury.   If they find the prisoner
guilty, the judge pronounces the sentence affixed by
law.   This arrangement, the best ever imagined,
leaves nothing to the judge but what is absolutely
required, and cannot easily be abused.   It is necessary, for the sake of regularity and accuracy of
judgments, that some one present should have that
knowledge of the laws, which can only be acquired
by long and exclusive study : and it is much better
that he should speak on the trial, than that he should
assist at the decision, for numbers are ready at the
bar to observe lest he misrepresent the law.

Notwithstanding this proper division, juries, in
the time of Charles II., were controlled and dictated

to by court judges, who were appointed and removed, in proportion to their subserviency. To prevent this abuse, an Act passed, early in the reign of King William, providing that judges should be appointed during good behaviour, and should be removable only by addresses from both Houses of Parliament,—an Act which completely answered its purpose of making the judicial power independent of the executive, and gave an authority to the name and character of an English judge, which it had never before possessed. We must not forget, however, that there is yet another security which is, perhaps, more valuable than any. The trial is public, and the accused is brought face to face with his accuser, before the country. This publicity controls both judge and jury.

Security of property is also well provided for. By a law of Edward I. it was enacted, that no aids or taxes should be taken from the subject, but by common assent of the realm. What this means we shall see in a following chapter. It having been found, notwithstanding this law, that the King, by means of the Star Chamber, was able to impose arbitrary penalties, it was enacted in the law which abolished that tribunal, that it should not be lawful for the King in council, by English bill, or any arbitrary way whatsoever, to call in question the property of the subject.

The courts in Westminster Hall, the circuit of the judges in the country, the body of the magistrates, consisting of the principal gentlemen of the county in which they act, giving their perpetual attendance at home, and meeting in quarter and petty sessions to administer the law gratuitously,*

---

* I have inserted this word, as we hear the unpaid magistrates so highly praised for disinterestedness. They have power, however, for their trouble, and a power which the barons of old struggled so hard to possess and exercise.

are all instruments engaged in executing that noble
article of the Great Charter,—' We will not deny,
nor delay, nor sell right or justice to anyone.' We
have reason to rejoice in the observation of De
Lolme, who remarked with pleasure, within the
precincts of the King's residence at Windsor, inscribed in an enclosed space, — ' Whoever tres-
passes on these grounds, will be prosecuted according to law ; ' thus claiming for the King the common
security of the poorest cottager in the land. Nor
has it been found, that the exalted station of the
royal family has ever enabled them to trespass on
the property, or disturb the private rights of individuals.*

* See Note (E) at the end of the volume.

CHAPTER XIII.

PERSONAL LIBERTY.

'Per me ho adottata nell' intero la legge d' Inghilterra, ed a
mi attengo; nè fo mai nessuno scritto che non potesse liberissima-
mente e senza biasimo nessuno dell' autore essere stampato nella
beata e veramente sola libera Inghilterra. Opinioni, quanti se ne
vuole: individui offesi, nessuni: costumi, rispettati sempre. Questo
sono stato, e saranno sempre le sole mie leggi; nè altro se ne
può ragionevolmente ammettere, nè rispettare.'

ALFIERI, *Vita*, t. ii. p. 133.

NEXT to civil liberty, in the order I have laid
down, comes personal liberty. By personal liberty,
I mean the freedom from restraint upon actions
which are not criminal in themselves. The chief
liberties of this class are the freedom of speaking
and writing, and freedom of conscience in matters
of religion. The absence of all exclusive personal
privileges, such as signorial rights, exemption from
taxes, monopoly of civil and military offices, must
be reckoned also in this class; for that which is a
privilege to one class of men is a restraint upon
another.

The liberty of speaking and writing was allowed
in ancient times, not only in free States, but wherever despotism fell into the hands of a mild sovereign; and so palling to the ear is the continual
monotony of praise, that in the absolute kingdom
of Persia, where the sovereign is thought to be the
very image of the Divinity, a jester was always
kept, whose business it was to tell the truth, and
yet to tell it in such a way that the King might,
if he pleased, laugh at the fable, and neglect the
moral. The fool of modern kings was a creature

invented for the same purpose. Such were the de-
vices which sovereigns adopted for the sake of hearing a little free observation, at a time when nations
were divided into the court and the country. The
court never spoke of the King's actions but to praise
them, and the country never spoke of them at all.
Such was still the state of Europe when Machiavel
wrote 'The Prince,' and he takes it for granted,
in that much-debated work, that the mass of the
people can be kept wholly ignorant of the real character of their sovereign. The progress of knowledge has overturned the basis of his whole system,
and were Machiavel to write at this day, he would
probably recommend to kings a totally different line
of conduct.

The policy pursued by the governments of Europe in later times has been extremely various.
Austria and Spain long assumed as a principle that,
as a general freedom of discussion must produce
much calumny on private persons, much seditious
writing against authority, and much matter offensive to morality and religion, it is prudent for the
State, and humane to the writers, to place the press
under the guardianship of censors appointed by the
government. By this method, it was asserted, all
fair and temperate discussion may be allowed; libels
are crushed in the egg, before they have worked
mischief; and public justice is spared the necessity
of inflicting severe punishment. But in fact there
is no method of restraining the abuse of the press
previous to publication which does not control the
use: the imperfect civilisation of Austria and Spain
bear witness to this truth. The government of
France, without sanctioning so strict a system of
ignorance as that of Spain, refused to allow publication without restraint. But the mitigated pro-
hibitions of the French censors in some degree
contributed to spread the false notions which ob-

tained vogue at the beginning of their revolution. Everything might be attacked by an equivocal jest, although nothing could be combated by direct reasoning; and the able writers of the last century soon found that the best institutions were as open to a sneer as the grossest abuses.　General declamation and affected sentiment were allowed, till the opinions of men fell into general confusion.　At length the throne was shaken, the altar sapped, and a mine ready to burst under their foundations, before anyone had had a fair opportunity of urging an argument in their behalf.　The policy of England has been, since the Revolution, completely the reverse both of the Spanish and the French.　During the reign of Elizabeth, as we have seen, the most severe punishments were awarded to libellers. During the reign of James I. and the early part of Charles I., a censorship was established by means of a License Act.　Cromwell adopted the same policy, which was continued by Charles and James. The License Act of the latter expired in 1694, and has never been renewed.　The government of England thus deliberately, not in the heat of the revolution itself, but without clamour, without affectation, without fear, and at once, adopted a free press. The principle then sanctioned is, that as speaking and writing and printing are things in themselves indifferent, every person may do as he pleases, till, by writing what is calumnious or seditious, he offend against the laws.　That a great advantage is afforded to personal liberty by the existence of a free press, is what no man can doubt.　Reflection may convince us that this liberty is also beneficial to the community at large.　Genius can never exert its powers to their full extent when its flight is limited and its direction prescribed.　Truth can never be ascertained when all discussion is regulated by those who hold the reins of government, to whom the discovery of truth is not always acceptable. Neither is it true, as some foreigners imagine, that no government can withstand the daily attacks of the press. Men know when they are prosperous, and although they love to grumble at their rulers, the most brilliant rhetoric will not persuade a nation already in possession of liberty that it is wise to risk a civil war in order to obtain a change in the form of government. Popular clamour, if it be no more than clamour, is more noisy than formidable, and by a wise, beneficent government may be safely endured. The slanderous whisper of the Emperor of Rome's courtiers was ten times more dangerous to a good minister than is the angry hubbub of the King of England's people.

The right of petition is another right by which men are enabled to express their opinions, and to set forth their grievances. When Charles II. was engaged in a contest with his Parliament, this right was much discountenanced; and it was therefore declared by the Bill of Rights — ‘That it is the right of the subject to petition the King, and that all commitments and prosecutions for such petitioning are illegal.’ This right is still a very important one.

The rights we have now been stating, viz. those of printing and petitioning, invest the people with no actual power or authority. But they are of infinite importance in controlling and guiding the executive power. The influence of a free press, however, has never been so thoroughly felt as it is now, and therefore, till I come to recent times, I shall defer any further observation respecting it.

We come next to religious liberty, upon which subject the authors of the Revolution did as much as they could, and by their maxims laid the foundation of much more.

We have seen how little of the spirit of charity and forbearance mixed with the reformation of Henry VIII. It is painful to think that Cranmer continued the same severity during the short reign of Edward, and that an unfortunate woman was burnt for some incomprehensible refinement respecting a mystery of our faith.

When the Papal power was for the second time overthrown by the accession of Elizabeth, no progress was made towards the establishment of religious liberty. From this time dates the great schism amongst the English Protestants, known, according to their respective parties, by the names of Puritans and Conformists. A congregation of refugees, settled at Frankfort in the reign of Queen Mary, omitted in their worship the Litany, and some other parts of King Edward's liturgy. A Dr. Coxe arriving there from England, interrupted the service by a loud response, omitted in the new form of prayer. After some contest, and some expedients not quite worthy of the cause of religion, he succeeded in driving his opponents from the place, and establishing the liturgy of Edward. Other congregations, however, had made similar reforms, and when the exiles returned to England there arose an open difference between the Conformists, among whom were Grindal, Parker, &c., and the Puritans, who reckoned among them John Knox, Bale, Fox the author of the 'Book of Martyrs,' &c. The chief deviations introduced by the Puritans in practice respected the use of the surplice, the cope, the cross in baptism, and kneeling at the communion; but in principle there was a much wider schism. The Conformists acknowledged the Church of Rome as a true church, though corrupted; and they maintained that the King, as supreme head of the Church, had authority to correct all abuses of order and worship. The Puritans abjured the Church of Rome

G

altogether, and contended that it belonged not to the King, but to assemblies of the reformed clergy, to pronounce upon ceremonies and worship.[*]

It is not surprising that Elizabeth should have warmly espoused the cause of the Conformists. Naturally inclined to the splendours of the Roman Catholic service, and fully impressed with the fulness of her authority in the Church as well as in the State, she proceeded to punish the adverse sect. In doing this she acted upon a principle common to both sides,—that uniformity of faith and uniformity of worship were absolutely necessary. Agreeably to these notions, she obtained an Act of Parliament for instituting a Court of High Commission, and invested them with powers of fine and imprisonment which the law had not granted. She offered bishoprics to Miles Coverdale, Knox, and others of the Puritan faith, but in vain ; nothing, she found, could shake their constancy. Many of the most upright reformers attested their sincerity by their deaths. Barrowe, Greenwood, and Penry were amongst the most distinguished of the reformers capitally punished for their religious or ecclesiastical faith.

James I., very soon after his accession, gave a sufficient warning that he was an enemy to toleration. For, having appointed a Conference at Hampton Court between the Conformists and the Puritans, he took upon himself to manage the controversy for the former, and after three days' dispute, speaking amid the applause and flattery of the clergy, he turned to their opponents and said, ‘ If this be all your party have to object to the established religion of this kingdom, I will make them conform, or expel them out of the land.'

He was as good as his word. The Court of High Commission required the Dissenters to appear before

* Neale's ‘History of the Puritans,' vol. i. p. 144. See Note (F) at the end of the volume.

them, and to affirm solemnly upon oath that which they could not conscientiously believe. Ruinous fines and long imprisonments were the penalties of disobedience. One person, accused of denying the divinity of Christ, and another charged with sixteen heretical opinions, were burnt alive.

Oliver Cromwell was raised by a sect which, the first in England, perhaps in Europe, made toleration a part of its doctrine. But it was a toleration of opinions, like the Presbyterian toleration of vestments, intended chiefly for their own convenience. Cromwell himself, who probably carried as far as any man of his day a wish for indulgence, yet in the Instrument of Government, after a solemn declaration in favour of religious liberty, finishes the article on this subject by expressly excluding Papists and Prelatists from the benefit of the general freedom. Thus, with liberality in profession, the law, in fact, authorises persecution.

The declaration of Charles II., from Breda, offered new hopes of a mild and conciliatory system. But such hopes were grievously baffled by the laws passed soon after his accession. Those who attended any meeting for religious purposes 'in any other manner than was allowed by the liturgy or practice of the Church of England,' were punished for the first offence by £5 fine and three months' imprisonment; for the second, by £10 fine and six months' imprisonment; and for the third, by transportation, and death in case of return.* By the Five Mile Act, dissenting clergymen were forbidden to preach within five miles of a market-town. During the last years of Charles, these laws against Dissenters were rigorously enforced.

At length, by the Act of 1 William and Mary, c. 18, intituled 'An Act for exempting their Majes-

* See note (G) at the end of the volume.

ties' Protestant subjects, dissenting from the Church of England, from the penalties of certain laws,' commonly called the Toleration Act, all persons who took the oaths of allegiance and supremacy, and subscribed the declaration against Popery, were exempted from penalties; and meeting-houses were regularly registered, provided the service was performed with doors unlocked. Since that time the Protestant Dissenters of England have been allowed to perform their worship in the manner which they think most acceptable to God. At the same period, an attempt was renewed, which had been made in the reign of Charles II., to bring about a reconciliation between the Conformists and Dissenters. In this pious work, called the 'Comprehension,' Tillotson and Burnet took an earnest and Christian share. They proposed to amend the liturgy in several points; to divide the services; to leave out parts of the prayers which had given offence, and, by a few wise and reasonable concessions, to restore to the Church a large multitude of her banished children. Articles for this purpose were prepared; but the clergy, in convocation, defeated these benevolent schemes, and insisted on exclusion and discord.

Among the concessions made to religious liberty, there were none in favour of the Roman Catholics. On the contrary, new laws were passed, of excessive severity, tending to render the Roman Catholics poor and ignorant, heaping penalty upon penalty, and making them, as it were, slaves among a nation of freemen. Yet it must not be supposed that a nation so humane as the English acted in this harsh and unusual spirit of bitterness without deep provocation. The reigns of Elizabeth, of James I., of Charles II., and of James II. had been disturbed by Roman Catholic plots more or less sanguinary, some using as their means the assassination of the sovereign, others the introduction of a foreign army,

but all tending to extinguish the liberties, and destroy the independence, of England. That the
precautions adopted by the English Parliament were
wise, I will not affirm; but I cannot deny that they
were the result of many injuries.

Under the head of Personal Liberty should be
placed eligibility to offices civil and military. The
policy of the great States of the world has been often
narrow, illiberal, and unjust, upon this branch of
true freedom. Rome excluded for centuries her
plebeian genius and valour from the rewards due to
distinguished services. Modern France, at first, by
custom of administration, and afterwards by positive
edict, closed the door of military eminence to all
ambition that was not of noble descent. Venice
gave the command of her fleets to her patricians,
and of her armies to strangers. England rejects all
these odious distinctions of class and birth. The
ploughman's son may climb to the command of her
military and naval forces; to the post of Lord High
Chancellor, or the dignity of Archbishop of Canterbury. This just and wise equality has amply
rewarded, by its effects, the State which established
it. Not only has England reaped the benefit of
talents which would otherwise have been lost in obscurity, but, by this impartial share in the dignities
of the State, society, instead of forming two hostile
classes of noble and plebeian, has been united in one
compact power. In a well-known conference between the Lords and Commons, it was stated, by Lord
Somers, and other managers on the part of the
Lords, that there can scarcely be a more unhappy
condition for an Englishman, than to be rendered
incapable of serving his country in any civil or
military office. It must be observed, however, that
religious disabilities have been well known to the
law of England. Protestant Dissenters were excluded from office by the Test and Corporation Acts.

And although, for more than a century, they have
been tacitly admitted, by an Indemnity Bill passed
every year, in favour of any who may have omitted
to take the oaths, their freedom cannot be said to
have been complete before the year 1828.   The
Roman Catholics, it has already been observed, were
likewise excluded from all power.   By the various
Acts of Charles II., William III., and Anne, all
offices, civil and military, and even the doors of the
Houses of Lords and Commons, were shut against
them.   It was not till 1829 that these barriers were
opened, and Roman Catholics admitted to Parliament, and the leading offices of the State.

CHAPTER XIV.

POLITICAL LIBERTY.

'I believe the love of political liberty is *not* an error; but, if it is one, I am sure I shall never be converted from it, and I hope you never will. If it be an illusion, it is one that has brought forth more of the best qualities and exertions of the human mind than all other causes put together; and it serves to give an interest in the affairs of the world, which without it would be insipid.'—*Fox, Letter to Lord Holland.*

THE two kinds of liberty of which we have spoken, viz. civil and personal liberty, have existed to a certain degree in States which we usually term despotic. The monarchies of modern Europe have all been more or less governed by fixed laws, deriving their sanction from prescription. The monarchy of Prussia, which is altogether unlimited, allowed, from the time of Frederick II., great latitude of religious and political discussion.

It is clear, however, that the definition of liberty, which describes a man as free who is governed by laws, is incomplete. So long as the supreme power of the State is placed in hands over which the people have no control, the tenure of civil and personal liberty must be frail and uncertain. The only efficient remedy against oppression is for the people to retain a share of that supreme power in their own possession. This is called political liberty. And what is called a love of liberty, means the wish that a man feels to have a voice in the disposal of his own property, and in the formation of the laws by which his natural freedom is to be restrained. It is a passion inspired, as Algernon Sidney truly says, by Nature herself. In the manner of exercising this power, and satisfying this desire of the people, and in the portion of control retained by them, free States have differed; and in these forms consist their respective constitutions.

Authors who have written upon these subjects have distinguished three powers, viz. the Judicial, the Legislative, and the Executive. These powers, they maintain, ought to be separated. But the Legislative and the Executive never have been, and never can be so, thoroughly. The Judicial, indeed, which, properly exercised, means nothing more than applying general rules or laws to particular cases, with a careful exercise of discrimination, may be so separated; and we have already seen that, in the English Constitution, this division has been very wisely made.

The Judicial Power in England is, as we have seen, placed in the hands of persons rendered independent of the Crown by the law of William III., which makes them removable only upon an address by the two Houses of Parliament. Since this time the character of English judges has been held in deserved estimation:—of their personal integrity, and their conscientious attachment to the law, no doubts or suspicions have been entertained. The corruption of Tressilian and the unprincipled violence of Jeffreys, have never been repeated. The utmost that can be said is, that, historically speaking, the judicial bias in political causes has been naturally and inevitably in favour of the Crown. Anyone who follows the State trials, will perceive that the judges, in their interpretations of law, and still more in their sentences, reflect too lively an image of the inclination of the Government of the day; mild when the minister is moderate, severe when he is intemperate. Such has been the fault of the judges of England; but one which, seldom pushed to any great extent, even in language,

and never to any violent or palpable misconstruction of law, is perhaps as slight a stain upon the
ermine of justice as human nature will permit.
Happily, too, precedents are now so numerous, and
so carefully recorded, that a judge cannot, in the
face of the Bar and of the country, very greatly
deviate from the line of duty. Hence, the confidence of the people in the impartial distribution of
justice still remains entire; so much so, indeed, that
he who takes a view of our imperfect code, together
with the attachment borne to it by the people, will
see that the honest administration of the law re-
conciles the country to many defects in the law
itself.

The two other Powers may be properly called
the Executive and the Deliberative. The term
Legislative implies merely making laws, which, in
no State that I remember, has been totally disjoined
from the Executive. These two powers are, in fact,
in every constitution, continually influencing and
acting upon each other.   In Parliament composed
of King, Lords, and Commons, resides the supreme
government of this nation : the two Houses of Parliament constitute the great council of the King; and
upon whatever subject it is his prerogative to act,
it is their privilege to advise. Acts of executive
government, however, belong to the King; and
should Parliament not interfere, his orders are sufficient.   In legislation, nothing is valid, unless by
the concurrence of all three.

The three branches of the legislature form what
has been called the balance of the constitution : it
would have been more just to have compared them
to what is called in mechanics, a combination of
forces; for the combined impression, the *vis im-
pressa* received from the three powers, decides the
direction of the whole.

The House of Commons, as it has before been

observed, was intended to represent the people at
large; and up to the time of the Revolution, it
had been found to do so sufficiently well. Even
the pensioner Parliament of Charles II. had, in its
last days, spoken fairly the sense of the people.
In the beginning of William's reign, therefore, the
House of Commons may be considered as a just
representative of the nation.

The next element of the legislature was the
House of Lords.

The Peerage serves two great purposes in our
constitution.

First, it is a great and splendid reward for national services, whether by sea or land, in the navy
or the army, in the king's council or on the judge's
bench: it places a stamp upon eminent merit, and
constitutes the posterity of the ennobled person a
perpetual image of his achievements, and a memorial of their recompense. Secondly, the House
of Peers collectively form a council for weighing,
with caution and deliberation, the resolutions of the
House of Commons. If the more popular assembly
is sometimes led away, as it is natural it should be,
by sudden impulses or temporary clamour, this
hereditary senate may interpose its grave and
thoughtful opinions, to suspend the effect of an
intemperate vote. In the possession of such an
assembly, indeed, consists the difference between a
constitution of pure democracy and one of mutual control. The United States of North America,
therefore, which is strictly a government of mutual
control, is not without its Senate, as well as its
House of Representatives.

Such is the Parliament or deliberative power of
England.

The next object of importance to a State is, to
place, in hands worthy to hold it, the power of negotiating treaties; of deciding upon foreign relations;

of directing, in time of war, the operations of fleets
and armies; and, in short, all that is called the
Executive Power.   This power has been generally
disposed of in one of two ways.

The first is, that of putting it into the hands of
one person, called an Emperor, Sultan, or King,
without any control.   The obvious disadvantage of
this mode is, that talent is not hereditary; and, as
it was well put by Lord Halifax, 'no man chooses
a coachman because his father was a coachman before him.'   It is a necessary consequence of this
form of government, that the peace and security of
the State entirely depend upon one ill-educated
man; for it is extremely difficult, if not impossible, that, in an absolute monarchy, a king should
receive a good education.   All his passions and all
his follies are indulged; his ignorance is called
genius, and his imbecility wisdom.*   But, above
all, no object can be offered to him that can excite labour or emulation.   Other men, whether
nobles or artisans, can only be distinguished from
amongst their equals by the excellence of their
moral character, the superiority of their talents, the
wealth they have inherited or acquired, or the advantages they have derived from industry.   But a
king, without any exertion, moral or intellectual,
is placed above every one.   Hence, in utter dearth
of all useful ambition, he tries to be celebrated by
driving,† or fiddling, or some other art of easy at-
tainment; or else, which is much worse, he aims
at fame by commanding armies, and destroying pro-
vinces.   The State, in the meanwhile, totally under
his guidance, becomes weak with his weakness,
vicious with his vice, poor with his extravagance,

* 'Bred up in ignorance and sloth,
   And ev'ry vice that nurses both.'—*Swift.*
† 'Il excelle à conduire un char dans la carrière.'—*Racine.* See
also Bacon's *Essays.*

and wretched from his ambition. Absolute monarchy, then, is a scheme for making one man worse than the rest of the nation, and then obliging the whole nation to follow his direction and example.

Another method of providing for the government, which is at least more plausible, is that of putting the executive power in the hands of a citizen, elected to office for a certain period, and subject to the control of the people at large.

The inconvenience of this method is, that he who has once attained to so high a station, and has become in undisputed pre-eminence the first person in the State, naturally endeavours to retain power for a longer time than it was granted, and even for his life. But even if he should unite, what is very seldom united, a desire of performing great actions with a just fear of infringing the liberties of his country, yet the minds of men are naturally so suspicious that, no sooner has an eminently gifted citizen raised himself above his fellows, than they suspect him of a desire of making himself absolute, and dispense with his services, that they may not be obliged to pay them with their liberty. On one or other of these rocks, if not both, nearly all democracies have split. Athens banished her best citizens by the ostracism. Rome drove from her Camillus, Coriolanus, Marius, and, above all, Scipio; and yet fell at last a victim to Cæsar's military power, and his ambition to be king. Holland, after numerous contentions, sank under the sovereignty of the Prince of Orange. Sparta and Venice are mentioned by Machiavel as exceptions to the general rule. But Venice also bought her security dear; for it was only obtained by a custom of excluding from military command all her own citizens, and giving to strangers the richest prizes a State has to bestow. The method adopted by Sparta was somewhat similar to that of England, to which we shall now pass.

The executive power of England is placed nominally in the hands of an hereditary king. His powers are known and defined by law, and are therefore less liable to be exceeded than those of any extraordinary office not known to the Constitution. This was the argument most ably urged by Whitelocke and his coadjutors to the Protector Cromwell, to induce him to accept the title of King.* At the same time, the current of law, and the established reverence paid to majesty, form a complete bar to any great man who might wish to make himself absolute. So confirmed is public opinion, that a victorious general never dreams of overthrowing the liberties of his country. The Duke of Marlborough was dismissed from his command as easily as an ensign; and the Duke of Wellington returned from all his victories and pre-eminences to occupy an office of inferior importance in a cabinet which had not to boast either of singular popularity or commanding genius.

But whilst the King's prerogative forms on the one side an almost invincible barrier to the ambition of any subject who might wish to become sovereign of the State in which he was born a citizen, it is on the other side restricted by the general control of the people. Thus the King has, by his prerogative, the command of the army; but that army is only maintained by virtue of a law to punish mutiny and desertion, passed from year to year. The King has a right to declare war; but if the House of Commons denies supplies, he cannot carry it on for a week. The King may make a treaty of peace; but if it is dishonourable to the country, the ministers who signed it may be impeached. Nor is the King's personal command any excuse for a wrong administration of power. The Earl of Danby was im-

* See the conferences on this subject. They are to be found in the Parliamentary History.

peached for a letter which contained a postscript in
the King's own hand, declaring it was written by
his order.   The maxim of the Constitution is, that
the King cannot act without advisers responsible by
law; and so far is this maxim carried, that a commitment by the King, although he is the fountain of
justice, was held' to be void, because there was no
minister responsible for it.

From the doctrine of the responsibility of ministers, it follows that they ought to enjoy the confidence of the Commons.   Otherwise their measures
will be thwarted, their promises will be distrusted;
and, finding all their steps obstructed, their efforts
will be directed to the overthrow of the Constitution.
This actually happened in the reigns of Charles I. and
Charles II.   There was but one mode of preventing
a recurrence of the evil.   It was by giving to the
King a revenue so limited, that he should always be
obliged to assemble his Parliament to carry on the
ordinary expenses of his government.   On this point,
more important than any provision of the Bill of
Rights, a warm contest took place at the Revolution
in the House of Commons.   The Tories, wishing to
please the new King, argued, against all justice and
reason, that the revenue which had been given to
James for his life belonged *de jure* to William for
his life.   The Whigs successfully resisted this pretension; and passed a vote, granting £420,000 to
the King, by monthly payments.   The Commons
soon afterwards had all the accounts of King James's
reign laid before them.   It appeared that his government, without any war, cost, on an average,
£1,700,000 a year; a revenue of only £1,200,000
a year was given to William, with the expenses and
debt of a formidable war to be provided for.

By this arrangement, the Crown was made dependent on Parliament ever after.   Without even offer-
ing any advice, by a mere symptom of an intention

to stop the supplies, the whole system of the King might be defeated, and his ministers dismissed from the council-board. Hence the House of Commons has the power to control most certainly and effectually the acts of the supreme magistrate. Whatever struggles have been made since, have been made within the House of Commons. Ambitious men, instead of attempting, according to their several views, to abolish the monarchy, or dispense with Parliaments, have either sought to reach the King's closet through the favour of the people's representatives, or to serve the Crown by corrupting that assembly, and poisoning the sources from which their authority was derived. But whatever may have been said of the prevalence of the latter of these methods of government, it is certain that, for some time after the Revolution, power was retained longest by those statesmen whose political principles were stamped by the approbation of their country. A friend of liberty was no longer forced to the alternative of defying the authority of his sovereign, or perishing by the axe of the executioner; the same sentiments which he had spoken to the people, he was able to repeat to the King; and the same measures which he had recommended as an individual member of Parliament, he was afterwards empowered to propose as the adviser of his sovereign. Thus harmony was produced between the different, and hitherto jarring, parts of our Constitution; while the means by which that harmony was attained gave, at the same time, a vent to emulation, liberty to the people, authority to Parliament, a boundary to the ambition of political leaders, and stability to the throne. In this manner were the great principles of English liberty brought into action by the Revolution of 1688, whose authors, unambitious of the fame of founding a new form of government, obtained for

the nation the full benefit of those venerable rights
and liberties, for which their ancestors and themselves had toiled and suffered. This great work,
thus gloriously completed, was at once a lesson to
the great to avoid oppression, and to the people to
practise moderation.

We have now gone through the different parts
of that form of government which some paradoxical
men have had the conceit to undervalue. Those
who have been shaken by nothing that they have
read in history, and who still maintain that liberty
cannot flourish under our barbarous and feudal
monarchy, may yet perhaps be struck by the following passage from an impartial judge.

M. de Talleyrand, in speaking of America, after
remarking the partiality which the Americans entertained for English maxims and manners, goes on
thus:—'Nor should one be astonished to find this
assimilation towards England in a country, the dis-
tinguishing features of whose form of government,
whether in the federal union, or in the separate
States, are impressed with so strong a resemblance
to the great lineaments of the English constitution.
Upon what does individual liberty rest at this day
in America? Upon the same foundations as English
liberty; upon the Habeas Corpus and the trial by
jury. Assist at the sittings of Congress, and at those
of the legislatures of the separate States; attend
to the discussions in the framing of national laws:
whence are taken their quotations, their analogies,
their examples? From the English laws; from the
customs of Great Britain; from the rules of Parliament. Enter into the courts of justice: what
authorities do they cite? The statutes, the judgments, the decisions of the English courts. To no
purpose do the names of republic and of monarchy
appear to place between the two governments dis-

tinctions which it is not allowable to confound: it
is clear to every man who examines his ideas to the
bottom, that in the representative constitution of
England, there is something republican; as there is
something monarchical in the executive power of the
Americans.'

CHAPTER XV.

LAWYERS.

' Rex sub lege.'—Bracton.

AMONG other cavillings at the practice of our Constitution, there has been raised a cry against the influence of lawyers. From the earliest times, however, that influence has been beneficial to the country. Bracton, who was a judge in the reign of Henry III., and Fortescue, who was chief justice in that of Henry VI., are among the earliest authorities in favour of the liberties of the country. In the beginning of the contest with the Stuarts, the names of Coke and Selden appear with auspicious lustre on the side of freedom. In the second contest with the Stuarts, among a host of lawyers, with the venerable Serjeant Maynard at their head, appears the virtuous, the temperate, the wise and venerated Somers. From him we pass to Lord Cowper, a Whig chancellor, who yet opposed the Bill of Pains and Penalties against Atterbury, as an unnecessary violation of justice. The next in succession, as a friend to liberty, is Lord Camden, who, by his admirable judgments on the question of general warrants and on libel, saved the country from the slavish doctrines with which it was threatened to be inundated.

In the House of Commons, the members who have taken a chief part in the debates have generally been lawyers. This is the natural result of their habits of speaking, and we see them on one side of the House as well as on the other. On the side of freedom we may reckon a series of bright names.

that began with the beginning of our Constitution, and, I trust, will continue to its close.

It were needless to come down to more recent examples, were it not that I should be sorry to omit any opportunity of expressing my admiration for that great genius whose sword and buckler protected justice and freedom during the disastrous period of the French Revolution. Defended by him, the Government found, in the meanest individual whom they attacked, the tongue of Cicero and the soul of Hampden, an invincible orator and an undaunted patriot. May the recollection of those contests, and those triumphs, brighten the last days of this illustrious man, and excite those who have embraced the same studies to seek for a similar inspiration! *

Such instances might persuade us that the study of the law, by giving men a better knowledge of their rights, gives them a stronger desire to preserve them, and, by affording them a nearer view of our Constitution, enables them the better to appreciate and cherish its excellences. Unfortunately, however, there are instances, on the other side, of men who, attracted by the brilliant rewards in the profession of the law which the Crown has to give, have made themselves the tools of tyranny and corruption. But this is by no means an exclusive attribute of lawyers. The mean Lord Strafford, who sold his country for an office and a peerage, was a country gentleman; and the false Lord Bolingbroke, who betrayed his benefactor, and endeavoured to restore a race of despots, was a wit and a man of fashion.

* Lord Erskine was yet living when this passage was written.

CHAPTER XVI.

RISE OF PUBLIC CREDIT UPON THE BASIS OF A FREE CONSTITUTION.

'I know nothing more remarkable in the government of Genoa than the bank of St. George, made up of such branches of the revenues as have been set apart and appropriated to the discharging of several sums that have been borrowed from private persons during exigencies. They have never thought of violating public credit, or of alienating the revenues to other uses than to what they have been thus assigned.'—*Addison's Remarks on Italy.*

Soon after the restoration of Charles II., a scheme was proposed to him by Sir George Downing, the whole merit of which consisted in laying down a rule for the exact and regular payment of interest for all money the King should borrow. With the view of affording to merchants security for the performance of this agreement, Downing, with the consent of the King, introduced a clause into a bill of supply, appropriating to the different purposes therein mentioned the money granted in the bill. Clarendon, who relates the affair, was highly indignant at this new check upon the prerogative, and, along with others, remonstrated in strong terms with the King. The rest of the story I will relate in Clarendon's own words. 'He (King Charles) enlarged more in discourse, and told them "that this would be an encouragement to lend money, by making the payment with interest so certain and fixed, that there could be no security in the kingdom like it, when it should be out of any man's power to cause any money that should be lent to-morrow to be paid before that which was lent yesterday, but that all should be infallibly paid in order; by which the Exchequer (which was now bankrupt, and without any credit) would be quickly in that reputation, that all men would deposit their money there; and that he hoped, in a few years, by observing the method he now proposed, he would make his Exchequer the best and the greatest bank in Europe, and where all Europe would, when it was once understood, pay in their money for the certain profit it would yield, and the indubitable certainty that they should receive their money." And, with this discourse, the vain man (Sir George Downing) who had lived many years in Holland, and would be thought to have made himself master of all their policy, had amused the King and his two friends, undertaking to erect the King's Exchequer into the same degree of credit that the Bank of Amsterdam stood upon, the institution whereof he undertook to know, and from thence to make it evident, "that all that should be transplanted into England, and all nations would sooner send their money into the Exchequer, than into Amsterdam, or Genoa, or Venice." And it cannot be enough wondered at that this intoxication prevailed so far, that no argument would be heard against it, the King having, upon those notions, and with the advice of those counsellors, in his own thoughts new modelled the whole government of his Treasury, in which he resolved to have no more superior officers. But this was only reserved within his own breast, and not communicated to any but those who devised the project, without weighing that the security for moneys so deposited in banks is the republic itself, which must expire before that security can fail; *which can never be depended on in a monarchy, where the monarch's sole word can cancel all those formal provisions which can be made* (as hath since been too evident), by vacating those assignations which have been made upon that and the like Acts of Parliament, for such time as the present

necessities have made counsellable; which would not
then be admitted to be possible.'*

From the above passage of Lord Clarendon, it is
evident he thought public credit incompatible with
arbitrary monarchy. His opinion was fully justified
by the subsequent conduct of the King, whom he
counselled. Charles II. was accustomed to borrow
money from the bankers, payable on receipt of the
taxes, very much in the manner of our present Exchequer bills, but at 8 or 10 per cent. interest instead
of 3 or 4. At the commencement of the second
Dutch war, when the taxes came in, he closed the
door of the Exchequer, and refused to pay. Such
conduct, it is evident, must be quite fatal to so sen-
sitive a plant as public credit, which can only grow
under the temperate influence of just and free laws.
The infamy of this swindling transaction of Charles
was in some measure repaired in the reign of William III., when a large portion, at least of the sum
owing, was funded as stock, and made to form part
of the national debt.

With the revolution came an expensive war
against the most powerful monarch in Europe, and
the nation had to support the choice it had made of
a sovereign by sacrifices of every kind. In this
situation, the party that governed the country be-
thought themselves of making use of those resources
of public credit which had already been found of
powerful effect in Holland and in Venice. Thus the
Bank of England was established a few years after
the Revolution. About the same time, the silver
currency was restored to a just standard, a measure
which for a time created a scarcity of coin in the
country: a general stoppage of trade took place;
and the paper of the Bank of England, soon after
its establishment, fell to 20 per cent. discount. In
order to remedy these evils, Mr. Montague, Chancellor of the Exchequer, who may be considered the

* Clarendon, Hist. Reb., vol. i. pp. 316, 317.

eb. ivl.   THE BASIS OF A FREE CONSTITUTION.   103

founder of our financial system, collected all the
debts outstanding, which amounted to five millions,
imposed taxes for the payment of the whole, and, in
order to relieve the want of currency, issued bills
payable on the receipt of the taxes, since called
Exchequer bills.   Public credit revived, the capital
of the Bank was increased, and the currency became
sufficient for the wants of the country.

From this time loans were made of a vast increasing amount with great facility, and generally
at a low interest, by which the nation was enabled
to resist her enemies.   The French wondered at
the prodigious efforts that were made by so small a
power, and the abundance with which money was
poured into the treasury.   They saw, to their dismay, that, while Louis could hardly obtain, by the
most humiliating means, sums sufficient to provide
his armies, Great Britain, firm and undismayed,
found for ever fresh resources in the wealth and
confidence of her merchants.   Books were written,
projects drawn up, edicts prepared, which were
to give to France the same facilities as her rival;
every plan that fiscal ingenuity could strike out,
every calculation that laborious arithmetic could
form. was proposed, and tried, and found wanting;
and for this simple reason, that, in all their projects
drawn up in imitation of England, one little element
was omitted, *videlicet*, her free constitution.*

All the money voted by the House of Commons
is, at present, strictly tied up to special purposes, by
an Act of Appropriation passed at the end of every
session of Parliament: the very measure which excited the loyal horror of Lord Clarendon.

* Among other schemes, the
King of France ordered that
every coin should pass for a nominal value higher than it had
hitherto passed for.   Addison
wittily said that he might as well

have ordered that every grena-
dier of six feet high should in
future pass for seven feet high,
and thus think to increase the
strength of his army.—*Freeholder.*

CHAPTER XVII.

PARTY.

'Party is a body of men united for promoting, by their joint endeavours, the national interest, upon some particular principle, in which they are all agreed. Men thinking freely will, in particular instances, think differently. But still, as the greater part of the measures which arise in the course of public business are related to, or dependent on, some great *leading general principles in government*, a man must be peculiarly unfortunate in the choice of his political company if he does not agree with them, at least nine times in ten. And this is all that ever was required for a character of the greatest uniformity and steadiness in connection. How men can proceed without connection at all, is to me utterly incomprehensible. Of what sort of materials must that man be made, how must he be tempered and put together, who can sit whole years in Parliament, with five hundred and fifty of his fellow-citizens, amidst the storm of such tempestuous passions, in the sharp conflict of so many wits and tempers and characters, in the agitation of such mighty questions, in the discussion of such vast and ponderous interests, without seeing any one sort of men, whose character, conduct, or disposition would lead him to associate himself with them, to aid and be aided in any one system of public utility ?'—*Burke.*

THE reign of Queen Anne is as remarkable for the violent contentions, as that of George I. for the complete ascendency, of party. It is worth while to consider the effects both of the contention and the triumph. Let us first, however, endeavour in a few words to explain the existence of party-divisions, and to vindicate the integrity of those who avow that they belong to party. The general defence of political connection, indeed, may be left where Mr. Burke has placed it. There can be nothing more striking, or more sound, than his writings on this subject. But, although his reasoning never has been and never can be answered, a certain degree of favour still attends the man who declares himself

not to belong to party, as if he were clearing himself from the imputation of dishonesty or selfishness.

The division of England into two great parties
began, as I conceive, and still continues, in consequence of wide and irreconcilable differences of
opinion.

The Tories, at the commencement of the reign of
James L, looked upon the exaltation of the Crown
as their favourite object. Allowing, as they now
do, that the King is entrusted with his power for
the public good, they yet thought that public good
required complete freedom in the exercise of his
prerogative, so long as the law is not infringed.
While he remained, therefore, within the legal
bounds assigned to him, they were, to say the least,
extremely unwilling to control his power. If he
stept beyond them, or placed the country in great
danger, they were ready to oppose the Crown by
their votes in Parliament, or in any other legal
manner. It followed from their doctrine, however,
that their tendency always was to support the King
in the first place, in all his measures, and to refuse their sanction only when those measures had
placed the country in peril so imminent, that they
were obliged reluctantly to disclose their own
opinions.

The Whigs looked towards the people, whose
welfare is the end and object of all government.
They maintained that, as the King's advisers are
responsible for his measures, it is the duty of Parliament to examine and pronounce whether those
measures are wise and salutary. They were, therefore, ready to interfere with any exercise of the
prerogative which they thought unwise or improper; and to insist (too haughtily, perhaps, at times)
upon the adoption of that line of policy which they
considered as best adapted to the wants and wishes
of the country.

Such appears to me a just general representation of Whig and Tory opinions, from the commencement of the reign of James I. to the end of that of George II.

If I have made a fair statement, it was inevitable that the two parties should separate, and remain divided.

Let me now suppose a young Member of Parliament coming to London at the beginning of the reign of Queen Anne. He adopts, let us suppose, the opinions of the Tories. He votes generally, but not always, with that party. He naturally becomes acquainted with some of them. He talks over the questions that are coming on for some time before. These conversations lead to a more intimate union; his opinions are listened to, and his doubts melt away in the course of amicable discussion. Sometimes, when the measure is one of party policy rather than of principle, he surrenders his own opinion to that of the statesman most respected by the society of which he is a member. He thinks it more probable that several able, and a large body of patriotic men, *arguing from the same principles as himself*, should form a right decision, than that he alone in the whole House of Commons should, from given general principles, have derived a true conclusion. He is, in short, a party man. Thus it is that, without any violation of conscience, party is formed and consolidated, and men acquire that kind of '*esprit monacal*' which, according to the remark of a very sagacious foreigner,* prevails in the political confederacies of England.

Let us now proceed to the effects of party contests.

Among the bad effects of party is to be reckoned the want of candour it necessarily produces. Few

* The Abbé Galiani.

men can enter into the heat of political contention, backed by a body of friends, who animate and support each other, without attributing to their adversaries bad intentions and corrupt motives, of which they are no more capable than themselves.

Another evil is, that men become unwilling to give way to the natural bent of their minds, when their understandings would lead them to admit any error upon which their adversaries have insisted, or to render them liable to reproach for weakness and inconsistency.   Obstinacy in supporting wrong, because an admission of what was right and true would give a triumph to opposition, has led many a minister of England into a course injurious to the country.

In attributing this evil to party, I by no means intend to lay upon the same cause the blame of the exaggeration which accompanies political discussion.   Such exaggeration I believe to be inevitable. It is true, indeed, that every statesman has at times occasion to weigh with some degree of doubt the reasons for or against a measure which he afterwards supports or opposes, with as much warmth and confidence as if there could not be two opinions on the subject.   But it does not follow that it would be right or useful to produce in public all the arguments which have gone through his mind before he came to a decision.   What would be the effect, for instance, of the speech of a minister proposing an address in support of a new war, who should lay a stress upon the hazards by which it would be attended, and the new burthens it must infallibly produce?   Nothing, it is evident, but discouragement, and perhaps a disgraceful treaty.   For the slightest words which a man lets fall in opposition to his ultimate opinion, are of more weight against that opinion than the strongest arguments he can use in its favour.   Those who agree with him are all

disheartened, and those who differ from him are
all encouraged. Nor does this proceed from the
factitious spirit of party, but from human nature
herself. Public affairs are so constituted, that the
truth scarcely ever lies entirely on one side; and
the human mind is so formed, that it must either
embrace one side only, or sink into inaction.

Nor do I impute to party the corruption by which
votes in Parliament are obtained. Some persons,
I know, imagine that the minister has recourse to
corruption only because it is necessary to strengthen
himself against the Opposition. But it is evident
that, in a free government like ours, the ministers
will always make use of the influence of patronage
that is in their hands to procure themselves adherents. For a minister knows very well that he
must have adherents. He cannot reasonably found
his administration on the support which he may be
able to obtain by his arguments in favour of each
particular measure. Now, of the two ways of pro-
curing adherents—the attachment of interest and
that of party—party is by far the best. Many a
man, I fear, would abandon his opinions, and fall
off from his principles, for the sake of office, who
yet will not desert a party to which he is engaged
by passion and affection, as well as by reason.

Party, therefore, instead of being the cause of
corrupt and undue influence, is often a substitute
for it. Some, indeed, think it possible that the
world may be governed by pure intention and the
force of argument only. But it is well said by Mr.
Wilberforce, when speaking of religion, ' Man is
not a being of mere intellect. *Video meliora pro-
boque, deteriora sequor*, is a complaint which, alas!
we might all of us daily utter. The slightest solicitation of appetite is often able to draw us to act
in opposition to our clearest judgment, our highest
interests, and most resolute determination.' ' These

observations,' proceeds the enlightened author, 'hold
equally in every instance, according to its measure,
wherein there is a call for laborious, painful, and
continued exertions, from which we are likely to be
deterred by obstacles, or seduced by the solicitation
of pleasure.   What, then, is to be done in the case
of any such arduous and necessary undertaking?
The answer is obvious:—You should endeavour
not only to convince the understanding, but also to
affect the heart ; and for this end you must secure
the reinforcement of the passions.' *

   The good effects of party in this country are numerous and weighty.   One of the chief of them is
that it gives a substance to the shadowy opinions of
politicians, and attaches them permanently to steady
and lasting principles.   The true party-man finds
in his own mind certain general rules of politics,
like the general rules of morals, by which he decides every new and doubtful case.   The belief that
those principles are just, enables him to withstand
the seductions of interest, and the ingenuity of projects : his conduct acquires somewhat of the firmness of integrity and wisdom.

   The union of many in the same views enables a
party to carry measures which would not otherwise
gain attention.   There often occurs a proposal eminently useful, yet not calculated to catch popular
favour, which, by the stout and strong working of
a party, at length becomes law ; that which is an
overmatch for the strength of an individual, is accomplished by the united force of numbers.   The
waggon arrives at last at its destination ; but a
loose horse will probably return to the place
from which he set out.   It likewise often happens
that party succeeds where the people have failed.
The enthusiasm of a whole nation is in its nature

---

* Wilberforce's Practical View of Christianity, p. 60.

evanescent. If successfully resisted at first, it often
sinks into apathy, and the country remains passive,
though not satisfied, under the weight of a defeat.
But a party is pledged; the character of the individuals belonging to it depends upon their consistency; their principles are handed down from
father to son, and become the mould from which
successive generations receive the form and pressure
of their politics. It may be observed, on the other
side, that many instances can be quoted of parties
who, on coming into power, have shrunk from their
original professions; but they are not so frequent
as those of a complete and radical change in the
popular voice with respect to the objects of its pre-
dilection or aversion.

The greatest benefit of all that is conferred by
party is, perhaps, that it embodies the various opinions of the nation for the time being. Those
opinions are at times so violent, that, had they not
a vent in Parliament, they would break the ma-
chine to pieces. Happily the people, when they
overturned Sir Robert Walpole, placed confidence
(a confidence little justified, perhaps) in his opponents; and when Lord North appeared to have
ruined his country, the nation looked for safety to
Lord Rockingham and Mr. Fox. There may be
a revolution in this country; but it is hardly possible that the country should not first try what may
be done by a change of counsels. Thus the great
and final reason of nations, the right of resistance,
is not likely to be used till better and safer means
have been tried. To possess such means is a great
advantage for the nation which can employ them.

In reckoning up the bad effects of party, I have
not spoken of the animosities and violent contentions it produces. Mock philosophers are always
making lamentations over political divisions, and
contested elections.

Men of noble minds know that they are the work-shop of national liberty, and national prosperity.

It is from the heat and hammering of the stithy that freedom receives its shape, its temper, and its strength.

CHAPTER XVIII.

WILLIAM AND MARY.—ANNE.

'Un roi fait ailleurs entrer aveuglément ses peuples dans toutes ses vues; mais à Londres un roi doit entrer dans celles de son peuple.'—*Voltaire, Siècle de Louis XIV.*

LET us now proceed to the history of the two parties from the Revolution to the reign of George I.

We have seen that the Whigs refused to grant King William a permanent income that might render him independent of his people; and he dissolved the Parliament in 1690 with some disgust. The next House of Commons was a Tory one; and Sir John Trevor, a violent Tory, was made First Commissioner of the Treasury. He undertook to distribute bribes in such a manner as to secure the votes of the majority; being the first systematic corruption after the Revolution. Trevor was afterwards punished for bribery in a question relating to the Orphans Bill. There arose at this time a fierce struggle between Whigs and Tories for the favour of the King, and the confidence of the people. The dismissal of Monmouth and Warrington attested and established the success of the Tories. The Tory party were supported by the small proprietors of land and the gentry of the country, who feared a bias to innovation on the part of the Whigs both in politics and religion. On the other hand, the Whigs were esteemed by the people as having been the original opposers of arbitrary power, and had the credit, as well as the responsibility, of the new settlement. In order to support it, they came forward with their wealth

in a time of embarrassment, and also prevailed upon
their friends in the city, which was then, as in
former times, a stronghold of liberty, to lend largely
to the government. By these means, the Whigs attached men of great wealth to the new establishment,
and distinguished themselves to their advantage
from the Tories, who were unwilling, or unable,
to advance considerable sums. Hence the King, who
had placed his confidence in Ranelagh, Rochester,
and Seymour, afterwards discovered an inclination
to trust the Whigs, raised Somers and Shrews-
bury to high situations, and gave his tardy consent
to the Triennial Bill. After the peace of Ryswick,
the Whigs defended the maintaining of the Dutch
Guards, in which perhaps they were right, though
the line they took exposed them to much popular
odium. The defeat of this favourite wish of our
deliverer is a proof how extremely weak the royal
authority was at this period. It would not be so
easy perhaps to defend the Whig party in their
transactions respecting a new East India Company.
Still less can they escape blame for having suffered
in silence the conclusion of the treaty of partition.
By this treaty, William imprudently trusted himself to the faith of the French King, and unwarrant-
ably disposed of the whole of the Spanish monarchy
during the life of the reigning sovereign. The
partition, thus previously arranged, at once provoked the Spaniards and enraged the Emperor. It
was rash in policy, unfounded in justice, and impracticable in execution. With arms thus imprudently furnished by their adversaries, the country
party violently attacked the Whigs in the House of
Commons: Orford and Somers were removed and
disgraced: a Tory ministry was established, and
was the last of King William.

Queen Anne came to the throne with violent prejudices in favour of Tory politics, both in Church and

I

State, and severe bills against occasional conformity
were received with applause by a House of Commons
composed chiefly of that party. But the natural
inclinations of the Queen yielded to the advice of
Marlborough, who, though himself a Tory, became
convinced that Lord Rochester would not actively
support the war, and that the Whigs alone sympathised with the sentiments of King William as expressed in the last speech that he delivered to his
Parliament. Feeling that a vigorous opposition to
the arms of Louis XIV. could alone save the liberties of Europe, Marlborough advised his mistress to
give her countenance to the Whig party. Lord
Cowper was made Lord Chancellor; but still the
Queen hesitated to give her consent to the admission
into her councils of persons whose politics she detested; and year after year passed in struggles at
court to obtain the higher offices of State for Sunder-
land and Somers. It would not be just to ascribe
these demands of the Whig leaders to the mere love
of office : their ambition was of a higher kind. They
aspired to rule the State according to their own system of policy, but they found that all their efforts
were thwarted by the wilful negligence of the Tories,
who filled less conspicuous places in the administration. Godolphin tells us, that there was not a Tory
in any ministerial office who did not require to be
spoken to ten times over before he would execute
anything that had been ordered, and then it was
done with all the difficulty and slowness imaginable.
This conduct, dangerous if not treasonable in the
midst of a perilous war, certainly goes far to justify
the importunity of the Whigs to remove Sir C.
Hedges from the post of Secretary of State, in order
to give him a more permanent and profitable but
less responsible office.*

* See Conduct of the Duchess of Marlborough. Coxe's 'Life of
Marlborough.'

The Whigs held their power by a precarious tenure. The Queen, originally adverse to them, was rendered implacable by their haughty invasion of the cabinet; and she was daily excited to little acts of hostility by Mrs. Masham, who had succeeded the Duchess of Marlborough in the government of her weak head and ignoble heart. There needed only a popular and plausible occasion for discarding the general who rendered the name of England illustrious by his victories, and the statesman whose reputation was founded equally on his wisdom and his love of liberty. The occasion soon happened: Marlborough and Somers fell: Harley and St. John rose upon their ruin: and nothing but the personal rivalry of these two unprincipled men saved the Hanover succession.

It must be owned, that the Whigs gave heedlessly a handle to the designs of their enemies. The trial of Dr. Sacheverel was imprudent. Under an established government it was not wise to proclaim without necessity the doctrine of resistance; nor could there be much peril in leaving a fanatical clergyman to vaunt his absurdities unmolested. The solemnity of an impeachment, the marshalling of all the forces of the State against a private individual, could not fail to excite afresh that cry in favour of the High Church which ought never to have been awakened. In consequence of the popularity of Sacheverel, and the well-known opinions of the Queen, a House of Commons was obtained completely favourable to the Tories. And here begins the history of those last four years of Queen Anne, in which the press was restrained, intolerance favoured, our allies, deserted, our enemies encouraged, and a disadvantageous peace concluded. Indeed, had not Queen Anne died before the measures of the Jacobites were prepared, the Elector of Hanover might never

have been able to ascend the throne, to which the
Act of Settlement had called him.

We have now gone over the struggles of party
during the times of the first two sovereigns who
reigned after the Revolution.   They were times in
which political integrity was rare, and political animosities violent, but the people were admitted as an
umpire between the contending forces; and, upon
the whole, the rise and fall of each party seems to
have been proportioned to its merits.   In so saying,
I must except the elevation of Harley and of St.
John : men who were base enough to flatter Marlborough for the purpose of lulling and supplanting
him, ought to have remained in obscurity.   With
this exception, however, the contest between the two
parties was a contest between two lines of policy, in
which the welfare of the State was involved, and
between two great principles, on one or other of
which the foundations of the English government
must be made to depend.   Men of great talents,
vast property, and long experience, distinguished
themselves on one side or the other ; and to which-
ever side the nation leant, more practical liberty,
more personal security, and more tranquillity from
religious persecution, as well as more fame and consideration abroad, were enjoyed by the nation than
had ever been known in England.

CHAPTER XIX.

IMPEACHMENT.—BILLS OF PAINS AND PENALTIES.

'The Parliament have also power to punish any who judge for man and not for the Lord; who respect persons or take gifts, or any way misdemean themselves in their offices.'—*Whitelocke, Notes on the King's Writ.*

It is absolutely necessary to the preservation of an established form of government, that there should exist a legal method of bringing to punishment those who endeavour to subvert it. For this reason the executive magistrate is always entrusted with the means of proceeding to a trial against persons who conspire against his or their lawful authority.

In the same way, and for the same reasons, there must exist in a free State a method of accusing those persons who have abused the authority confided to them for the purpose of usurping undue power, or corrupting the citizens, or obtaining ends adverse to the general interest of the community. In this case the discretionary power of proceeding to trial cannot rest with the executive magistrate, for he is generally the party complained of; it must reside in the popular branch of the State. It is therefore wisely provided in our government, that the House of Commons should have the right of impeachment. This extraordinary power, thus confided to the representatives of the people, enables them to denounce, as guilty of high treason, all who shall violate the law upon this subject. It enables them also to denounce, as guilty of high crimes and misdemeanours, all ministers of State whose conduct is injurious to the interest of the nation. Some, I know, have maintained that

an impeachment can only lie against an indictable
offence; but this doctrine is in plain contradiction to
three out of four of the impeachments which have
taken place.   To take one instance only :—In the
case of the ministers who signed the Treaty of Partition, the House of Commons resolved on April 1,
1701, ' That William Earl of Portland, by negotiating and concluding the Treaty of Partition (which
was destructive to the trade of this kingdom, and
dangerous to the peace of Europe), is guilty and
shall be impeached of high crimes and misdemeanours.'—Now what petty jury could take upon them
to say that a treaty was destructive to the trade of
England; or to bring in a verdict of guilty on a
charge of endangering the peace of Europe ?

The same thing may be said of the impeachments
against Oxford and Bolingbroke for signing the
Treaty of Utrecht.   Those who argue that impeachments can only be brought for an indictable offence,
say, ' It is true a jury could not try these offences ;
but that is only an objection to the jurisdiction ;
every misconduct in office is a misdemeanour at common law.'   This answer, it is evident, reduces the
difference to nothing ; for if certain offences can be
prosecuted by impeachment only, it does not matter
whether the cause is to be found in the want of law,
or the defect of jurisdiction, to bring them before
any other court.

It is impossible for the King to stop the progress
of an impeachment.   His pardon under the great
seal cannot be pleaded in bar of trial.   His prerogative of prorogation, or even of dissolution, may
suspend, but does not put an end to the proceedings.
These two securities for justice were contended for
during the trial of the Earl of Danby, in the reign
of Charles II.; the first was established at the
Revolution, and the second confirmed during the
impeachment of Mr. Hastings.

It is much more difficult, in a free State, to establish impartial judges than to find courageous accusers.
There can hardly be any body of men who are at
once qualified to form an opinion on political questions, and not disqualified by having formed one
before they are called upon to judge. This latter
fault, it must be owned, is found in our House of
Lords. It is difficult, if not impossible, to bring a
principal minister before them, on whose conduct
they have not already pronounced judgment in their
own minds. For this reason we find, that when the
Lords are in favour of the accused, Lords and Commons generally conspire to produce a quarrel between
the Houses, and thus avoid giving judgment. So it
happened in the cases of Lord Danby, Lord Somers,
and many others. The experience of later times has
not made impeachments more easy in the trial, or
more impartial in judgment. The impeachment of
Hastings was a long punishment; and in the last
case of impeachment the Lords were found to vote
more from a sense of political or personal friendship
than from a sense of justice; and some came to the
decision without having heard a word of the evidence. Impeachment, upon the whole, is rather a
scarecrow to frighten public delinquents, than a real
security for public justice. In former times it drove
many a bad minister from the council-board; at
present that end is attained, when it is attained, by
simpler means. Yet, perhaps, the bloodless result
of impeachments is one of the modes by which the
lenity of our parties towards each other has been
preserved.

Bills of attainder and bills of pains and penalties,
passed by Parliament, are of a very different nature
from impeachments. They have been generally, if
not always, used on occasions of great moment and
urgency. Two circumstances seem to be requisite
to all bills of this kind:—First, That it is impos-

sible to convict the offender by due course of law.
Secondly, That his escape would be in the highest
degree injurious to the State. Great indeed must
be the mischief that would arise from the impunity
of a criminal, to overbalance the evil of shaking
the common security of the subject, disturbing the
regular course of justice, and affording an example
of punishment inflicted on one who cannot be convicted of a crime.

Instances of bills of attainder and bills of pains
and penalties are, unfortunately, too numerous on our
statute-book. But, in early times, bills of attainder,
however unjust in their operation in particular instances, had not the character they have at present.
Originally, the high court of Parliament was not a
court only in name, but was chiefly employed in
deciding causes, and particularly in judging all the
great criminals whose power placed them beyond the
reach of a jury. The offences for which such criminals were condemned were, however, offences of
which a jury might legally have taken cognisance.
Thus it was with the Spencers, the adherents of
Richard III., and others. The reign of Henry VIII.
opens to us a more alarming scene. A bill of attainder was passed against Empson and Dudley at the
accession of that king, for the exactions of which
they had been guilty under the reign of his father.
As these exactions had been sanctioned by an Act
of Parliament, there was surely great injustice in
condemning those who had acted under it to a capital
punishment. The act of attainder was also unnecessary; for Empson and Dudley had been previously
convicted of treason at Guildhall, for an attempt to
maintain themselves by force.* So strong was the
popular feeling against them, however, that they
probably met with as little justice from a jury as
from a Parliament.

* State Trials. Burnet's Hist. Reformation.

In the same reign of Henry VIII., Queen Catherine Howard was condemned to lose her head, by a bill of attainder, for incontinency before her marriage with the King.   When the bill was in progress, the Lords, by the desire of Henry, sent a message to her, to ask her if she had anything to say in her defence. She, however, confessed her guilt; and in those times she did not think of complaining that she was to suffer death for a crime unknown to the laws.

In the year 1539, a most dangerous precedent was made.   The Marchioness of Exeter and the Countess of Salisbury refusing to answer the accusation against them, were attainted by Act of Parliament. 'About the justice of doing this,' says Burnet, 'there was some debate; and to clear it, Cromwell sent for the judges, and asked their opinions, Whether a man might be attainted in Parliament, without being brought to make his answer?   They said it was a dangerous question; that the Parliament ought to be an example to all inferior courts; and that when any person was charged with a crime, he, by the common rule of justice and equity, should be heard to plead for himself.   But the Parliament being the supreme court of the nation, what way soever they proceeded, it must be good in law; and it could never be questioned whether the party was brought to answer or not.' * The precedent thus begun was soon made worse, as all bad precedents are; in this case, however, the person was well chosen: it was Cromwell himself.   Instead of declining to plead, he petitioned to be heard; but his request was refused, and an attainder passed on the mere assertion of his enemies.

Of the bill of attainder against Strafford I have before spoken.   There can be no excuse for the manner in which the bill was forced through.   It must

* Burnet, Hist. Ref., p. 265.

be observed, however, that few cases of State necessity can be imagined so strong as that which could
be urged for the condemnation of Strafford.   Some
of the moderate among the Presbyterian party * were
for sparing his life; but they were hurried on by
others of a more bloody temperament.   The bill of
banishment against Clarendon had this strong foundation, that he had withdrawn himself from justice:
yet this ground seems to me not to be sufficient for
such a proceeding.   I am not, however, disposed
very greatly to blame the act of attainder against Sir
John Fenwick.   A person accused of high treason,
and about to be tried in the due course of law for
that offence, who pretends he is going to reveal his
treason, and takes advantage of his fraud to spirit
away a witness, seems to me to have removed himself beyond the pale of all law.   His crime was one
of the most dangerous nature.

There is not so much to be said in favour of the
bill of pains and penalties against Atterbury.   It
is urged in justification, that Walpole could have
brought evidence enough against him to have convicted him of high treason in a court of law.   Whether
he could have done so or not, it remains as a stain
upon his memory for ever, that, for the purpose of
banishing this busy priest, he should have induced
Parliament to condemn him upon the evidence of
letters not in his own hand, and after the death of
the person supposed to have written them.

The protest signed by Lord Cowper and thirty-
nine other Peers on this occasion, contains a sound
and satisfactory doctrine on the subject of all bills
of this nature.

'We are of opinion,' say these Lords, 'that no
law ought to be passed on purpose to enact that anyone be guilty in law, and punished as such, but

* The Earl of Bedford, Mr. Pym, Mr. Selden, &c.

where such an extraordinary proceeding is evidently necessary for the preservation of the State.

' We clearly take it to be a very strong objection to this mode of proceeding, that rules of law made for the security of the subject are of no use to him in it, and that the conclusion from hence is very strong; that, therefore, it ought not to be taken up, but where clearly necessary, as before affirmed; and we do desire to explain ourselves so far, upon the cases of necessity excepted, as to say we do not intend to include a necessity, arising purely from an impossibility of convicting any other way.'

Setting aside bills of pains and penalties as of dangerous example, it may be alleged that the regular power of impeachment is the security for the responsibility of the ministers of the Crown. As the power of refusing supplies enables the House of Commons to insist that no persons should be advisers of the Crown as ministers who do not enjoy the confidence of the House of Commons, so the power of impeachment is a security against high crimes and misdemeanours on the part of persons who possess that confidence. The impeachment of Lord Melville, who possessed fully the confidence of the House of Commons, may be quoted as a case in point. But it must also be truly said that these two powers of the House of Commons, namely, that of refusing supplies and of impeachment, have proved so efficient, that it was quite enough they should be understood to exist, in order to procure all the advantages they were intended to secure. A refusal or even a delay of supplies on the part of the House of Commons would alarm the country, and shake public credit; the impeachment of a minister may be voted in Parliament, but could hardly in practice be prosecuted to conviction. These terrors have had their day, and their disuse is the proof, not of their uselessness, but of their efficacy. .

CHAPTER XX.

GEORGE THE FIRST AND GEORGE THE SECOND.

' I shall continue, during the short remainder of my life, most steadily attached to the ancient freedom of my country (as it was practically enjoyed under those honest old gentlemen, George the First and Second), and your grateful servant,
'JOHN HORNE TOOKE.'
Mr. Horne Tooke's Address to the Electors
of Westminster, June 26, 1802.

THE tranquil accession of the House of Hanover to the throne of these realms is the greatest miracle of our history. The ministry of Queen Anne, great part of the Church, and almost all the country gentlemen, were against this violation of the rules of legitimacy, merely in order to preserve the civil and religious liberty of the country; it was the triumph of the enlightened few over the bigotry of millions.

The accession of George I. was the era when government by party was fully established in England. During the reign of William, Whigs and Tories had been employed together by the King; and although the distinctions of a Whig ministry and a Tory ministry were more decidedly marked during the reign of Anne, yet Marlborough and Godolphin, who formed great part of the strength of the Whig ministry, were Tories; and Harley and St. John, who put themselves at the head of the Tory administration, had held, a short time before, subordinate offices under the Whigs. But the complete downfal of the Tory administration, who had signed the peace of Utrecht, and the well-founded suspicion which attached to the whole

party, of favouring the claim of James II.'s son,
placed George I. entirely in the hands of the
Whigs. At the same period, the financial difficulties which followed the winding-up of the war,
and the great practical talents of Walpole as a
statesman, contributed to give a greater importance
to the House of Commons than ever, and to place
within that House, if I may so express myself, the
centre of gravity of the State. Besides these causes,
much weight and authority, according to the opinion
of Speaker Onslow, were added to the House of
Commons by the Septennial Act.

We now find, therefore, a party ruling the country through the House of Commons; a species of
government which has been assailed with vehe-
mence, with plausibility, eloquence, and wit, by
Swift, and Bolingbroke, and the whole Tory party
in the reigns of George I. and II.; by Lord Bute
and the King's friends in the commencement of the
reign of George III., and by a party of Parliamentary reformers at a later period. The sum
of their objections to it is this:—That it mixes
and confounds the functions of the King with those
of the House of Commons; that the King hereby
loses his prerogative of choosing his own servants,
and becomes a slave to his powerful subjects;
whilst, on the other hand, the House of Commons,
by interfering in the executive government, open
their door to corruption, and, instead of being the
vigilant guardians of the public purse, become the
accomplices of an ambitious oligarchy. Now this
objection, if good, is fatal to our whole constitution; for we have seen, in reviewing the reign of
Charles I., that a King whose servants are quite
independent of Parliament, and a Parliament which
is adverse to all abuses of power, cannot exist together: submission from one of the parties, or civil
war, must ensue.

The question, then, for us to consider is, not whether the government of the two first Princes of the House of Brunswick was a corruption of the old English constitution, but whether it was upon the whole a good or an evil form of government.

The first consideration that must strike us is, that the liberty of the subject was maintained. The chief exceptions to this remark are, the suspension of the *Habeas Corpus* Act on the discovery of Layer's plot, and the attainder of Bishop Atterbury. Of the latter I have already spoken. The suspension of the *Habeas Corpus* Act on Layer's plot has always seemed to me unnecessary; but it is impossible to form any correct judgment on this point, and it must not be forgotten that all the chief Jacobites of England were at that time intriguing at Rome to bring in the Pretender. These exceptions to the general liberty of the subject are trifling and temporary; few periods in the history of any nation have been so little disturbed by violations of personal freedom as that of the administration of Walpole.

Another remark nearly allied to the former is, that the triumph of party was not marked in England as it has been in nearly every republic that ever existed, ancient or modern, by a cruel and unsparing persecution of their adversaries. The history of the divisions of the parties of aristocracy and democracy in the minor States of Greece,—of the parties of Marius and Sylla, of Cæsar and Antony and Octavius at Rome,—of the Guelfs and the Ghibelines, the Bianchi and the Neri, in Italy, —of the Catholics and the Huguenots in France,— is a history of proscriptions, confiscations, massacres, and murders; but the reign of the first Prince of the House of Hanover, is a time when little severity, and still less rancour, is to be found. Although many of the Tories were known to be adverse to the Protestant

settlement, yet little was done against them, besides
the banishment of Bolingbroke, Ormond, and Atterbury. The temper of Walpole inclined him to
mildness and moderation. He knew many who
corresponded with the Pretender, of whom he took
no notice. It is said that, one day, Wyndham, or
Shippen, made a violent speech, which excited a
murmur, and a cry of ' Tower !' ' Tower !' among
his opponents. Sir Robert Walpole rose : ' I know
the honourable gentleman expects me to move
that he be sent to the Tower; I shall disappoint
his expectations, however, for I shall do no such
thing.'

The strength of Walpole's administration lying
chiefly with the House of Lords and the aristocratic
part of the country, he was enabled to carry on for
many years a pacific system. Peace, at all times
a blessing, was then most desirable. The politic
union between England and France took away all
the fears so long inspired by the overgrown ambition of Louis XIV. of seeing Europe enslaved, and
a king forced upon us by foreign powers. Thus
the country, undisturbed either by invasions of
liberty at home, or by wars abroad, enjoyed a
respite from the violent contests in which she had
so long been engaged. And, upon the whole, the
people had reason to be satisfied with the government of Walpole. Montesquieu, who has most
contributed to spread an admiration of the English
constitution over the Continent, and to hold it out
as a fit model for imitation, took his notions of it
from this period. At the same time, however, there
was a fault in the temper of Walpole's government, the most fatal of any to the permanence of
a spirit of freedom in a nation. With the view
of soothing the angry passions which disturbed the
early part of his career, he gradually weakened,
and had nearly extinguished, every large and liberal

feeling in politics. To maintain 'our happy establishment' was the great end of his administration; an object which, however praiseworthy,
was little calculated to excite vigour of thought, or
energy of character. For this, perhaps, no blame
is justly imputable to him. What we may complain
of, with truth, is, that in his choice of means he
showed a low opinion of human nature, and ad-
dressed himself rather to the interested views of
individuals, than to any public sense of the benefit
of the whole. Thus he went on depraving the
times in which he lived, and the times again depraving him, till the State was divided into a number of low parties and petty chiefs.

The administration of Walpole fell at last by
unjust clamours about the right of search, and
a general impatience for change. No government
can withstand a combination of the stupid and
the foolish, or, as Henry VIII. termed them, the
'dull party' and the 'rash party.' In England, the
Tory party had always had the benefit of the weight
and influence of the stupid part of the nation. The
unlettered squires embraced with cordiality the notion
of the divine right of kings. Addison has given a
perfect picture of one of them in a number of the
'Freeholder.' The dog that has the sagacity to
worry a dissenter, the squire's complaints of the progress of trade and commerce, and his resolution to
resist any government that is not for non-resistance,
are characteristic of the Tory country-gentlemen of
that day. Even at the time of the dissolution of
Walpole's administration, Pulteney, in talking of
the disposal of places, said, that the Tories, not being
men of calculation, or acquainted with foreign languages, did not pretend to the higher offices of the
State. The Whigs, on the other hand, had in their
origin derived some support from the folly of mankind. The wisdom of Somers, and the steady pa-

triotism of Lord Cavendish, did not excite so much
enthusiasm as the handsome person of the Duke
of Monmouth; and the story of the warming-pan
brought as many adherents to the cause of the Revolution, as the *Habeas Corpus* Act and the Bill of
Rights. The foolish were, however, naturally es-
tranged from Walpole by his calm conduct, and the
unpretending wisdom of his measures. They united
themselves with the stupid, and formed, as might
have been expected, an overwhelming majority in
the nation.

It is astonishing to see how little, after twenty-
five years of power, could be brought against Walpole, even when his enemies were in office. His
conduct in the South Sea business appears upon the
whole to have been extremely judicious. Corruption
in boroughs to an extent at which their posterity
would not blush, is indeed related by the Secret
Committee. Large sums, too, the disposal of which
his agents persisted in keeping secret, are unac-
counted for. The attempt to indemnify them from
all proceedings in order to get evidence from them
against their principal, failed in the House of Lords.

The effect of the long stagnation of public spirit
in the country is lamentably seen in the changes of
ministry which took place after the resignation of
Walpole. Principle seems to have made no part of
the faith of statesmen; and all political contention
was reduced to a scramble for office, between little
bands of men whose rank and fortune only rendered
their conduct more contemptible. Lord Melcombe's
diary affords a faithful and very disgusting picture
of the manner in which these small factions rose
alternately one upon the other, forming every day
new combinations, and varying their connections in
every possible way, without ever deviating into an
honest and consistent line of public rectitude.

It is singular, and at the same time melancholy to

K

observe how much influence was retained by a person so totally devoid of clearness of head, and even
of common manly spirit, as the Duke of Newcastle.
By intriguing to overturn Walpole, his colleague,
and by bargaining in boroughs, he became the most
powerful amongst the Whigs.   But his incapacity
and dishonesty were one of the chief causes of the
ruin of the party, who did not for a long time recover
the disgrace of having served under such a chief.

There is one man, however, whose life forms an
exception to these remarks, and who did much to
waken the country from the lethargy into which it
was plunged.   I mean, of course, Lord Chatham.
He was in almost every respect the reverse of Walpole.   Walpole lowered the tone of public men, till
it became unequal to any generous effort : Chatham
raised his voice against selfishness and corruption,
and his invectives even now make the cheeks tingle
with indignation.   Walpole acted upon the love of
ease, the prudence, and the timidity of mankind :
Chatham appealed to their energy, their integrity,
and their love of freedom.   It must be acknowledged
that Walpole had some merits which Lord Chatham
wanted.   He pursued from the beginning one steady
and, upon the whole, useful line of State-policy :
Lord Chatham acted from the impulse of the moment;
and if he followed his feeling of the day, he little
cared how inconsistent it might be with his former
sentiments.   Walpole seemed to aim at what was
most expedient; Chatham, at what was most striking:
the former secured the guarantee of France to the
Protestant succession ; the latter attacked her pos-
sessions and humbled her name.   Walpole looked to
prosperity, Chatham to glory; the one carefully
amassed the means which the other magnificently dis-
sipated.   Walpole was successful nearly to the end
of his life.   The cause of his long power is to be
found both in the steadiness of his conduct, and his

care to unite together a large and respected party in favour of his government.   Lord Chatham succeeded in nothing after the accession of George III.   He had neither sufficient consistency of character to inspire confidence in those who were to act with him, nor did he set a proper value on the importance of party in this country.   If Walpole had thought too much of individuals, Lord Chatham consulted them too little.   Provided he made up his mind to a measure, he seems to have thought that he could always find men to carry it into effect.   His temper made him reject or quarrel with those who were best fitted by integrity and general views to assist him, but who differed with him in the smallest point; and he sought aid from others who flattered, ridiculed, betrayed, and supplanted him.

Hence it was that the political character of England was not raised out of the mire into which it had fallen, by the splendid talents, generous virtues, and lofty views of the first William Pitt, Earl of Chatham.

CHAPTER XXL

GEORGE THE THIRD.—BEGINNING OF HIS REIGN.— AMERICAN WAR.

'Moreover, I have a maxim, that the extinction of party is the origin of faction.—Letter of Horace Walpole to Mr. Montague, Dec. 11, 1760.

WHEN George III. came to the throne, little apparent alteration took place in the internal government of the country. An Act was passed to continue the judges in their offices notwithstanding the demise of the Crown. Although it was obvious that such an Act diminished in no way the power of George III., but only took away one means of influence from his successor, yet this measure was represented as an act of unparalleled generosity on the part of the young King. As a proof of royal patriotism, it is nothing; and as an addition to the liberties of the subject, it is not worth mentioning. The Act of William III., which made the judges independent of the pleasure of the Crown, and gave them their offices during good behaviour, was the true security for their independence. What has been done since has been merely ornament.

The important feature of the new reign was the experiment of a new project of government. Among other disastrous consequences of the want of public spirit in England, was a total neglect of the political education of the young King; hence he came to be placed in the hands of men who had but recently shaken from their minds their allegiance to the House of Stuart. It occurred to these persons that, in the general blight of political virtue and public

confidence, an opportunity was afforded for raising
the household standard of the sovereign, and rallying
around his person the old relics of the Jacobite party,
with the addition of all who, in the calculation of
chances, might think the favour of the sovereign as
good an interest as the countenance of any minister
whatever. To form and consolidate this party, they
studiously spread all the doctrines which place the
whole virtue of a monarchy in the supreme sanctity
of the royal person. They endeavoured to obtain a
certain number of seats in the House of Commons,
which, with the help of a proportionate quantity
of patronage, might make the tenure of any ministry uncertain. They made loud professions of
honesty and of conscience, which, when examined,
consisted in an obstinate adherence to certain narrow-
minded tenets, and did not prevent the most shameful violations of sincerity and truth, whenever it
suited their purpose to deceive and to betray. They
assiduously planted their maxims of government in
the mind of their royal pupil; and as he was naturally slow, obedient, good-tempered, and firm, he
too easily admitted, and too constantly retained, the
lessons of his early masters.

Almost everything conspired to favour the projects of this mischievous faction. The disunion of
the Whigs; the contemptible character of the Duke
of Newcastle; the inconsistency and vanity of Lord
Chatham; the decay of Jacobitism; the predilec-
tion of the people in favour of the young King, the
first of his family born in England, all strengthened
the new sect. The prejudice of the nation against
Lord Bute, as a Scotchman, was the only set-off
against a host of favourable circumstances.

The system had flourished for some years in full
vigour, when Mr. Burke gave the powerful exposi-
tion and the sound and statesmanlike refutation of
it, which we read in the 'Thoughts on the present

Discontents.' This, which is one of the few standard works on the practical art of government
which the world possesses, did not and could not
immediately destroy the monster which it attacked.
But it rendered a service to this country scarcely
less essential, by instilling into the minds of young
politicians, who at that time were greatly increasing in number throughout the country, those wise
and beneficial principles which their Whig ancestors had practised, but which the old intriguers of
that day had entirely forgotten.

The American War, disastrous as it was to the
councils and to the arms of the country, was eminently useful in reviving the spirit of liberty. The
speeches of Lord Chatham, the speech on conci-
liation with America of Mr. Burke, and above all
the fervid eloquence of Mr. Fox, revived the genius
of the Whig party, and made them truly that 'con-
servatory of free principles' which they must ever
be, if they aspire to their proper place in the Commonwealth.

CHAPTER XXII.

THE SENSE OF JUSTICE.

'Sous quelque idée de légèreté et d'inconsidération qu'on se plaise
à nous représenter le peuple, j'ai éprouvé que souvent il embrasse à
la vérité, certaines vues, vers lesquelles il se porte avec chaleur, ou
plutôt avec fureur; mais que ces vues ont pourtant toujours pour
objet quelque intérêt commun, et d'une certaine généralité, jamais
un intérêt purement particulier, comme peuvent être les ressentimens
et les passions d'un seul homme, ou d'un petit nombre de personnes.
Je hasarde même de dire, que sur ce point le juge le moins faillible
est la voix de ce peuple même.'—*Sully*, 1. 14.

ONE of the conditions necessary for the maintenance of that species of freedom which excludes all
arbitrary power, is, that the people should be ready
to take part with the weak oppressed, against the
powerful oppressor. Madame de Staël remarks of
the French people of her own day, that they perceive immediately where power lies, and always
range themselves on that side. The truth of this
observation may be demonstrated by referring to
the events of the Revolution, or attending to what
happens in any one year in France. The quality
essential to freedom, however, is one directly the
reverse. The people ought to feel a continual
jealousy of power; and when they see any man borne
down unjustly, they ought to perceive immediately,
that the cause of that man is the cause of the whole
nation.

This is happily the case with the English people.
Nothing but the sympathy of the people could have
raised to such importance and celebrity the cause of
Hampden, when he refused to pay a few shillings to
the Crown. The imprisonment of a Mr. Francis
Jenkes, for making a patriotic speech in the Common Council of London, roused the indignation

of all lovers of their country, and was the immediate
cause of the Habeas Corpus Act.

Such, too, was the case of John Wilkes. Mr.
Wilkes, though detested and despised by good men,
as a hypocrite in public and a profligate in private
life, was defended by all who loved their country,
when arbitrary measures were resorted to for the
purpose of oppressing him. He was arrested by
virtue of a general warrant, wherein his name was
not mentioned, and he was designated only as the
author of the 'North Briton,' No. 45. At the same
time his papers were seized, and he was by this
means discovered to be the author of an obscene
libel, called the 'Essay on Woman.' It is evident
that the authority to issue general warrants was a
very dangerous power, and might have been used
to renew those arbitrary arrests which took place
under the Stuarts. Hence all the friends of freedom espoused the cause of Wilkes. Lord Chatham,
then Mr. Pitt, spoke with abhorrence of the man
and of his works, but with indignation of the means
that had been used to oppress him; and the people
who would have rejoiced to have seen him legally
punished, would not allow him to be unjustly persecuted. They felt not for Wilkes, but for the
law; they would have praised the jury which convicted him; they censured the minister who oppressed him; and in the cry of Wilkes and Liberty,
they adopted a contemptible person for the sake
of a sacred principle. A motion against general
warrants was defeated by a small majority in the
House of Commons; but Wilkes obtained at length
large damages against the ministers who had abused
their power, and put an end to general warrants for
ever. So I trust it may always be, when any
individual, however humble, however odious, or
however despicable, is pursued by illegal or unjust
methods!

CHAPTER XXIII.

OF AN EXTREME REMEDY AGAINST THE ABUSES OF POWER ; AND OF MODERATION IN THE USE OF THE REMEDY.

. . . Esto
Liberque ac sapiens.—*Persius.*

As a very numerous body are found incapable of transacting foreign affairs with that secrecy, or of deciding upon them with that celerity, which the foreign relations of a State so often require, every wise State has found it expedient to transfer a large portion of power out of the hands of large numbers, and to entrust it to a single person or select council. Hence the great council of Venice was, by the advice of the wisest senators, excluded by degrees from all deliberations which required delicacy and despatch. Hence the Republic of Holland found it necessary to name a few persons to whom all foreign negotiations were confided.

But for whatever purpose power may be confided to a few persons, or however worthy they may be of the trust reposed in them, human nature is such, that there ought always to remain with the people an extreme remedy by which they may punish the abuse, or restrain the power itself that has been abused. In States really free this extreme remedy will always be found to exist, either by custom or by law. Thus the Roman people, when they felt themselves aggrieved, retired to the *Mons Sacer,* or refused to be inscribed as soldiers in the army that was about to march against the foreign enemy. There could not be apparently two more dangerous expedients ; but such was the moderation of the

Roman people, that I know not they ever pushed
their resistance beyond the bounds of reason. Indeed, the long period that elapsed before the
plebeians could be elected to any office in the
State, and the many years that followed after the
law passed allowing them to be military tribunes,
before any plebeian was really chosen, are sufficient
proofs of their temperance, both in advancing a
claim and in making use of a right.

The English have, in the same manner, an extreme remedy. If the king abuses a just, or attempts to exercise an oppressive power, the representatives of the people have the right to refuse
the money required to carry on the government.
This remedy, however, was for a long time far
from being so efficacious as those employed by the
Roman people. In spite of the resistance of the
nation, Charles II. and James found means, with
the aid of packed Parliaments, and drafts on the
French treasury, to slip the bridle from their necks.
In fact, until the expulsion of the Stuarts, our kings
enjoyed a revenue independent of Parliament, which
enabled them to keep their Commons out of sight in
ordinary times. The parliamentary check was made
perfect at the Revolution; but the influence of the
Crown in the body which ought to exercise it, has
continually deadened its effect. The voice of the
people, however, has sometimes enforced the constitutional interference of the House of Commons.
The most remarkable instance, perhaps, of the use
of this right took place at the end of the American
war. The House of Commons declared, by a resolution, that the further prosecution of offensive war
on the continent of North America tended to
weaken this country, and to prevent a reconciliation
with America. An address in conformity to this vote
having been carried to the throne, and the King
having returned a gracious answer, complying with

the address, the House of Commons voted that they should consider as enemies of his Majesty and this country all those who should advise the further prosecution of the war in North America, for the purpose of reducing the revolted colonies to obedience by force.   In this, as in a few other instances, although the word *supplies* is not mentioned, it must always be understood; and there is, in fact, a tacit menace of refusing supplies in every interference of the House of Commons with the exercise of the prerogative.

This power, it is quite clear, would enable the House of Commons, if so disposed, to declare themselves the sovereigns, and to take away every efficient prerogative from the Crown; but such is the moderation of the English people, that they have never desired so formidable an increase of their own power or that of their representatives.   At the Revolution, when the whole question was open, they did not take away a single grain of the powers necessary to maintain the monarchy.   So, at the present day, the true reason why the Crown maintains its prerogative and the House of Lords their privileges unimpaired lies in the temper of the nation.   The country has a deep-rooted affection for kingly government, and would highly resent any attempt to change or destroy this keystone of the Constitution: nor, as far as I can observe, is this sentiment confined to particular orders of men; it pervades the whole country from one end to the other.

CHAPTER XXIV.

CRIMINAL LAW.

'The discretion of a judge is the law of tyrants: it is always unknown: it is different in different men: It is casual, and depends upon
constitution, temper, passion. In the best, it is oftentimes caprice; in
the worst, it is every vice, folly, and passion to which human nature
is liable.'—*Lord Camden.*

UNTIL the years which followed the peace of 1815,
our legislators were so much engrossed by political
events, that criminal law met with little attention.
Thus a merchant or squire went into the House
of Commons, exasperated by the loss of his broad-
cloth, or the robbery of his fish, and immediately
endeavoured to restrain the crime by severe penalties. Mr. Burke used to relate that, being
stopt one night as he was leaving the House of
Commons, and requested by the clerk at the table to
stay to make a House, asked what was the business
in question.—'Oh! sir,' said the clerk, 'it's only a
new capital felony.' Hence it was that, every man
judging that to be the most deadly offence by which
he was himself a sufferer, the Parliament permitted
the statute-book to be loaded with the penalty of
death for upwards of two hundred offences. Among
the crimes so punishable, we find the offences of
cutting down a tree; being found with the face
blackened upon the high road; being in company
with the persons called gipsies. These continued
to be capital crimes till the year 1820, and one of
them at least still longer.

These extreme cases are not, however, the most
mischievous. The absurdity of the law is an anti-

dote to its cruelty. There were other offences, punishable with death, which are really in themselves very serious crimes, but not of so atrocious a character as to reconcile any humane man to their being visited with so severe a penalty. Of this kind are many offences against the bankrupt laws; privately stealing from the person; stealing from a dwelling-house to the amount of 40s.; privately stealing from a shop to the amount of 5s.; and many others. The mischiefs produced by these sanguinary laws were not however, as might have been expected, a very great frequency of capital punishment, and general insensibility in the people.

The evils peculiarly felt were two :—First, as it is justly stated by Mr. Justice Blackstone, there is a general disposition not to convict of a crime to which an inordinate punishment is affixed. Cases were innumerable in which juries have found goods of great value, and even £10 and £20 notes, to be under forty or five shillings value, in order not to convict a thief of a capital offence.[*]

Mr. Harmer, who had been solicitor for two thousand persons condemned to death, informed the Criminal Law Committee that an old offender always preferred being tried for a capital offence, as it gave him a better chance of an acquittal. It is instructive to reflect that something of the same kind happened at Athens. A criminal, when convicted, was asked before the people how he would be punished; and an old offender always named the most severe punishment, to excite compassion in his judges. It was partly because Socrates, instead of following this custom, replied that his sentence ought to be that he should be kept all his life at the expense of the State, that he was condemned to death.

Notwithstanding this well-known disposition of

<hr/>

* See the excellent speech of Mr. Buxton on the Forgery Bill, 1821.

human nature, so accustomed were we to rely on the
efficacy of capital punishments, that in any discussion on repealing a criminal law, the question in
many men's minds always was, not whether the
offence was actually prevented by that law, but
whether the offence is sufficiently grave to deserve
that it should be prevented by so severe a method.
People are apt to consult their own sense of this
matter, instead of looking to that of jurymen.

Secondly. Another great evil in the former state
of the law was its uncertainty. Two men, for instance, were tried at Launceston for sheep-stealing:
both were found guilty; one was condemned to
death, and the other to be transported for seven
years. It is evident there is no proportion in the
punishments. What is the reason? The one had a
good character, the other a bad one. So that in
England a man was hanged, not for the crime of
which he was found guilty, but for the general
course of his life. Now this is a matter upon which
the prisoner was not tried. Such a system leads to
injustice, cruelty, and confusion. It takes away the
only motive for capital punishment, viz. the benefit
of example. It does little or nothing towards the re-
pression of the crime punished. It makes the punishment of death useless, and therefore cruel; for
every criminal will hope that his character will not be
found so bad as to make him forfeit his life. It
puts a man upon his trial for actions which the law
does not profess to try, and upon which he cannot
be prepared with a defence. Thus it happened a
few years ago, that a man of notoriously bad character, after going through a course of larceny and
burglary with impunity, was at last, to the great surprise of his neighbours, his jury, and his prosecutor,
hanged for cutting down young trees.[*]

[*] See the evidence respecting this case given before the Criminal
Law Committee.

Many persons however, till a recent period, thought it extremely dangerous to admit that our law was in such a state as to require reform. Absolute sovereigns have not been affected by this danger. The King of Prussia (Frederick the Great), during part of his long reign, placed his whole system of law under discussion, and during a remaining portion a project of new laws was under the eye of the public for general criticism and consideration; the King thus taking away from the authority of the old law without substituting anything in its place. Catherine of Russia, and Napoleon, were the authors of new codes. Many of the sovereigns of Europe have altered their whole criminal jurisprudence. Why is it, that all these governments have undertaken the task without fear or hesitation, and that a party in England was so long fearful of any innovation whatever in our old system? The reason I believe to be this,—that a very large portion of the higher ranks in England never have understood, and never will understand, the real security of the English Government. These persons, seeing authority continually attacked, imagined that the throne would be subverted, if any part of our bad laws were removed. They were not aware that the real foundation of royalty and aristocracy in England is the opinion the people have of their utility to the country, and that the retaining any absurd or bigoted or cruel statute, instead of preserving, undermines and destroys the respect paid to the assemblies which have the charge of improving and amending, as well as of strengthening and preserving, the volume of our laws.

The question of secondary punishments is the most difficult of any. The words of Mr. Harmer afford perhaps the best rule, shortly expressed, on this subject. 'If I were asked,' said this gentleman, in an examination before a committee of the House of Commons, 'what description of punishments would, in my opinion, be productive of benefit, I would answer, Such as might force the delinquent into a course of discipline wholly opposite to his habits. Idleness is assuredly a part of his character, which industry would counteract. Set him to labour. He is probably debauched, and abstinence would be advantageous to both his mind and his body : apply it. He has been accustomed to dissolute companions, separation from whom would essentially ameliorate him : keep him in solitude. He has hitherto rioted in uncontrolled liberty of action. I propose that he should be subjected to restraint, and the observance of a proper decorum.'

CHAPTER XXV.

PUBLIC SCHOOLS.

' As it is in the body, so it is in the mind ; practice makes it what
it is ; and most even of those excellences, which are looked on as natural endowments, will be found, when examined into more narrowly,
to be the product of exercise, and to be raised to that pitch only by
repeated actions.'—*Locke, of the Conduct of the Understanding.*

THE education of youth, which has employed so
many pens, produced so many sublime writings, and
undergone so little practical alteration, is not to be
thoroughly discussed in a few words. Some remarks,
suggested rather by observation of the world than
by any original speculation, may perhaps be allowed.

Men of enlarged views, and hearts glowing with
the love of mankind, have often conceived that
youth might be taught more knowledge than is distributed and less vice than is permitted or winked
at in the public schools of England. With this project in their heads, and the most laudable love of
their children in their hearts, many parents have
given their children a private education. They
have instructed them in ten branches of knowledge
instead of two, and have preserved their morals and
their health during the first eighteen, or perhaps
twenty years of their life. But how often have we
seen these promising flowers drop off without being
succeeded by fruit in due season! The lessons
which are learnt by a boy in the lingering and lifeless manner of a private study, without the excite-
ment of emulation, perhaps without the fear of
correction, make no lasting impression on the mind.
The restraint of a nursery of twenty years, gives a
zest to the pleasures and the vices for an indulgence
in which boyhood alone can be any palliation. The

L

period when the talents and strength of the man
ought to be unfolded is wasted in the new pursuits
of idleness and debauchery. At the same time, the
habits contracted at home, where the young patrician
met with no equal, unfit him for the rub of the great
world, and fix for ever those defects of temper which
early contradiction and early society might have ex-
tirpated. Such is often, though not certainly, the
result of an education intended to produce a prodigy
of perfection, and laid out with the hope of giving
its unhappy object a pre-eminence over the ill-trained
generation of his equals and contemporaries. The
mistake in these instances seems to arise from the
want of considering, that the object of education is
not only to store the mind, but to form the character.
It is of little use that a boy has a smattering of mi-
neralogy, and is very fluent at botanical names ; it
will be of no avail to him to talk of argil and poly-
andria, if he cries when he loses at marbles, and is
lifeless or timid when he is obliged to play a game at
cricket. Now, a public school does form the character.
It brings a boy from home, where he is a darling, where
his folly is wit, and his obstinacy spirit, to a place
where he takes rank according to his real powers
and talents. If he is sulky, he is neglected ; if he is
angry, he gets a box on the ear. His character, in
short, is prepared for the buffetings of grown men,—
for the fagging of a lawyer, or the fighting of a sol-
dier. Now, this is of much more importance than
the acquisition of mere knowledge. Many men only
begin to acquire their knowledge between twenty
and thirty, few men change their characters after
twenty. Considering the question in this view, it
is of little importance to enumerate the names of
eminent men in England who have not been brought
up at public schools. Many of these rose from
middle life, and to them my argument does not apply.
The son of a tradesman or a farmer meets hardships
enough, without being sent to any school : he is

ordered to serve a customer, or look after the hay-
makers; and learns practical life much sooner than
any gentleman's son can possibly do. If the view
that has been here opened is a right one, parents
ought to beware how they withhold from their sons,
if sufficiently strong and healthy, the advantages of
a public school. The democratic character of the
nobility of England, the democracy of the aristocracy,
if I may be allowed so to call it, is very much to be
attributed to the gregarious education they receive.
In this manner, her public schools form a part of the
constitution of the country. If they produce some
vice, and a good deal of rudeness, they subdue pride,
selfishness, and conceit; they create emulation,
friendship, a love of truth, and a manly strength of
mind. Let anyone watch the education of a youth
of high expectations in Austria or Spain: he will see
him followed everywhere by a servile flatterer, under
the name of a preceptor, learning nothing but the
varnish and the falsehood of the world,—the idol of
his parents, and the torment of their friends. Men
of sense, who have undergone this dangerous ordeal,
all speak with envy and admiration of the public
schools of England.

Let it be granted, however, that more may be
taught by private tuition. I am far from agreeing
that, for this reason, the boy of the private tutor
will have any advantage over the boy of the public
school. His knowledge will be out of place; his
exertions of mind will fail of their effect, because
they will not fit in with the minds of other men.
His superiority in some branches of learning will
be unheeded, and his inferiority in others will make
him ridiculous. Upon the whole, there is perhaps
no point from which a man can start, in any profession or pursuit, so advantageous as a complete and
thorough knowledge of what is known by other
young men, among whom he wishes to excel.

It being conceded that a boy of high expectations ought to be brought up at school, I am
not disposed to contend that the education of our
public schools is exactly what is right, or that it
is all that is right. These schools were instituted
at a time when all knowledge was contained in the
Greek and Latin classics, and no sound opinion
or polished taste was to be found out of the learned
languages. From this groundwork, however, the
moderns have raised a prodigious edifice, both of
science and of literature, of the whole of which our
school education, from eight to eighteen, took till
lately no notice whatever. The first thing, however,
it must be admitted, is to learn how to learn: '*Il faut
apprendre à apprendre*;' and for this it is requisite
that the first thing taught should be difficult to acquire and be retained when it is acquired. I know
nothing so good for this purpose as the Latin grammar. Boys, it is said, do not understand it. They
do understand, however, that a nominative case goes
before the verb; and they come in a short time to
learn where each part of speech must be placed, and
how it depends upon another. If Mr. Locke is right
in his estimate of the importance of words, this is a
point of great consequence. And who can doubt
that he is right? It is to a dogged application to
the Latin grammar perhaps that the precision of
men, when compared to women, in this country, is
in great part to be attributed.*

The Latin grammar learnt, easy prose, then the
poetry of Virgil, some arithmetic, the Greek grammar, Homer, some geometry, and a little geography,
might come in their due order. Above all, I would
make boys learn faithfully an abridgment of the
History of England, and of the first and last volumes
of Blackstone.

* I hear with pleasure that the masters of our public schools have agreed upon an improved Latin grammar. (1864.)

French should be learnt early, in order to acquire the pronunciation, and because it is the general language of Europe; German and other languages, as far as it is possible. It will be sufficient to lay a foundation for learning, at a more mature age, those parts of knowledge that are likely to be sought voluntarily, and may be acquired easily.

I know not whether it would be practicable to introduce improvements of the kind I have mentioned into our great public schools. If the masters should resist, what could be easier than to make a foundation for a certain number of boys, with the qualifications of being the sons of poor officers, who might afterwards choose their profession; and to institute at the same place a school where education might be conducted in a manner suitable to the knowledge of the present age?*

As it is at present, there is no doubt that women of the higher ranks have much more knowledge and information, when their education is attended to, than men have. But I cannot see any reason why our boys should not, while they have the advantages of public schools, at the same time be taught to do a sum in the rule-of-three, and make themselves masters of the fact that James I. was not the son of Queen Elizabeth.†

* This is done to some extent at Wellington College. (1864.)

† All the improvements suggested in this chapter, written forty-five years ago, are either made or making, and the process will be greatly accelerated by the excellent Report of the Public Schools Commission. (1864.)

CHAPTER XXVL

POOR-LAWS.

' Generally it is to be foreseen (*provided*) that the population of a kingdom, especially if it be not mown down by wars, exceed not the stock of the kingdom by which it is to be maintained.'—*Bacon.*

THERE was nothing, perhaps, in the whole state of England, which forty years ago was more threatening to its tranquillity, and the permanence of its Constitution, than the administration of the poor-laws. The perversion which had been made of them from the original meaning of the statute of Elizabeth, had at length fallen most heavily upon those who thought to draw from that abuse a selfish gain.

The statute of the 49th of Elizabeth seems to have had its rise in a general increase of idle poor throughout the country. The notion that this increase was owing to the dissolution of the monasteries is now given up ; it having been clearly shown that the same complaint was made in Spain about the same time.* It is more probable that the introduction of legal order, and the cessation of internal war not long before, both in England and Spain, threw upon society a great number of vagabonds, who were accustomed to live by vagrancy and plunder. The Act of Elizabeth directed that the old and impotent should be provided for, and that the strong and healthy should be set to work. The first of these two directions is the law of a tender and humane people, and will, I hope, ever remain upon the statute-book of England. The

* This important fact was first brought to light in the 'Edinburgh Review.'

second direction is not equally easy of execution.
A few casual beggars, indeed, might be provided for
in this way; but when, from stoppage of trade, or
any other cause, there exists a superabundant population, it is manifest that any work which could be
done by the unemployed, would only be augmenting
the stock of a market already overflowing. When
this was found to be actually the case, the overseers,
instead of furnishing work, supplied the unemployed
with money. With the fluctuations of commerce,
the issue of a fictitious currency, the vast increase
of taxes, and, above all, in the years of scarcity
during the great war, a new difficulty arose:—men
who had large families found themselves unable to
support them, although they were themselves employed, from the very low rate of wages compared
with the price of food. Instead of a rise of wages,
the natural and obvious remedy for such an evil, it
was agreed that a certain sum of money should be
paid for the support of each child at the house of
his father. In this provision, introduced under the
pressure of temporary distress, the farmer saw a
means of reducing the price of labour. Having the
market of labourers overstocked, and therefore at
his command, he refused to give to the unmarried
labourer more than was sufficient to support life;
he gave the same to the married labourer, and paid
out of the poor-rates the exact sum necessary for
the subsistence of the labourer's children. By this
scheme the ignorant employer thought he had reduced the price of labour to the lowest possible;
and there have not been wanting men of enlightened
minds disposed to exalt the scheme as the perfection
of rural economy. The natural consequence of such
a scheme, however, was in the first place to lower
the character of the labourer : to make him pass his
life in dependence, and see himself, instead of being
able to rear an industrious family from the savings

of his wages, reduced to the condition of a public mendicant. This consequence, perhaps, might not have given any disquiet to the employer; but there is another as certain and as necessary: and that is, that marriages will no longer be regulated by the demand for labour; and that a labourer, seeing that his children will be fed out of the public fund, will marry when it suits his inclination, without a penny in his pocket. Hence an immense growing population, with a defective and diminishing market; a rapid supply, without any adequate demand. And there existed forty years ago no apparent reason why the evil should not continue to increase, until, at length, the whole profits of cultivating the land were swallowed up by the expense of maintaining a colony of useless mouths. If that had happened, the farmer and the labourers must have fallen together; and there would have been thrown upon society a number of people ignorant of all duties, deprived of all sense of independence, and accustomed to derive their means of subsistence without labour from the public funds. Such a result, it is manifest, would have been more calamitous than any revolution that has yet happened in the world. Happily, the farmers at length felt the evil themselves, and endeavoured, by one way or another, to apply a remedy.

The evils of the poor-laws at length became so great as to incline men to wish for their total repeal. But I am inclined to think that, great as was the mischief of the former system, the entire abolition of the poor-laws would have been still greater. In a country subject to such violent transitions from the revolutions of trade and commerce, it would be cruel and inhuman to expose the labouring classes to the ruin that would follow a period of agricultural or manufacturing distress. The poor-laws required to be pruned, not rooted up: the use of the knife, and not of the axe. Happily the true remedy was at length applied.

CHAPTER XXVII.

WAR WITH THE FRENCH REPUBLIC.

'It is imprudent to attack a people who are divided amongst themselves, with a view of conquering them, in consequence of their disunion.

' There was such disunion in the Roman republic between the people and the nobility, that the inhabitants of Veii, together with the Etruscans, thought that they could extinguish the Roman name by taking advantage of these dissensions. Having raised an army therefore, and made incursions upon the territory of Rome, the senate sent against them Cneius Manlius and Marcus Fabius, whose army encamping near the enemy, the people of Veii did not cease from attacking, both by arms and by reproaches, the Roman name; and such was their rashness and insolence, that the Romans, who were disunited, became united, and engaging the enemy, defeated and routed them. We see therefore how much men deceive themselves, as we have before observed, in the line of conduct they adopt, and how it frequently happens that, in thinking to obtain an object, they lose it. The people of Veii believed, that by attacking the Romans disunited, they should defeat them; and the attack, on the contrary, caused the union of the Romans, and their own ruin: for the causes of dissension in republics are generally idleness and peace; the causes of union are fear and war. . . . The people of Veii therefore were deceived in their opinion, and were, in short, in one day overcome by the Romans. And so for the future will be deceived whoever, in a similar way, and for a similar cause, shall think to oppress a nation.'—*Machiavel, Discourses.*

THE war against France, undertaken in 1793, exemplified at its commencement the wise observations which I have quoted from Machiavel. The more apparent the attempts of the Allied Powers to regulate her internal government, the greater her vigour, the more brilliant her victories, the more extensive her conquests. At length, tempted by military trophies and successful treaties, she confided herself to a sovereign who, abusing his genius and his force, endeavoured to make himself despotic lord of the whole continent of Europe. The Whig

ministry of 1806 found it impossible to make peace
with him; and, with few exceptions, all parties in
England agreed in thinking the continuance of the
war just and necessary. The Spanish people, in
1808, rose in the same cause which the French
people had defended in 1793—the cause of national
independence. At length, drunk with unexampled
power and glory, and irritated by a perpetual thirst
of action, the Emperor of France carried his great
army of conquerors to perish amid the frosts of
Russia. The nations roused themselves, restored
national governments, and hurled the conqueror from
the throne. The republic had triumphed, the universal monarchy was defeated. In other words, the
kings of Europe made war on the people of France,
and were beaten: at a later time the nations of
Europe made war on the Sovereign of France, and
were successful.

CHAPTER XXVIII.

LIBERTY THE GREAT SOURCE OF THE WEALTH OF NATIONS, AND ESPECIALLY OF THAT OF ENGLAND.

'Liberty, the parent of commerce; the parent of wealth; the parent of knowledge; the parent of every virtue!'—*Speech of Sir James Mackintosh, on the Foreign Enlistment Bill.*

THE object of political economy, it is well known, is the wealth of nations. Quesnay, who is generally styled the inventor of this branch of knowledge, considered agricultural labour as the only source of public wealth: Smith superseded him, and taught that wealth consisted in all material products. He therefore called the labour which raised such products from the earth, or which added a value to them by industry, productive labour; while he styled the labour which neither created such products, nor added a value to them, unproductive. The first class included agriculturists and manufacturers; the second, kings, judges, clergy, soldiers, actors, &c. M. Say has since amended this definition, and has proposed to include under the head of productive labour, all labour which is useful, whether of body or mind. Thus he considers the labour of a professor of civil law as valuable as that of a weaver of stockings. M. Say, however, though he makes this distinction, very soon loses sight of it, and in the rest of his work we find little traces of the opinion. The opinion of Adam Smith still remains the corner-stone of his own system, and of that of his disciples.

Without discussing these definitions, which are not very scientific, I conceive the object of political economy to be, to remove obstacles that may impede the progress of a nation to wealth.

In entering upon the enquiry how this object may best be effected, let us take a view of those States which history or a recent time exhibits to our view as peculiarly prosperous, or peculiarly wretched. In the latter, we should perceive a languor, a distaste to labour, an indifference to emulation, narrow parsimony, and a wretched way of living; in the former, we should observe incessant activity, vigorous enterprise, the arts flourishing, learning encouraged, comfort and ease diffused through every class. Proceeding to enquire into the circumstances which produced this difference, we should find liberty to be the great exciting cause of industry in the States whose prosperity has been the most remarkable.

It appears certain, that wherever the spirit of the Government itself has not repressed the love of gain, as at Sparta, the industry of free citizens has excelled the efforts of slaves, deprived of motives by the jealousy of their masters. Let us turn our eyes to the proud merchants of Florence, Venice, and Holland, making their little States the envy and terror of great monarchies. Let us refer, on the other hand, to the people of France, living in wretched dependence on arbitrary taxes, and forced to conceal their food from dread of their Government. Let us pause a moment to consider what was, forty years ago, the different situation of England and Spain. By the report of a committee of the Cortes, it appeared that the utmost amount of taxation which, in their judgment, Spain could bear, was about £6,000,000; in the same year, England and Scotland cannot have paid less than £60,000,000, and, including poor-rates and county-rates, nearer £70,000,000. What was the cause of this prodigious difference of wealth? Was it that the English laws on trade and commerce were so greatly superior in wisdom to those of the Spaniards? This can hardly be alleged to be the case: our own laws on these subjects were, up to the

peace of 1814, the products of protection and prohibition, the most absurd and irrational of any system of national economy. Is it that Spain entirely neglected the new lights of the age? On the contrary,
she endowed a professorship of political economy in
the University of Salamanca; a step which was not
taken so early, that I know, by any other great State
in Europe.   She has had, in the course of the last
century, ministers who had the most enlightened
views of public wealth; but despotism blasted all
their efforts, and every tree they planted, after a few
feeble shoots, withered and died beneath its poisonous
influence;—the very desire of accumulation was
wanting, for all the privileges of civilisation, the
expanded mind and generous knowledge of freemen,
were forbidden by the Inquisition. England, on the
other hand, blest with equal laws, and affording scope
for the expansion of the best faculties of man, has
been rewarded for her liberality by the efforts which
industry, genius, and talent will always make when
not impeded by despotic or bad government.

But let us listen on this subject to two great
orators, at a period when the exertions of the country to retrieve its losses during the American War
had been crowned with unexampled success.   Mr.
Pitt, the minister, said—

'Such are the circumstances which appear to me
to have contributed most immediately to our present
prosperity.   But these again are connected with
others yet more important.   They are obviously and
necessarily connected with the duration of peace, the
continuance of which, on a secure and permanent
footing, must ever be the first object of the foreign
policy of this country.   They are connected still
more with its internal tranquillity, and with the
natural effects of a free but well-regulated government.   What is it which has produced, in the last
hundred years, so rapid an advance beyond what can

be traced in any other period of our history? What but that, during that time, under the mild and just government of the illustrious princes of the family now on the throne, a general calm has prevailed through the country beyond what was ever before experienced? And we have also enjoyed, in greater purity and perfection, the benefit of those original principles of our Constitution, which were ascertained and established by the memorable events that closed the century preceding? This is the great and governing cause, the operation of which has given scope to all the other circumstances which I have enumerated. It is this union of liberty with law which, by raising a barrier equally firm against the encroachments of power and the violence of popular commotion, affords to property its just security, produces the exertion of genius and labour, the extent and solidity of credit, the circulation and increase of capital; which forms and upholds the national character, and sets in motion all the springs which actuate the great mass of the community through all its various descriptions. The laborious industry of those useful and extensive classes, the peasantry and yeomanry of the country; the skill and ingenuity of the artificer; the experiments and improvements of the wealthy proprietor of land; the bold speculations and successful adventures of the opulent merchant and enterprising manufacturer;—these are all to be traced to the same course, and all derive from hence both their encouragement and their reward. On this point, therefore, let us principally fix our attention; let us preserve this first and most essential object, and every other is in our power! Let us remember that the love of the Constitution, though it acts as a sort of natural instinct in the hearts of Englishmen, is strengthened by reason and reflection, and every day confirmed by experience; that it is a Constitution which we do not merely admire

from traditional reverence, which we do not flatter
from prejudice or habit, but which we cherish and
value because we know that it practically secures
the tranquillity and welfare both of individuals and
of the public, and provides, beyond any other frame
of government which has ever existed, for the real
and useful ends which form at once the only true
foundation and only rational object of all political
societies.'

Mr. Fox, the leader of Opposition, on the other
hand, ' took occasion to pay a compliment to the
eloquence of Mr. Pitt, and to the philosophical principles of government on which he had argued. He
said the right hon. gentleman had enumerated the
causes of national prosperity with truth and splendour. He subscribed to his statement cordially,
and, if he did not himself go over the same ground,
it was because he had nothing to add to what had
been already said. But he begged to be understood
that these reasons were all applicable to the prosperity of the country, not merely to the prosperity
of the revenue. The right hon. gentleman had fairly
said that, above all, they were to be ascribed to the
happy form of our Constitution.'*

We may be satisfied with the testimony of two
such witnesses to the fact, that our free constitution
is the source of our prosperity.

The first and main cause of the wealth of nations,
then, is liberty. Passing from this part of the subject, the next great incentive to industry is order.
This can only be procured by the union of religion,
morality, and law. It is order which assures to
every one the tranquil possession of the wealth that
he may have acquired; it is the regular authority
of the law which confers a value on a house in
Middlesex above one in Turkey. Who would lay

out his capital in purchasing the fee-simple of the finest estate in the wilds of Tartary?

Connected with order, and the respect paid to property by the law, is good faith on the part of the Government. Any man would prefer the security of a banker of Amsterdam to that of an Arab chief; or the word of a London coal-merchant, to the most solemn bond of the Sultan of Bokhara. These three things, therefore, may be considered as the true springs of national wealth—freedom, order, and public faith.

Next to these great motive powers, is a wise disposition of the economical laws of the nation. Tho whole of the precepts, however, to be given on this subject resolve themselves into one—remove all obstacles to industry. As far as wealth is concerned, the fewer restrictions the better. This is the great truth proved by Smith, and his coadjutors in France and England, in opposition to the absurdities of the mercantile system.

'Laissez faire, et laissez passer,' said the French merchant to Colbert; and after two centuries of struggle against restrictions, monopolies, protections, bounties, differential duties, and regulations for directing industry and fixing wages, we can say nothing more wise or more concise.

CHAPTER XXIX.

NATIONAL DEBT.

' The common people do not work for pleasure generally, but from
necessity.   Cheapness of provisions makes them more idle ; less work
is then done, it is then more in demand, proportionally, and of course
the price rises.   Dearness of provisions obliges the manufacturer to
work more days and more hours ; thus more work is done than equals
the usual demand ; of course it becomes cheaper, and the manufactures in consequence.'—*Franklin's Political Fragments.*

' It may now be affirmed, without fear of contradiction, that we
find it as easy to pay the interest of eight hundred millions, as our
ancestors found it a century ago to pay the interest of eighty millions.'—*Macaulay's History,* vol. vi., ed. of 1864.

THE capital of the national debt, at the accession of
George I., and when all the accounts of the great
War of the Succession may be supposed to have
been settled, amounted to £54,000,000, the interest
to £3,351,000.   Sir Robert Walpole instituted a
sinking fund, on which great eulogiums were made,
and of which great hopes were entertained.   In
1739 the capital of the debt was £46,954,000, the
interest £1,963,000 ; so that he diminished the interest about £1,400,000, and the capital about
£7,000,000.   The Spanish War, however, which
commenced in 1739, increased the capital of the debt
by £31,300,000, and the interest by £1,096,000.
The peace which followed diminished the capital by
£3,700,000, and the interest by £664,000.   But in
1763, after the Seven Years' War, the national debt
amounted to £146,000,000.

From that time to the breaking out of the American War, the national debt was diminished by
£10,739,000.

At the close of the American War the national
debt amounted to £257,000,000.

M

The celebrated sinking fund of Mr. Pitt, established in 1786, reduced the national debt, during the peace, by £4,751,000, and the interest by £143,000.

On the 5th of January, 1817, after the close of the war, the national debt amounted to £848,282,247.

In four years from that time, that is, on the 5th of January, 1821, the debt amounted to £845,100,931, being a diminution of little more than three millions.*

During more than a year of this time a new sinking fund had been in operation, voted by Parliament to amount to £5,000,000 a year.

Such has been the alternate progress of national debt and sinking fund—the one advancing by giant steps, and the other, although much vaunted, never having, in the course of a century, made half the progress that was made by the national debt in the single year 1815. He must be a sanguine man indeed who expects the sinking fund to overtake his opponent.

Such being the state of the case, it is more than ever necessary to examine what this debt is, what are its effects on the prosperity of the country, and what is likely to be the ultimate result. This last enquiry is indeed one of great uncertainty. Causes the most unlooked-for may intervene, and entirely change the direction of political events.

The first operation of the national debt is as follows :—The minister borrows, we will say, £300, of a merchant who has the money in his coffers. He engages to pay £15 of interest. For this purpose he lays a tax of £5 on a landed proprietor, another £5 on a farmer, and another £5 on a tradesman, all supposed for the present to have equal incomes, and to pay the tax equally. The first operation of the tax is generally the following :—The farmer and

* Account of the Total Amount of the National Debt of England and Ireland, presented to the House of Commons, Sess. 1821.

tradesman add the tax to the price of their commodity. Thus the tradesman pays a part of the tax of the farmer, and the farmer part of that of the tradesman. A tax, it is evident, still remains upon the shoulders of each. The tradesman and farmer must therefore either work harder, and produce more of their own commodity, or they must be contented with less profits, retrench their expenses, and buy less of the commodities of their neighbour. The first takes place in a flourishing condition of a community, and the second in a poor, weak, and exhausted state. It is by the continual efforts of men to produce more, and to accumulate, that a country rises to prosperity; it is by the saving and narrowing of accumulation and expense that a nation falls into decay.

There is another manner in which a tax is paid that is still worse. It is by diminishing the profits of a particular trade. Thus, if a tax of great amount had been laid on shoe-buckles, the sellers of that article, unable to obtain the payment of the tax, would have been obliged to content themselves with less profit. The trade which is thus unequally taxed is soon abandoned.

We must not lose sight, however, either of the landed proprietor or the stockholder. The proprietor, it is evident, must pay, besides his own part, a part of the tax of the farmer and the tradesman, and he has no means of repaying himself. For this reason the economists supposed that the proprietors of land paid all the taxes. But they may, if they please, retrench their consumption, and that too with much more ease than the tradesman; as a livery-servant is more easily parted with than an artisan.

The stockholder, in the meantime, if he is a consumer, pays to the tradesman and the farmer part of the tax which is raised for his benefit. But he has greater facilities of avoiding expense than any other branch of the community.

There can be little doubt that, for a certain time,
a national debt is beneficial in its effects.   It pro-
motes a rapid circulation of money ; it brings new
capitalists into the market, with more enterprise and
more invention than the old proprietors of land ; it
obliges the labourer to work harder, and at the same
time produces new demands for labour.   But when
the national taxes have increased to a certain amount,
these effects are nearly reversed.   Prices are so pro-
digiously increased to the consumer, that all prudent
men retrench both their consumption and their em-
ployment of labour.   The greater proportion of the
general income of the country is transferred from
the hands of men who have the means of laying it
out in agriculture or manufactures, into the hands of
great merchants whose capital overflows the market,
and returns again upon the land in the shape of
mortgages.   There is, at the same time, a great want
of money in some quarters, and a great abundance
in others.   Such are the effects of a large national
debt upon individuals.   But there is another view
in which this debt is an unmixed evil.   I mean, as
it impairs and exhausts the resources of the State.
The expenses of former wars render it at last difficult
for a nation to raise taxes for its defence.   So much
of the rent of the landholder is taken from him, that
the minister dares not ask for more, as it would be
equivalent to the confiscation of the land itself.

Mr. Hume has speculated with great ingenuity on
the consequence of the national debt arriving at this
pitch.   He supposes that one of three methods must
be resorted to.   The first is, that the scheme of some
projector should be adopted, which could only tend
to increase the confusion and dismay, and the nation
would thus ' die of the doctor.'   The next is a
national bankruptcy—a plan that he seems to look
upon with some approbation.   The third, and last, is,
that the nation should persevere in paying the full

interest. He speculates on such a determination, and compares it in the following manner with his two former suppositions :—' These two events, supposed above, are calamitous, but not the most calamitous. Thousands are thereby sacrificed to the supply of millions. But we are not without danger that the contrary event may take place, and that millions may be sacrificed for ever to the temporary safety of thousands. Our popular government, perhaps, will render it dangerous for any man to venture on so desperate an expedient as that of a voluntary bankruptcy. And though the House of Lords be altogether composed of proprietors of land, and the House of Commons chiefly, and consequently can neither of them be supposed to have great property in the funds; yet the connection of the members may be so great with the proprietors, as to render them more tenacious of public faith than prudence, policy, or even justice, strictly speaking, requires. . . . The balance of power in Europe, our grandfathers, our fathers, and we, have all esteemed too unequal to be preserved without our attention and assistance. But our children, weary of the struggle, and fettered with encumbrances, may sit down secure, and see their neighbours oppressed and conquered ; till at last they themselves and their creditors lie both at the mercy of the conqueror.' *   The picture of things at home he draws in the following manner :—' No expedient remains for preventing or suppressing insurrections but mercenary armies: no expedient at all remains for resisting tyranny: elections are swayed by bribery and corruption alone : and the middle power between king and people being totally removed, a grievous despotism will prevail. The landholders, despised for their

---

* This course, thus foreseen by Mr. Hume, has been lately recommended as a new and a wise policy; but it is, in fact, the policy of the Tories, in the reign of Queen Anne. (1864.)

poverty, and hated for their oppressions, will be utterly unable to make any opposition to it.'*

If we look to foreign nations, we shall see that Venice, after wars of glory, arrived, in the beginning of the last century, at that stage of decay of which Mr. Hume speaks. Her revenue was not sufficient to pay the interest of her debt. She suspended payment, but still was unable to support the expense of her government. It requires, however, more space than we have here, to examine the complicated causes of her downfall.

Holland was also borne down in her latter years by the weight of her debt. It is still enormous in proportion to her wealth and population.

France began the Revolution with a debt she could not support. By a summary process, in the middle of the war, she virtually abolished the greater part of it. No country, however, has yet been precisely in the situation of England. Commerce and credit are not confined to a spot, but run through every vein in her body; and a national bankruptcy would give a sudden check to industry, the effects of which would not easily be repaired. Very mistaken notions prevail with respect to the good effects which would follow from applying a sponge to the debt. Of these mistakes, none is more mischievous than the notion which many entertain and inculcate, that the labourer who receives 18s. a week, of which several are consumed by the taxes on beer, &c., would, if these taxes were taken off, receive the same 18s., and obtain more than twice as much for them. The real price of labour, it must be recollected, is regulated by the supply and demand. The money-price, of course, will vary with the money-price of the provisions, house-rent, clothes, candles, &c., which are required for the

* Hume's Essays. Essay on Public Credit.

maintenance of the labourer.   If the demand for
labour remains the same, and by a reduction of
taxes the articles which the labourer uses are reduced in price from 18s. to 8s., his wages will fall
from 18s. to 8s.   But it will be said that the
farmer and manufacturer, having more capital to
lay out on labour, the reduction of taxes will bring
an increased demand.   This, indeed, may ultimately
be the case; but it is not likely that such effect
would follow a sudden stoppage of the payment of
the dividends.   So many consumers are spread over
this country, who derive their income, either directly
or indirectly, from the funds, that the first effect of
a national bankruptcy would be a great diminution
of demand, and a general depreciation of agricultural and manufactured produce throughout the
country.

Happily, we have not at present any reason to
fear that we shall be placed in the ugly alternative
of national bankruptcy or national ruin.   But we
must not, for this reason, undervalue the evil of a
great national debt.   An income-tax of two shillings
in the pound would not be more than sufficient to pay
the interest of sums borrowed to pay the expense of
our American and French wars, and no one would
think lightly of the burthen of that tax greatly
increased in order to defray the expenses of fresh
wars.

CHAPTER XXX.

THAT A FREE GOVERNMENT REQUIRES PERPETUAL JEALOUSY, AND FREQUENT RENOVATION.

' Le gouvernement d'Angleterre est plus sage parce qu'il y a un corps qui l'examine continuellement, et qui s'examine continuellement lui-même : et telles sont ses erreurs, qu'elles ne sont jamais longues, et que par l'esprit d'attention qu'elles donnent à la nation, elles sont souvent utiles.'—*Montesquieu, Grandeur et Décadence des Romains,* chap. viii.

ALL experience of human nature teaches us the fact, that men who possess a superiority, real or imaginary, over their fellow-creatures, will abuse the advantages they enjoy. A man cannot drive a one-horse chaise without looking down upon those who walk on foot; much less can a mortal be entrusted with the uncontrolled guidance of an empire, and not be guilty of insolence or oppression towards those who are styled his subjects.

The History we have been reviewing is pregnant with examples of the encroachments of power, and the decline of virtue in those who are appointed to govern. The House of Tudor enlarged their prerogative beyond the boundaries of all former times; the House of Stuart improved upon those bad precedents, and claimed, *de jure,* that despotic authority which the Tudors had exercised *de facto.* When this sin was washed away in the blood of the royal martyr, Cromwell, who had been appointed to command the forces of a free Commonwealth against an ambitious Sovereign, made use of the influence he had obtained to set up his own authority still higher than that of England's hereditary kings. When Charles II. was restored to the throne of his father, by the indulgence of a forgiving nation, he imposed upon her a yoke at once more galling and more degrading than that of any former monarch. William III. passed his life in continual struggles with his subjects to obtain new prerogatives or prevent fresh restrictions on the royal power. When, by the accession of the House of Hanover, the Whigs at length became completely triumphant, they also fell off from virtue, and the martyrs and patriots of the seventeenth century were succeeded in the eighteenth by a race of pettifoggers and peculators. Nothing can show more clearly the necessity of perpetual jealousy than the corruption of the Whig party: inheriting all the great principles of liberty, and forming the only free government of any importance in Europe, power proved to them a Capua, and success induced them to forget the means and neglect the qualities by which they had obtained it.

It is true, that the continual agitation of public questions in England has in it something very alarming to persons at a distance. I remember when the question of the Liberty of the Press was discussed in the Spanish Cortes of 1811, an orator, who spoke against a free press, held out the fate of England as a warning, and asked the assembly if they wished to see as many factions, and as many tumults, as prevailed in Great Britain. But these things are more dreadful in appearance than in reality. Tavern-speeches, contested elections, fieldmeetings, and tumultuary processions, often seem to portend the instant destruction of the order of society; but the sound and the smoke are greater than the mischief, and the people, accustomed to the noise, pursue their occupations with as much composure as the crew of a frigate manœuvre the vessel amid the roar of the wind. The evils of

despotism, through less striking, occasion far more
suffering : the one is like an eruption of the skin,
of little importance, though visible to every eye ;
the other is a mortal, deep-seated disease, which
unseen attacks the noblest and most vital parts of
the frame.

These observations apply, in my opinion, to the
agitated question of Parliamentary Reform. It appears to many, even in England, that the discussion of this subject is fraught with the mightiest
dangers, and cannot terminate but in the convulsion of society. It appears to me, on the contrary,
that these discussions arising out of the state of the
people, and carried on with the whole nation for
an audience, so far from being mischievous, tend to
excite that spirit of enquiry and investigation which
is necessary to the freedom of the State.

Whether Reform is carried or not, it cannot but
be of the utmost service to direct the attention of
the people to the conduct of the House of Commons,
and to oblige them to become, either by their constitution or by the fear of shame, the vigilant
guardians of the public interests. The discussion
of the question of Reform will beneficially serve to
prevent that stagnation of the public mind, and that
blind confidence in the depositories of power, which
are fatal to a free State.*

One melancholy reflection seems to result from
what has been said. Liberty, which requires perpetual agitation, perpetual jealousy, and perpetual
change, must be exposed to more hazards, and
therefore be less durable in its nature than despotism, which to subsist requires only to be un-
altered. A despotism, indeed, which is founded
upon ignorance, and which carefully excludes the
external light, may, if not invaded from without,

* Written in 1821, but applicable in some degree to 1865.

be the most permanent of all governments; for the
debasement of the people, which is one of its means
of immediate government, is likewise a security
against any future change. It would seem, indeed,
that freedom, like all the best and finest produc-
tions of this world, is one of the most frail and
transitory. But let not despotism boast her advantage: half a century of freedom within the circuit of a few miles of rock, brings to perfection
more of the greatest qualities of our nature, displays
more fully the capacity of man, exhibits more
examples of heroism and magnanimity, and emits
more of the divine light of poetry and philosophy,
than thousands of years and millions of people collected in the greatest empire of the world can ever
see accomplished in the darkness of despotism.

CHAPTER XXXI.

CONSTITUTION OF THE HOUSE OF COMMONS.

> ' It is true that what is settled by custom, though it be not good,
> at least it is fit. And those things which have gone long together
> are, as it were, confederate within themselves. Whereas new things
> piece not so well; but though they help by their utility, yet they
> trouble by their unconformity. All this is true if time stood still;
> which contrariwise moveth so round, that a froward retention of
> custom is as turbulent a thing as an innovation ; and they that
> reverence too much old times are but a scorn to the new. It were
> good, therefore, that men in their innovations would follow the ex-
> ample of time itself, which, indeed, innovateth greatly, but quietly.'
> —*Lord Bacon.*

WE have hitherto said scarcely anything of the constitution of the House of Commons. From the time
of Edward I. it has been composed of knights who
represented the freeholders or landed property of
counties, and of citizens and burgesses, who represented the commercial interests of cities and boroughs.
What these boroughs so distinguished were, is a
question lost in remote antiquity. It appears clear,
however, that the writ sent to the sheriff merely
directed him to send to Parliament burgesses for the
boroughs within his county, and that the sheriff issued his precept to such of the places called boroughs
as he thought fit. Whether they were so called
from charter or prescription is uncertain. This
service being attended by wages to the members,
was considered as a burden ; and several boroughs
petitioned and obtained leave to be relieved from it.
During the contest of the Houses of York and
Lancaster, however, the House of Commons having
become of more importance, and having not unfre-

quently a voice in the disposal of the crown, the
privilege of electing members to have a seat in it
grew into a desirable privilege. The Charter of
Wenlock, granted by Edward IV., which is said to
be the first in which the privilege of sending members
to Parliament is expressly mentioned, grants that
privilege as a matter of favour, and as a reward of
services performed by the proprietor of the borough.
A little before this, the right of voting at county
elections was restrained to 40s. freeholders, on account, it is said, of the tumults and affrays which
were likely to occur at those elections—a proof that
they were already objects of interest. The kings of
the House of Tudor, it will be recollected, although
they raised themselves above the people, acted not
without, but through the Parliament. The House
of Commons began to debate according to present
forms under the sovereigns of this family. During
the reign of Elizabeth, it happened, for the first
time, that a member was found guilty of bribing the
returning officer. In the reign of James, after
four hundred years' discontinuance, Agmondesham
was restored to the privilege of sending members.
Wendover and Marlow were restored at the same
time. Amongst the arguments in favour of their
right, we find the following, in an abstract of the
case drawn in 21 Jac. I.*—' Thirdly, the use in
these ancient times being, that the burgesses, attending in Parliament, were maintained at the charge of
the boroughs; when the boroughs grew poor, the
boroughs only for that reason neglected to send their
burgesses to the Parliament; therefore, now seeing
they were contented to undergo that burthen, or to
choose such burgesses as should bear their own
charges, there was no reason to deny that petition.
Lastly, it was urged in behalf of the burgesses, that

---

* Browne Willis, Notitia Parliamentaria, vol. i. p. 120.

the liberty of sending burgesses to Parliament is a
liberty of that nature and quality, that it cannot be
lost by neglect of any borough; for every burgess so
sent is a member of the great council of the kingdom,
maintained at the charge of the borough; and if
such a neglect may be permitted in one borough, so
may it be in more, and consequently in all the
boroughs in England; and then it might follow that,
for want of burgesses, there would be no Parliament.'

In consequence of this decision, there was returned, for Wendover, Mr. John Hampden, 'who
beareth the charge.' In this and the succeeding
reign, the following boroughs were restored by Parliament: —

Ilchester . .	. 18 Jac. I.
Agmondesham	. 21 Jac. I.
Wendover .	. Ditto.
Great Marlow .	. Ditto.
Cockermouth .	. 16 Car. I.
Okehampton .	. Ditto.
Honiton . .	. Ditto.
Ashburton .	. Ditto.
Milborne Port .	. Ditto.
Malton . .	. Ditto.
Northallerton .	. Ditto.
Seaford . .	. Ditto.

Twenty-four were restored by the Sovereign himself:
these apparently were willing to bear the charge.
Fifty-one boroughs that had sent members have
never been restored at all. From the reign of Henry
VIII. to the accession of Charles I., the House of
Commons received an addition of 156 members. In
Cornwall alone, Edward VI. added 12 members,
Mary 4, and Elizabeth 10.

Cornwall, it appears, was chosen as the best place
to fix these members, because the Crown, in right

of the duchy, had great influence there, by means both of mines and lands. These additions clearly show the desire of the Crown to obtain dependents within the House of Commons. Such unhealthy excrescences, however, did not prevent the Petition of Right, or guard the throne from the Roundheads.

At a time when projects were teeming on all subjects, for the amendment of the whole body of the law, of the Church, of the State, and even of the calendar, it was not to be expected that the House of Commons should be without its reformer. Especially it was to be expected that a plan should be recommended for making representation equal and uniform. Accordingly, a proposal of this nature came from the masters of all reforms of that day—the army. The plan was adopted in its chief principles by Cromwell in the two Parliaments he called after becoming Protector; but neither the temper of the times, nor the genius of the man, permitted the experiment to be made in such a manner as to give it the slightest value. From the first of these two Parliaments Cromwell experienced a decided opposition to his authority; and it was dissolved because it presumed to discuss the question whether the government should be in a single person. In the second, after various means used to influence the electors, no person was allowed to enter without a certificate from the Council of State, and thus 100 members were excluded. Richard Cromwell, either discouraged by these essays, or yielding to the growing partiality for old forms and methods, assembled a Parliament in the ancient manner. Lord Shaftesbury, however, who was the first after the Restoration to violate the independence of Parliament, by insisting that all returns should be judged of in Chancery, was also the first to renew and keep alive the doctrine of Parliamentary reform. In a paper published after his death, he complains not only of the undue

length of Parliaments, and the corrupt practices of
boroughs, but insists on the great speculative grievance that Cornwall sent more members than Wales.
Some of his friends, and especially Mr. Samuel
Johnson, chaplain to Lord Russell, endeavoured to
move the question at the Revolution, but both the
great parties studiously avoided the discussion.
From that time to that of Lord Chatham, the principle of reform, though favoured by some illustrious
men, chiefly Tories, seems to have slept in peace ;
at the same time, however, the grievance greatly
increased.   Boroughs became more and more venal ;
and the number of placemen in a house of 556 members is said to have been not less than 200.   But
the people take little or no interest in the question
of reform, or indeed in any question purely constitutional, except when they are suffering real evils
from misgovernment.   It should be mentioned, however, that in 1745 a Tory motion for annual Parliaments, intended probably to shake the Hanover
succession, was rejected by a majority of only 32.

Lord Chatham, finding from experience how difficult it was to rouse the House of Commons to a due
sense of ministerial abuses, proposed, as a measure
of expediency, that a hundred members for counties
should be added to the representative body.   This
plan was obviously founded on utility only : in the
phrase of its illustrious author, it was a plan ' to infuse new life into the Constitution.'

The American war having placed the misrule of
our statesmen in a glaring light, Mr. Pitt, in 1781,
in 1782, and in 1785, made motions in the House
of Commons itself in favour of different plans of
reform ; all, however, professing to amend only a
part of the representation, and resting, like those
of his father, on the basis of utility and experience.
There were, however, other doctrines afloat.   Dr.
Jebb, and, after him, Mr. Cartwright, broached the

theory of personal representation; which, following
out the principles of Mr. Locke, pretended to establish, as a natural and indefeasible right, the claim
of every man to have a vote.   Neither this theory,
however, nor the plan of Mr. Pitt, which was supported by Horne Tooke and all the temperate
reformers of that day, met with any success.   Mr.
Pitt became at first cold, and then totally silent on
the subject.

The question slept till the French Revolution,
which disturbed everything, woke it anew.   A society, consisting of many of the ablest men of that
day, drew up the paper called the Petition of the
Friends of the People.   This was no less than a bill
of indictment against the governing assembly of
Great Britain.   The history and the state of the
boroughs is minutely detailed; and an elaborate
attempt is made to show that a few individuals have
the command of the House of Commons, and of
course it follows, of the persons and purses of every
man in Britain.   There is one part of this statement,
however, which is manifestly irrelevant to the subject.   A large number of county members and others
are enumerated as elected by the influence of peers
or certain wealthy commoners.   It is alleged, that
not only do 84 persons nominate directly 157 members, but that 70 others, by indirect influence, in
counties and large towns, return 150 more; and
thus a pretended proof is given, that a few persons
elect a majority of the House of Commons.   Now
every one who knows England, knows that the freeholders of the same political opinions in a county,
whether magistrates or shopkeepers, generally agree
to give their votes to the same candidate.   The
qualities which they seek for in a candidate, it is
also known, are, generally, not eloquence, or even
abilities, but sense, integrity, and property.   Property itself is supposed, in some manner, to be a

N

guarantee of character. It therefore happens, that
the person among them who has most land, if he has
other common requisites, is the member; and if that
person happens to be a Peer, then his brother or his
son. Thus it is not the tenants only of a man of
property, but his party in conjunction with his
tenants, who make him knight of the shire. A
complaint, therefore, that the eldest son of a certain
Peer is always returned member for a county in
which he has a large estate, instead of the wisest
shopkeeper or labourer in the county, is not a grievance fit to be stated to the House of Commons,
although it might make part of an essay on the
character of the English people, or of a general
treatise on human nature.

Laying this objection aside, however, the main
scope of the petition admits of this answer :—' You
complain of the formation of the House of Commons, such as it has existed from the Revolution to
the present time. You prove that the frame of our
government during that time has been a corrupt
combination for private purposes. But our fathers
and our grandfathers have told us, that during that
time they were very free and very happy. Their
testimony is confirmed by the ablest lawyers, the
greatest philosophers, the most enthusiastic poets
of the times. Your theory goes to overthrow the
testimony of Blackstone, Montesquieu, Thomson,
Cowper, and a hundred others, who have declared
England to be in their time in the enjoyment of
complete freedom. Now government is a matter of
experience, and not of speculation; we will, therefore, rest contented with things as they are.'

Such an objection as this appears to me to be
sound. For the complaint is made, not of a single
or particular grievance, but of the majority of the
governing body of the State, such, or nearly such,
as they had existed for a hundred years of liberty

and glory. To explain this further: if a petition
were presented complaining of the bankrupt laws, it
clearly would not be a good objection to say, ' Our
ancestors have been free and happy with the bankrupt laws, therefore we will not change them.' But
if a petition were presented, stating that the division
of our government into three powers was a most
absurd one ; that it was ridiculous to give one man
as much power as 658 representatives of the whole
people; that it was out of all reason to admit into
the House of Lords a spendthrift or an idiot, because
his father had been a statesman or a favourite; that
the veto of the king was a barbarous invention unworthy of a polished nation ; we should answer,
' The theory may be bad, but the practice has been
excellent.'

Mr. Fox, fully sensible of the weight of this
answer, came forward in 1797 and put the question
upon totally different grounds. He declared the
situation of the country to be so perilous as almost
to make him despair of the safety of the State. He
argued, that the conduct of the ministers had been
such as to bring the commonwealth to utter ruin ;
and no expedient remained but to recur to first
principles, and reconstitute the State. Admitting
the evil to have been fully as great as Mr. Fox
represented it, his reasoning was far from proving
the propriety of the remedy. For that evil certainly
did not arise from disregarding the voice of the
people in the American and French wars. ' Liberty
is in danger of becoming unpopular to Englishmen,'
says Mr. Burke, in the American war. ' In short,'
says Mr. Fox, during the French war, ' liberty is
not popular. The country is divided (very unequally, I admit) betwixt the majority, who are
subdued by fears or corrupted by hopes ; and the
minority, who are waiting sulkily for opportunities

N 2

of violent remedies.'* What a strange resource, then,
to make the Legislature more democratic!

But when we are examining the principles of the
English Government, it is necessary to endeavour,
as far as we are able, to lay down some general
rules for the formation of the assembly of the Commons of a limited monarchy. A few may suffice,
both for the author and the reader.

First, All parts of the country, and all classes of
the people, ought to have a share in elections. If
this is not the case, the excluded part or class of
the nation will become of no importance in the eyes
of the rest; its favour will never be courted in the
country, and its interests will never be vigilantly
guarded in the Legislature. Consequently, in proportion to the general freedom of the community
will be the discontent excited in the deprived class,
by the sentence of nullity and inactivity pronounced
upon them. Every system of uniform suffrage, except universal, contains this dark blot. And universal suffrage, in pretending to avoid it, gives the
whole power to the highest and the lowest, to money
and to multitude, and thus disfranchises the middle
class, the most disinterested, the most independent,
and the most unprejudiced of all. It is not necessary, however, although every class ought to have
an influence in elections, that every member of every
class should have a vote. A butcher at Hackney,
who gives his vote perhaps once in twelve years at
an election for the county of Middlesex, has scarcely
any advantage over another butcher at the same
place, who has no vote at all. And even if he had,
the interest of the State in these matters is the chief
thing to be consulted; and that is as well served by

* Letter to Lord Holland.
See also Mr. Fox's Speeches at
the beginning of the war, which
are full of avowals that he had
become unpopular by his opposition to it.

the suffrage of some of each class, as by that of all of each class.

It is an argument too against making the right of suffrage too common, that the privilege of giving a vote gains a value, from not being too generally possessed, or too frequently exercised : were it used every year, by everybody, it would be as little regarded as the golden pebbles were by the children of El Dorado.

Secondly, Enlightened men of every class should be capable of being elected. The highest in rank, excepting the Peers, should be admitted, because they give to a popular assembly new importance, and receive from it additional stability. Above all, their presence and concurrence unite the aristocracy and the people in a common sympathy, planing away the pride of the one, and the envy of the other. Men who have risen by commerce ought, most undoubtedly, to be capable of admission, both to give an encouragement to the honest exertions of all sorts of men, and to make every class feel intimately persuaded that they are represented in fact as well as in name. These two sorts of persons require only the legal permission to enter the Legislature : they are sure to find themselves there. But there is another class who ought to form a part of any good representative body, whose election is not so sure,— I mean those who are distinguished by their learning or their talents, but not by their fortune or their commerce with the world ; men who have devoted their youth to the acquirement of the knowledge of English law, laws of nations, history of the constitution, political economy ; but who are excluded by their want of pecuniary means, their temper, or their habits, from popular contests. For it is not to be denied that a body of 10,000 farmers or tradesmen will choose no man who is not known to them, either by his station in the country, or by a course of

popular harangues. If, then, you make none but
elections by large bodies, you either shut out the
aristocracy of talent from your assembly, and constitute them into a body hostile to your institutions,
or else you oblige them to become demagogues by
profession : things both of them very pernicious, and
very dangerous to the State. It is useful, therefore, to have some elections by persons who, from
their station in society, are acquainted with the characters of the men of talent of the day. This may
be done either by forming some elective bodies of a
few persons, with a high qualification, or by giving
to property a commanding influence in the return of
a proportion of members.

Thirdly, The grand principle of all, derived from
the two foregoing, is, that the representative body
should be the image of the represented : not that
it should represent property only, or multitude only,
or farmers, or merchants, or manufacturers only ;
not that it should govern with the pride of an in-
sulated aristocracy, or be carried to and fro by the
breath of transient popularity ; but that it should
unite somewhat of all these things, and blend these
various colours into one agreeable picture. The
House of Commons should be, as Mr. Pitt said,
an assembly united with the people by the closest
sympathies. Nor is it meant by this expression to
say, that it should be for ever following the upper-
most passion of the people. The decisions of the
House of Commons should be such as either to satisfy the people at the moment, or capable of satisfying them upon plain reasons, when the arguments
and the facts are laid before them. If the decisions
of the representative body are not fit to do this, not
only are they a bad House of Commons, but they
would form a bad senate or a bad privy council.
Let us now see whether the English House of Commons is formed upon principles similar to those I
have mentioned.

1st. The general scheme of the representation is evidently calculated to give the right of voting to persons of all classes. Landed property is represented in counties; commercial, in cities; and the boroughs contain various modes of suffrage, and are subject to various influences; in one place of a great landowner, in another of a club, in another of the multitude. These, too, are all so blended together—the towns have so much influence in county elections, and landed proprietors so much influence in the neighbouring city or town, that one kind of members does not feel much jealousy of another kind. It is always a great misfortune when they are pitted against each other.

But although no class is excluded from our constituent body, there were parts of the country which before the Reform Act were very inadequately represented. The county of Lancaster, and the county of York, comprising Manchester, Bolton, Leeds, Sheffield, Halifax, and Huddersfield, and containing 2,500,000 of inhabitants, were represented by four persons. This was evidently a practical grievance, and as such it was felt.

2nd. Enlightened men of every class have found their way at all times into the English House of Commons. Those who had property in land were candidates for their respective counties; those who had made their fortune by commerce or manufactures, easily established an interest in cities with which they had some connection, or in towns (there are many such) where, without bribery, the inhabitants required a man of fortune to support their public institutions, and give them his custom in laying out his income. There remains the aristocracy of talent, who before the Reform Act arrived at the House of Commons by means of the close boroughs, where they generally were nominated by Peers or Commoners who had the property of these boroughs in their hands. In this manner the greater part of our

distinguished statesmen have entered Parliament.
The use of such members to the House itself, and to
the country, is incalculable.   Their knowledge and
talents give a weight to the deliberations, and inspire a respect for Parliamentary discussion, which in
these times it is difficult for any assembly to obtain.
The speeches, too, of able and eloquent men produce
an effect on the country, which is reflected back
again on the Parliament; and thus the speech of
one member for a small borough was often of more
benefit to the cause of truth and justice than the
votes of twenty silent senators.

3rd. Did the Commons of England before the Reform Act represent the people? Perfectly well when
the people and the Government agreed; but when
they separated, the decisions of the House of Commons leant more to the side of the Government than
to that of the people. This may be proved by examining the history of the last two years of the American
war.   The majorities on these occasions were small,
and they consisted chiefly of borough members.
The same thing happened on the Walcheren expedition, and after the peace of Paris, on divisions relating to the scale of expenditure which the ministers
kept up.   The country was decidedly one way; and
the House of Commons, by small majorities, determined in the opposite direction.   The proof of
this is made by analysing the divisions, and seeing
how the county members have voted. Thus, on Mr.
Dunning's motion in 1780, ministers out of 215
members counted only 11 county members, whilst
their opponents out of 233 had 69.   The desertion
of 20 members was then sufficient to turn the scale.
On the Walcheren expedition, the English county
members against ministers were nearly as three to
two, but the majority of the whole House was in
favour of the administration.   In 1817, on the question of appointing a finance committee with less than

five placemen upon it, the county members divided
27 to 15 for the Opposition; the House at large, 178
to 136 for ministers.   On a motion for reducing two
Lords of the Admiralty, the county members were
35 to 16; the House, 208 to 152 the other way.
It thus appears that during two periods of crisis, the
county members, who, as we have seen, are men of
property, inclined to the Crown always from station,
and generally by party, have been in minorities upon
the popular side.   It is sufficiently clear, therefore,
that other parts of the House of Commons are far
indeed from representing the people.   The boroughs
especially are liable to this censure.   The boroughs
generally gave a large majority to ministers; but
the smaller boroughs gave five and six to one, and
the Cornish boroughs sixteen or seventeen to one in
their favour.   There is one kind of boroughs which
was known before the Reform Act, which was a chief
cause of this disorder.   This was a species of borough of which the seat was sold by the electors to
the highest bidder.   Many of those who represented
this kind of borough came into Parliament with what
were called commercial views.   These views were
to advance their own interests as much as possible at
the Treasury, and to vote on all questions and at all
seasons with the Treasury.   Many boroughs also had
what was called a patron—sometimes an attorney,
sometimes a baronet, and sometimes a peer, who sold
them in the market, and took fifty per cent. for his
trouble.

We have now arrived at the conclusion, that the
House of Commons did not adequately represent
the people, and that the small boroughs prevented
that vigilant stewardship of the public revenue which
is the bounden duty and peculiar function of that
assembly.   It follows, as an immediate consequence,
that the small boroughs betrayed the trust which
was reposed in them for the good of the community,

and that they might without injustice have been
deprived of the valuable privilege they possessed.
But we then come to another question.   It is not
certain, because we have a right to do this, that it
may not be better to bear the ills we have, or that
the remedy may not be worse than the disease.   Let
us then pass in review one or two of these remedies.

Let us, for instance, consider the effects of a plan
to divide the country into districts, and extend the
right of suffrage to all persons paying direct taxes.
If this plan were accompanied by a triennial bill, it
would certainly render the House of Commons an
assembly very obedient to the popular voice; but
there is some danger that many of the advantages of
representation would be lost.   The very scope and
object of representation is to obtain a select body,
who may not only have a sympathy with the people,
but who may, by the habits of business which their
number permits, and the judgment which their election implies, manage the interests of the country
somewhat better than each town and county could
do by petition and public meeting.   If you render
the House of Commons a mere echo of the popular
cry, you lose, on many questions, all the benefit of
having a body in some degree capable of directing
public opinion.   I am aware that this argument
may be easily pushed too far.   I can only repeat, to
explain my meaning, that the House of Commons
ought to make such decisions as are either agreeable
to the people at the time, or when they are not so,
the weight of argument should be so great as to convince the country, within a short time afterwards,
that the resolution or vote was adopted, not from
any corrupt or sinister motive, but from an enlarged
and sagacious view of the public interest.

Many arguments might be used to show that a
House of Commons elected by one class only would

not form a body so well fitted to represent the
people as one chosen by many different classes.   It
is sufficient to say, however, that there seems to be no
necessity for changing the whole frame of our representation.   For my own part, I cannot understand
how an Englishman can have read the histories of
Athens, of Sparta, of Venice, of France, of Spain—
how he can have looked into the history of the
world—how he can have thrown a single glance at
the governments existing in the world at the end of
the eighteenth century—how he can have weighed
the miserable result of the most benevolent plans,
and the most brilliant schemes of government, and
not cling the closer to his native home.   Whatever
may be said by theoretical writers, it is impossible
not to see that the laws afford a greater protection
to civil, personal, and political liberty in England,
than the general average of governments attain.

    ' The blessings of the constitution under which we
live ' is not, after all, an unmeaning phrase.   They
are acknowledged by foreign nations, and by the
great majority of the people of this country.   The
true coin of our freedom may be clipt and worn,
but still it is better than any paper security that
may be offered to us.   We speak, we write, we
think, we act, without fear of a Bastille or an Inquisition.   We wear liberty about us as a garment;
and the remains of the spirit of old times are of
sounder and better flavour than a new constitution,
however admirable, which requires new maxims of
conduct, and would produce new feelings of right
and justice.

    There was, however, another principle, or basis
upon which measures of reform might in 1821 have
been founded.

    We have seen that, towards the end of the
American, and after the conclusion of the French
war, the decisions of the House of Commons were

contrary to the well-known sense of the people.
But the majorities were small, and perhaps an instance will hardly be found of a majority of more
than one hundred, on a question on which the
country itself was not extremely divided. Now, as
it is a maxim of Newton and succeeding philosophers, not to admit more causes than are sufficient
to explain the phenomena; so also it ought to be
the maxim of a statesman, not to propose more innovations than are sufficient to cure the evil.

· I have elsewhere, however, fully explained my
opinion on this subject.*

I shall only state, in conclusion, that upon the
whole, the authority of our greatest statesmen has
leant to a partial, and not a general reform. Mr.
Pitt's first proposition was to add 100 members ·
to counties; he next moved for a committee; and
the last time he brought forward the subject, in conjunction with Mr. Wyvill and the great body of
reformers, he proposed to buy the franchises of 36
boroughs, and of some close corporations, who
should be willing to part with them. But he never
proposed to pull down the house in order to build
it up again from top to bottom after a modern plan.
Mr. Fox, during the war of the French revolution,
went much farther. But his sober opinions, as well
as those of a person illustrious by his own character, as well as by his friendship for Mr. Fox, may, I
think, be collected from the speech of Lord Grey,
on bringing forward a motion for a committee on the
state of the nation, in 1810.†

* See Speeches in the House of Commons on Reform, 1821–1822–
1831–1832.
† See concluding chapter.

CHAPTER XXXII.

STANDING ARMY.

> 'Nothing ought to be more guarded against in a free State than making the military power, when such a one is necessary to be kept on foot, a body too distinct from the people.'—*Blackstone,* b. i., c. 13.

In every free State, a Standing Army has been an object of attention and suspicion, and various methods have been resorted to, to prevent the dangers which might be expected to liberty from so formidable an instrument of power. In a view of the constitution of England, the subject of the standing army certainly ought not to be omitted.

In ancient times, the king had a right to call for the attendance of his military subjects in any war in which the kingdom might be engaged, but the term of service was never more than a summer, and the feudal troops ranged under the banners of their lords, retained their special allegiance, and added nothing to the civil authority of the king. Henry VII. is said to have been the first of our sovereigns who maintained a body guard for his own person. Henry VIII., and after him Queen Elizabeth, began the practice of sending lord lieutenants into the counties with authority to array and command a part of the population for the defence of the county.

From this institution arose the well-known pretension of Charles I. to the command of the militia; a pretension which, however countenanced by the practice of his immediate predecessors, had no authority in law. At the accession of Charles II.,

however, the question was decided by Parliament
in favour of the Crown; and a statute was passed,
enacting that the command of the militia, as well
as of all other forces raised, or to be raised, in the
kingdom, should reside in the king. Charles was
extremely jealous of this part of his prerogative;
and on one occasion, when a militia bill was passed
by the House of Commons, he said he would not
let the militia out of his hands, no, not for one
hour.   He made use of the power granted him by
Parliament to raise a standing army, varying in
numbers, according to the circumstances of peace
or war, and supported in times of peace by the
subsidies of Louis XIV.   He is said to have been
the first king of England who went to open his
Parliament under the protection of the sword.
James II. increased the standing army to 30,000
men, and endeavoured to make them the instruments of his designs by a strong infusion of Roman
Catholic officers; but the English soldiers disap-
pointed his expectations, and, by their shouts at the
acquittal of the bishops, convinced the tyrant that
his trouble had been thrown away.   At the Revolution, it was provided by law that no standing
army should be maintained in these kingdoms, unless by authority of Parliament.   Since that time,
an Act has passed every year, enabling the king
to punish mutiny, desertion, and other military
offences; the number of men to be maintained
during the year being always inserted in the body
of the Act.   Thus we are secured at least against
the renewal of an attempt similar to that made by
Charles and James to keep up a military force, in
defiance of the authority of Parliament, and by
means proceeding from other sources.   There is
not much gained, however, by this provision; the
cost of maintaining an army is so great, that it

could scarcely be defrayed otherwise than by Parliamentary funds.

During the reign of William, extreme jealousy of a standing army was shown by the House of Commons. After the peace of Ryswick, they obliged the king to dismiss his Dutch guards, though William sent down a message to the House of Commons, written with his own hand, imploring, in very earnest terms, that he might be allowed to retain his favourite veterans. But the Commons were inexorable. Nay, they voted at the same time that the whole standing army should be disbanded; but, upon consideration of the necessity of guards and garrisons, they in the following year agreed to vote 7,000 men for the defence of England, and 12,000 for Ireland. Let it be remarked, that, at this period, Louis XIV. was on the throne of France, supporting the title of the exiled king of England, and reviewing in his camp at Compiègne an army of 80,000 men, part of 450,000 whom he maintained during war. Some among us will perhaps be surprised at the boldness of the English House of Commons, both in thwarting their own, and in defying a foreign sovereign; yet we shall not perceive that they had any reason to repent of their rashness; for, during the succeeding war, the conqueror of Blenheim and Ramilies renewed for England the military glories of Crecy and Agincourt.

At the accession of the House of Hanover, the standing army appears to have been increased. Fifteen, sixteen, and seventeen thousand men were usually voted by the Parliament of England, and a separate establishment maintained in Ireland. This number seems to have been the average of the greater part of the last century. In our own days, the number has been much more largely increased.

A standing army being thus, as it were, engrafted upon the constitution of England, it remains to be seen what are its effects upon the government, and whether any real danger is to be apprehended from it. From the Revolution to the present day, there have never been wanting a certain number of persons, whether moved by patriotism or by faction, who have warned the country of the evils to be apprehended from a military establishment, and pointed out the subversion of the freedom of Rome and other popular States by a standing army, as an example for us to avoid. I am inclined to doubt, however, whether the parallel be a just one. Republics have been destroyed by standing armies, because armies have assisted their chiefs in establishing a perpetual dictatorship, and in overthrowing the senates and the laws in behalf of a military despotism: but in England, neither experience nor the present state of the country can excite any reasonable dread of the usurpation of a successful general. The monarchical form of our government seems to be a preventive of this evil. Neither is it much to be apprehended that the sovereign himself will make use of the standing army to cashier the Parliament, and subvert the constitution by force. Opinion is too much settled, and the institutions of the country are too vigorous, to admit of so desperate a project: the army itself likewise is too deeply connected with the other classes of the country, to concur in a scheme for putting down the established authorities of the realm. It is true, indeed, that the virtue of the army is, as Lord Chatham said, our chief protection against this danger; but seeing how the army is constructed, it is a sufficient security.

The open subversion of our liberties by the force of the standing army is then not impossible certainly, but extremely improbable. Yet we are not

to conclude that because there is little danger of the
army destroying our freedom, like the troops of
Marius or Cæsar, or of its becoming the servile
instrument of a king in a design of making himself
absolute, that therefore a large standing army may
not be a reasonable object, if not of alarm, yet of
some suspicion and jealousy.

CHAPTER XXXIII.

OF THE INFLUENCE OF JURIES IN INTERPRETING AND MODIFYING THE LAWS.

Virtue! without thee
There is no ruling eye, no nerve in States;
War has no vigour, and no safety peace;
Ev'n justice warps to party, laws oppress,
Wide through the land their weak protection fails,
First broke the balance, and then scorn'd the sword.
Thomson.

THE proposition, that good laws without virtue in the society where they are established are of little or no avail, is one so generally admitted, that it seems useless to waste a word respecting it. Perhaps there is not a more comprehensive or a more humane code of laws, than that which was provided in Spain for the government of the Indians of Mexico and Peru; but, unfortunately, the legislators were at Madrid, and the people to be protected working for their masters in America, without the power of enforcing their legal rights; so that the code was of no force or value whatsoever. The converse of the proposition I have selected, however, although perhaps not formally contradicted, is not so generally impressed upon our minds. Men are easily led to believe, that where liberty and wealth have flourished, there must be some very singular excellence, some unfailing virtue, inherent in the laws by which the State has been governed. It would be an easy task to prove, that neither at Athens, nor at Rome, nor at Florence, nor in Holland, has the form of laws reached to any great perfection. This would probably be admitted; and yet many would persevere in thinking that in England our ancestors had discovered some secret for making faultless laws. Blackstone has contributed much to spread this opinion. All that was established had, in his eye, a peculiar sanctity, and he praises the English Constitution with the enthusiasm of a scholar who is admitted to view the picture of a great master. The fault, indeed, was on the right side. If he refrained from pointing out many obvious improvements, he also kept alive that respect for our ancient liberties, which speculative statesmen find to be the greatest obstacle to their arbitrary innovations. It is impossible, however, to attempt any general view of the history of our government, and not to be struck with the modifications and forced interpretations which have been accepted, in order to make the law of the land agree with the security of the State and the safety of the subject.

The first instance I shall mention is the treason law. For three centuries, we have been accustomed to appeal to the Act of the 25 Edward III. as the perfection of wisdom and liberty on the subject of treason. Yet what is this law, when we come to examine it? The bold and spirited compact of a turbulent nobility with a feudal king, totally unfitted for a commercial and civilised society. It provides, that the penalties of treason shall apply to those only who conspire against the life of the King, or actually levy war against him.* Such a law as this, it is evident, was well calculated to protect the barons from being arrested for disaffection, and to give them the power of holding their private councils for rebellion undisturbed. In the progress of society, however, it was discovered, that a conspiracy to levy war, far from being an ordinary or light offence, was a crime of the utmost magnitude, dangerous alike to the safety of the King and the tranquillity of the

---

* Of the other offences made treason by the bill it is not necessary to take notice here.

country. What was to be done? It was obvious,
that a conspiracy to levy war was not treason by the
Act, for no men could have been so absurd as to have
specified the actual levying of war as treason, when
they had already included a conspiracy to levy war
under the head of compassing the King's death. If
a conspiracy to levy war amounted to compassing
the King's death, à fortiori the actual war must have
borne that meaning. Had they wished to include
this offence of conspiracy to levy war in their statute,
they would undoubtedly have said, levying war
against the King, or conspiring to levy war. Indeed,
so certain was the meaning of the law of Edward,
that a new law making a conspiracy to levy war
amount to high treason was enacted, and afterwards
repealed with other new treasons at the beginning of
the reign of Mary. In this dilemma, the lawyers
cut the Gordian knot. They decided, that ' compassing or imagining the death of the King,' meant
conspiring to depose him, or to imprison him, or to
use force for the purpose of making him change his
counsellors or his measures; for any of these acts
might lead to his death.* They interpreted the
offence of levying war against the King to mean a
riot for any general purpose, as to pull down inclo-
sures or meeting-houses. These violent constructions
of law, first imagined under the reign of the Tudors,
and put in force to shed the blood of good men
under the Stuarts, crept in and flourished till they
received the sanction of the upright and venerable
Judge Foster in the reign of George I. In those
times of mild government, however, the engine was
little wanted, and it was reserved for Mr. Pitt to

* Foster, the great authority
on these subjects, says, that conspiring to imprison the King, is
compassing his death; because
the graves of princes are near
their prisons. To stretch this
trite moral observation into a
snare for taking away a man's
life, under pretence of explain-
ing a law of the fourteenth century, is a refinement as absurd
as it is cruel.

direct it against the lives of his old supporters the
reformers, during the French revolutionary war.
But juries refused to carry the construction as far
as the minister desired.   It was proved, indeed, to
their satisfaction, that Hardy and others had joined
in associations which had no other object than to
overturn the institutions, one and all, by which the
throne was surrounded.   The Chief Justice declared
there could be no doubt respecting the construction
of the law.   But it was impossible to convict Hardy,
without making all political association in opposition
to the ministry liable to capital indictment, and the
prisoners were therefore acquitted.   After the peace
of 1815, some raving demagogues went beyond anything that appears of Hardy and the constitutional
society.   They resolved not to obey the laws, and
they recommended in their speeches physical force,
as the only means of obtaining redress.   Certain of
them were committed for high treason.   But the
Government, recollecting the lesson their predecessors had received, declined to prosecute for that
offence; and thus tacitly abandoned a pretension
dangerous to the safety of every man in the country.
At the same time, there can be no doubt that if an
accused person were proved to have levied troops for
the direct purpose of insurrection against the King,
a jury would find him guilty of high treason.   The
law of high treason, insufficient at first for the security of the State, and afterwards a snare for the
subject, has thus been worked out at last into a
barrier, alike providing for the stability of the
offended throne and the safety of the innocent
accused.

Let us now pass to the law of libel—the security
by which the liberty of the press is to be protected.
Blackstone tells us that libels, in the sense in which
we are speaking, are ' malicious defamations of any
person, and especially a magistrate, made public by

either printing, writing, signs, or pictures, in order
to provoke him to wrath, or expose him to public
hatred, contempt, and ridicule.' He tells us that
' the communication of a libel to any one person is a
publication in the eye of the law;' and that ' it is
immaterial, with respect to the essence of a libel,
whether the matter be true or false.' Thus, then,
a man may be punished for any writing on the conduct of a minister called a malicious defamation,
which may expose him to public hatred, contempt,
and ridicule; although the allegations contained in
it be true, and it has only been shown to one person.
To make this power more formidable, the judges
were wont formerly to maintain that they alone
had the power of deciding whether the writing
were libel or not; and that the jury were only
called upon to decide upon the fact of the publication. Here indeed is a law of tyrants! How has the
liberty of the press ever survived it?

The miracle is soon explained.—The prosecutor
on the part of the Crown formerly contented himself
with putting in the paper and proving the publication, leaving it to the judge to pronounce the writing
libellous. The counsel for the accused always dwelt
upon the hardship of convicting any man for the
publication of a writing without examining whether
that writing were innocent or pernicious. The jury
felt the injustice of the proceeding, and generally
acquitted the accused. The libel bill of Mr. Fox, of
1791, while it afforded a just protection to the public
press, was no less necessary to the Government
itself. By this bill, juries were constituted judges of
the law as well as of the fact; that is to say, they
were entitled to decide not only whether the writing
in question had been published or no, but also whether it were libellous. Thus the spirit of the people
produced the amendment of a bad law.

Many other cases might be mentioned, in which

the verdicts of juries have operated to check the execution of a cruel or oppressive law, and in the end to repeal or modify the law itself.   The direct perjuries of juries on the subject of criminal law have been already mentioned ; the verdicts given in cases of bankruptcy would afford many other instances of the same kind.   Thus, not only are juries in fact the real judges in England, but they possess a power no judge would venture to exercise, namely, that of refusing to put the law in force.   Undoubtedly this is a very dangerous authority, more especially as juries, consulting in secret, deciding without reason assigned, and separating without being afterwards responsible, are free from all control but that of their own consciences ; yet, exercised as it has been with temper and moderation, the discretion of juries has proved extremely salutary.   It has been the cause of amending many bad laws which judges would have administered with exact severity, and defended with professional bigotry ; and, above all, it has this important and useful consequence, that laws totally repugnant to the feelings of the community for which they are made, cannot long exist in England.

I have thought it useful to devote this chapter to an effect of the institution of trial by jury, hitherto little remarked ; but I am unwilling to conclude it without expressing, in the strongest manner, my own sense of the value of the institution itself.   It is to trial by jury, as much perhaps as even to representation, that the people owe the share they have in the government of the country ; it is to trial by jury also that the Government mainly owes the attachment of the people to the laws.

CHAPTER XXXIV.

INFLUENCE OF THE CROWN.

' Men are naturally propense to corruption ; and if he, whose will
and interest it is to corrupt them, be furnished with the means, he
will never fail to do it. Power, honours, riches, and the pleasures
that attend them, are the baits by which man are drawn to prefer a
personal interest before the public good ; and the number of those
who covet them is so great, that he who abounds in them will be
able to gain so many to his service as shall be sufficient to subdue
the rest. It is hard to find a tyranny in the world that has not been
introduced this way.'—*Algernon Sidney.*

THE celebrated resolution of 1780, ' That the influence of the Crown has increased, is increasing,
and ought to be diminished,' may seem to carry its
own refutation along with it. A House of Commons
that can vote a resolution so hostile to the Crown, it
may be said, can have little reason to dread its influence. This objection, however, would be more
specious than solid. The influence of the Crown
acts by slow but continual pressure ; the opinion of
the people, by sudden impulse. Thus a series of
measures injurious to the interests and honour of the
country are persisted in for a long time by mere
force of authority and the private advantages which
individuals acquire by supporting the system. At
length the evil is carried beyond bearing: the people
see they have been misled and benighted, and determine to dismiss their guides. But even then the
holders of power have innumerable means of soften-
ing, perhaps of totally averting their disgrace, and
they proceed for some time longer conducting the
nation through fresh difficulties, and involving the
State in new and greater perils. Thus it was in

1780: the party who had carried the abstract resolution before mentioned, found themselves in a minority a few weeks after, when they attempted to deduce from it a practical result.

The reign of Charles II. is said to have been the period when the plan of influencing the members of the House of Commons by gifts and favours of the Crown was first systematically framed.   The name of ' Pensioner Parliament,' given to the House which sate in that reign for seventeen years without dissolution, is a sufficient index of the general opinion concerning it.   Many of the poorer members sold their votes for a very small gratuity.   Offices and favours were granted to the speakers most worth buying ; the rest were glad of a sum of money.   The trifling sum of £10,000 was allowed by Lord Clifford for the purpose of buying members.   This was increased by Lord Danby.   By the report of a Committee of Secrecy, appointed in 1678, it appears that many members received money or favours of one kind or another for their votes.

There can be no doubt that the practice was continued during the reign of William.   Sir John Trevor was convicted, when Speaker, of receiving bribes from the City of London, to procure the passing of the Orphans Bill.   Mr. Hungerford was expelled for the same offence.

These facts show how unjust it is to charge Walpole with having been the first who governed England by corruption.   That he employed corruption among his means cannot, indeed, be doubted.   He did it with a coarseness which, by destroying the shame attendant upon it, overthrew the low barrier of virtue still subsisting, and extended the vice which thus openly displayed itself.   He is said to have affirmed that he did not care who made members of Parliament, so long as he was allowed to deal with them when they were made.   Perhaps these stories were unfounded; but they threw discredit on his government.

At the time of Lord North's administration, the influence of the Crown was exerted in the most profuse, most shameful, and most degrading manner. The friends and favourites of the minister were allowed to have a share in the loan, which they sold the moment after at a gain of ten per cent.* Mr. Fox, in his speeches, more than once accuses Lord North of having devoted £900,000 of a loan to conciliate support. It is remarkable that Mr. Fox allows, at the same time, that it is natural that a minister, in making a loan, should favour his own friends, and that it is not to be expected any minister will ever act otherwise. He does not venture to blame Lord North for this practice, but only for the abuse of it. Some members of Parliament actually received at that time a sum of money for their votes. Every office of government was a scene of confusion, waste, and prodigality, admirably adapted for the interests of all who wished to enrich themselves at the expense of honour, patriotism, and conscience. A cry for reform in the expenditure, louder than that which had overturned Walpole, was raised, and produced the resolution mentioned at the beginning of the chapter. The wish of the nation extended to parliamentary as well as economical reform. Mr. Pitt skilfully made himself the organ of both, and on the strength of his professions obtained that credit from the people which was denied to the party who, after a long and unpopular opposition to the American war, had lost the fruits of their exertions by joining the minister who carried it on.

After the close of the American war, Mr. Burke's Bills, and the regulations of Lord Shelburne, made a diminution of 216 places. Mr. Pitt abolished 200

* Rose's ' Influence of the Crown.'

inferior offices in the salt department, the salaries of
which amounted to £25,000 a year.[*]   In addition
to these, thirty-two placemen have been, since 1780,
excluded from Parliament by Mr. Burke's Bills,
and Mr. Rose adds to the list fifteen contractors.
Sinecures, too, have been abolished.

All these reductions of the means of influence,
however, are of little importance; public opinion
has far outgrown the influence of the Crown, and
has subdued everything to its own pervading omni-
potent authority.

[*] Rose on the Influence of the Crown.   Ed. Review, vol. xvi. p. 191.

CHAPTER XXXV.

LIBERTY OF THE PRESS.—PROBABLE FATE OF THE ENGLISH CONSTITUTION.

' If it be desired to know the immediate cause of all this free writing and free speaking, there cannot be assigned a truer than your own mild, free, and humane government: it is the liberty, Lords and Commons, which your own valorous and happy councils have purchased us; liberty, which is the nurse of all great wits. We can grow ignorant again, brutish, formal, and slavish, as ye found us; but you then must first become that which ye cannot be, oppressive, arbitrary, and tyrannous as they were from whom ye have freed us. That our hearts are now more capacious, our thoughts now more excited to the search and expectation of greatest and exactest things, is the issue of your own virtue propagated in us. Give me the liberty to know, to utter, and argue freely, according to conscience, above all liberties.'—*Milton.*

THERE is no enquiry more interesting than the examination into the present state of our laws and manners, with a view to ascertain the probable fate of our Constitution.

In considering this question there is no more broad foundation for hope and confidence than the Liberty of the Press. It seems difficult to conceive a people passing at once from the general diffusion of political knowledge to the utter darkness of despotism, and the prohibition of all discussion which such despotism would require.

But, in speaking of the press, let us always bear in mind that it is ill to talk of its liberty without its licentiousness. Every attempt to curb its licentiousness, otherwise than by the verdict of a jury, after an offence committed, must likewise restrain its liberty. To do one without the other, were as

difficult as to provide that the sun should bring our
flowers and fruits to perfection, but never scorch
our faces.

Many have a mistaken notion of what the press
is. They suppose it to be a regular independent
power, like the Crown or the House of Commons.
The press does nothing more than afford a means of
expressing, with able argument and in good language,
the opinions of large classes of society. For if these
opinions, however well sustained, are paradoxes confined to the individual who utters them, they fall as
harmless in the middle of thirty millions of people,
as they would do in a private party of three persons.
Thus it is that the true censor of the press is the
national mind; for it is not the sentiment of A., the
editor of one newspaper, or of B., the editor of
another, which controls the course of government.
These gentlemen are little, if at all, known; with
one or two exceptions, their names are never mentioned. It is their skill in embodying in a daily
journal the feelings and the reasonings which come
home to the business and the bosoms of large por-
tions of their countrymen, that obtains for their
writings fame and general acceptance. But it would
be vain for these persons, powerful as the daily press
is, to endeavour to make the people permanently
discontented with laws which they revered, and a
minister whom they respected. The newspaper
which took that erratic course would not be even read.
Equally vain would it be for a vicious, oppressive,
and odious Government to suppress the liberty of
printing. It was not the press which overturned
Charles I., nor could the Inquisition preserve to Fer-
dinand VII. his despotic power. The dark cabal, the
secret conspirator, the sudden tumult, the solitary
assassin, may all be found where the liberty of printing has never existed. And were a Government to
suppress it where it does exist, without taking away

the matter of sedition, more crime and less security
would probably be the result of their foolish panic
and powerless precaution.

In looking at the celebrated governments of antiquity, and those of modern times which have not
admitted a free press, it must strike every one that
they have declined, not from any vice inherent in
the institutions by which they were governed, but
by the gradual decay of national virtue, and the corruption of the people themselves, as well as of their
leaders.   In Sparta and in Rome this corruption
may, in the beginning, be attributed to an influx of
wealth acting upon a nation whose liberties and
whose morals were founded upon poverty and the
contempt of riches.   But the precipitate fall of a
State, like that of Rome, into an abyss of profligacy
and venality, can only happen when the whole people,
stained by political and moral vices, are delivered
from a sense of shame by the want of any effectual
restraint upon their actions.   In both these circumstances, England has the advantage of Rome.   Her
institutions are not founded on the postulate that her
manners must be rude and her legislators poor.   Commerce and industry of every kind have been favourites
of the law from the commencement.   Nor is it easy to
emancipate our rulers or our elective body from the
sense of shame.   Their actions are not submitted to
the opinions of a single city, but scanned publicly
by thirty millions of people — nay, by Europe, by
America, by the whole globe.   The nation itself is
too numerous to be generally seduced by the officers
of the Crown.   In a village of one hundred householders, two, or perhaps four, may be gained by
government influence; but the other ninety-six are
free to choose their politics and their newspaper.
Nor could any anonymous writer venture to appeal
to any but the good principles of our nature.   No
one has yet seen the newspaper or pamphlet which

openly defends the venality of judges, or the inflic-
tion of torture, any more than the tragedy which
holds up cowardice to our admiration, or endeavours
to make envy amiable in our eyes.   Even the worst
men love virtue in their studies.

In ordinary times, it is evident the exercise of
this censorship must be beneficial to the country.
No statesman can hope that his corrupt practices, his
jobs, his obliquities, his tergiversations, can escape
from a vigilance that never slumbers, and an industry
that never wearies.   Nor is it an important obstacle
to sound opinion, that the daily newspapers are the
advocates of party, rather than searchers after truth:
they act like lawyers pleading in a great national
cause; and the nation, like a jury, after hearing
both sides, may decide between them.   Neither are
the advantages to be derived from publicity merely
speculative.   We see instances of them every day.
One of the most remarkable effects of public opinion
that can be quoted is, perhaps, the personal integrity
of our statesmen with respect to money.   In the
time of Charles II., and a long time afterwards, the
greatest men in the country were not inaccessible to
what, in these days, we should call bribery.   In
the time of Lord North, many members of Parliament were influenced by money in its most gross
and palpable shape.   In these days it is impossible
not to allow that there is much more personal delicacy, more honesty, and, I will add, a higher sense
of honour, among our statesmen than formerly.

The greatest benefit, however, that we derive
from publicity, is that it corrects and neutralises the
vices of our institutions, even when they are not
immediately amended by it.   Thus, to come at once
to the greatest instance of this: the House of Commons was, before the Reform Act, so composed, that
had it been shut up, and had it admitted no influence
from without, the people would have found that its

spirit was so gone, its organs so decayed, its acts
so unpalatable, that they would have submitted to
such a government no longer.   But the talent of a
single member often outweighed the sense of the
whole House; and a minister, after protecting a
favourite abuse, year after year, by confident speeches
and overwhelming majorities, silently retreated, and
abandoned the ground on which he appeared to
have taken an impregnable position. The House
of Commons themselves, too, could not fail to be
influenced on great questions by the general opinion
of the people out of doors.   If they could have
met and discussed measures of State day after day,
made speeches that are to be read in Caithness and
in Cork, exposed their whole conduct and arguments to the view of the country, and yet have
paid no attention to the feelings of that country,
they would have been more or less than human.

Thus, in favour of the preservation of our free
Constitution, we have the general diffusion of the
light of knowledge, the long-settled habit of liberty,
and the security of funded property depending upon
that liberty.   We have a people of virtuous habits,
a high standard of morality, and more of the improvements and embellishments of life combined
with energy and purity than perhaps ever existed
together.   We have a political Constitution which
favours, instead of repressing, wealth, commerce,
learning, and the fine arts; we have the whole civilised world as the audience before whom our statesmen must defend their conduct.

These considerations seem to point out a way of
safety through all our dangers.   We have seen that
when our people strongly and manfully express their
opinion, their voice prevails.   If, then, they resist
with energy the slow creeping abuses and the violent
sudden innovations that weaken and deface the edifice of our freedom, it may be preserved entire.

But in order to this, our gentlemen, superior to childish fears, must submit to hear noisy orators without shrinking; they must cut away with a steady hand the disease which menaces the nobler parts of our political frame. In plain words, they must consent to reform what is barbarous, what is servile, what is corrupt in our institutions. They must make our government harmonise one part with another, and adapt itself to the state of knowledge in the nation. I would fain hope that it will be so: I trust that the people of this great community, supported by their gentry, will afford a spectacle worthy of the admiration of the world. I hope that the gentry will act honestly by their country, and that the country will not part with the blessings which it obtained by the endurance of all the miseries which can oppress a nation,—by suffering persecutions, by confronting tyranny, by encountering civil war, by submitting to martyrdom, by contending in open war against Powers that were the terror of the rest of Europe. I would fain believe that all ranks and classes of this country have still impressed upon their minds the sentiment of her immortal Milton—' Let not England forget her precedence of teaching nations how to live.'

CONCLUDING CHAPTER.

SUCH were the hopes, and such the doubts and fears, with which I regarded, about the year 1820, the future history of the English Government and Constitution.

In the preface to the work of which the present is a new edition, I said, ' Let Englishmen bear in mind that the old monarchies of the Continent were so vicious in structure, and so decayed in substance, as to require complete renovation, while the abuses of our Constitution are capable of amendments strictly conformable to its spirit, and eminently conducive to its preservation.'

Events have justified this distinction. France has undergone the Revolution which overthrew Charles the Tenth, and the Revolution which over-threw Louis-Philippe. Italy has effected a com-plete and happy revolution. Austria is undergoing an auspicious change in her constitution; Prussia has hardly commenced the process; Spain and Por-tugal have not fully completed it. England, on her side, has made many peaceful reforms, of which I propose in this chapter to trace the outline.

So long as the alarm created by the French Revolution lasted, the party which had sustained Lord North in the American war and Mr. Pitt in the French war remained unbroken. During nearly sixty years of power, that party had devoted all its energies to the suppression of colonial or domestic revolt, and the prosecution of war against a foreign enemy.

The few measures of a liberal character which

marked this epoch, Mr. Burke's Bills of Economical Reform, and the Abolition of the Slave Trade, were the fruit of the short intervals when office was held by the Whig party in 1782 and 1806.

But as the fear of foreign jacobinism and domestic disturbance subsided, the Whig party gained gradually upon public confidence. Still their triumph over ancient prejudices and compact party strength would have been remote, had not the great Tory body separated itself into two divisions.

The one using the name of Mr. Pitt abhorred his wise views regarding Catholic disabilities and commercial policy, and, according to the happy comparison of Mr. Canning, adored him only in the hours of his eclipse.

The other division, while retaining their old allegiance to the war policy of 1793, and the severe restrictive laws which accompanied it, yet saw in the altered circumstances of the time reasons for breaking down the barriers which separated one portion of the King's subjects from another, for appealing to tha reason rather than the passive submission of the people, and for letting 'persuasion do the work of fear.'

These different views occasioned from time to time much rumbling and jarring, and finally such an upheaving of the fiery element as to burst the solid mass and heavy level, which for more than half a century had lain incumbent upon the soil of Great Britain.

Of those who took the more enlightened view of the interests of their country, Mr. Canning, Mr. Huskisson, Lord Palmerston, and Mr. Grant were the first.

At a later period, Sir Robert Peel, Lord Aberdeen, Lord Lincoln, Mr. Gladstone, and Mr. Sidney Herbert found the Tory yoke intolerable, and joined the party of progress. In the same period the Radical

party, which during the war had been composed of
a few scattered remnants, became under Mr. Joseph
Hume a considerable, consistent, and active body.

The separations, the adhesions, and the forma-
tions took place at different times, and on different
questions.   But substantially the great changes
which have taken place during forty years, between
1823 and 1863, have been the work of these parties,
sometimes acting together, or, as more frequently
happened, co-operating from opposite benches and
advancing in different columns, but with equal
regard to the promotion of the great principles of
Reform.

The state of England in 1823 was not auspicious.
In 1817 the Habeas Corpus Act was suspended,
and spics were sent from the Home Office into the
manufacturing counties, who, acting according to
their nature, and not according to their instructions, stimulated the crimes which were afterwards
punished on the scaffold.[*]

In 1819, bills were introduced by Lord Castlereagh, described by him as measures 'of severe
coercion.'

The general state of the laws, finances, and trade
of England was most backward.   The criminal law
was full of capital penalties, some for very trifling
offences, such as cutting down a growing tree, or
being seen with the face blackened on the high-
road.   Foreign trade was cramped by monopolies
and restrictions.   Taxes were imposed on the necessaries of life; excise duties were very onerous, and
the duties of customs, extending to many hundred articles, produced vexation to merchants, and
narrowed the comforts of the people.

---

[*] See 'State Trials,' vol. xxxii.
p. 859, and ' Parliamentary Debates,' vol. xxxvi. pp. 1003 and
1018, with other references in
the 'State Trials,' loco cit.   Oliver, the spy, did all in his power
to promote insurrection.

Protestant Dissenters were only indirectly admitted to office. Roman Catholics and Jews were expressly excluded both from Parliament and from political offices. Parliamentary Reform was successfully opposed. Even when a corrupt borough was extinguished, the populous and flourishing borough of Leeds was not enfranchised, because it would be a novelty. The press was restricted by a fourpenny stamp on each newspaper, and prosecutions were rife against those who indulged in too great freedom of criticism.

The state of foreign affairs was very lamentable. The three great northern Powers, Russia, Austria, and Prussia, having succeeded to the Continental despotism of Napoleon without his genius (*impar Congressus Achilli*, as Lord Byron has it) had ordered that no liberty should be allowed, no reform introduced without their sanction.* In this spirit they had suppressed, in 1821 and 1823, the revolutions of Naples, Piedmont, and Spain; thus deceiving and betraying the people of Europe who had fought in 1813 and 1814 for liberty as well as independence. Against those atrocious acts England had protested feebly in 1821, forcibly in 1823,—in both cases fruitlessly.

As the Tory party were in power in 1823, it was natural that the task of innovation should commence on a question upon which Tory precedents would favour the aggressors.

The French Commercial Treaty of 1713 was made by the Tories, and pulled to pieces by the Whigs. The French Commercial Treaty of 1786 was concluded by the Tories, and opposed by the Whigs.

On this side, therefore, Mr. Canning and Mr. Huskisson, Mr. Peel and Mr. Robinson, commenced

* See Note H.

their attacks upon the outworks of the existing
system.

The silk manufacture had been bound in the
swaddling-clothes of the State from the days of its
infancy.

Mr. Huskisson took a liberal but at the same time
a very temperate course on this subject. The import
of foreign silk manufactures had been hitherto prohibited; he proposed to admit them after a preparation
of two years, with an import duty of thirty per cent.*

The next work taken in hand, but by the Whigs
and not by the Government, was the removal of
restrictions on religious liberty.

In 1828, the House of Commons consented to
repeal the Test and Corporation Acts, which were
a relic of intolerance, and inflicted an undeserved
stigma on Protestant Dissenters. This measure was
carried, in the first instance, against the weight of
the Government, though afterwards befriended by
Sir Robert Peel.

In the next year the disabilities which at once
oppressed and degraded the Roman Catholics of
England and Ireland were removed, on the proposition of the Duke of Wellington, Sir Robert Peel,
and Lord Lyndhurst. From the beginning of the
century, Mr. Fox and Mr. Pitt, Mr. Windham and
Lord Grenville, Mr. Sheridan and Mr. Canning,
Lord Castlereagh and Mr. Grattan, had proved in
Parliament the justice and the wisdom of admitting
Roman Catholics to all the benefits of the Constitution. But until Mr. O'Connell roused the physical
force of Ireland to a point of violence which was
almost rebellion, no concession could be obtained.
In 1829, that which had been contemptuously refused to reason and eloquence, was amply conceded
to menaces and masses.

* See Note L.

Sir Robert Peel, however, rendered ample justice to the Whigs, while he proposed the measure of which they had been the consistent advocates.

When the debate on the second reading of the Catholic Relief Bill was drawing to a close, and the triumph of the great cause of religious freedom was assured, Sir Robert Peel, at the conclusion of his speech, gave his generous testimony to the merits of his forerunners and his opponents. He said, 'One parting word, and I here close. I have received in the speech of my noble friend, the Member for Donegal, testimonies of approbation which are grateful to my heart; and they have been liberally awarded to me by gentlemen on the other side of the House, in a manner which does honour to the forbearance of party among us. They have, however, one and all, awarded to me a credit which I do not deserve, for settling this question. The credit belongs to others, and not to me. It belongs to Mr. Fox, to Mr. Grattan, to Mr. Plunkett, to the gentlemen opposite, and to an illustrious and right honourable friend of mine who is now no more. By their efforts, in spite of my opposition, it has proved victorious.' *

The political party which for sixty years had swayed, with very brief intervals, the destinies of the State; which had led the nation to the American and the French wars; which had resisted all reform and protected all abuse; which had maintained all that was bigoted and persecuted all that was liberal,—broke down under this great failure.

The light now burst in: after the general election the ministry was defeated, and Lord Grey, the new Prime Minister, proclaimed the advent of peace, retrenchment, and reform.

On the subject of peace the rising of Belgium

* Parliamentary Debates, new series, vol. xx. p. 1289.

gave an opportunity to Lord Grey of acting as a
minister on those principles of which he had been the
unavailing advocate in opposition.

The questions raised by the Belgian insurrection
were complicated; the Northern Powers beheld with
some alarm a revolution effected by popular tumult,
and the French Government had some difficulty in
restraining the national wish for annexation.

On the 21st of June, upon the opening of Parliament, the speech from the throne contained the following announcement:—'The discussions which have
taken place on the affairs of Belgium have not yet
been brought to a conclusion, but the most complete
agreement continues to subsist between the Powers
whose Plenipotentiaries have been engaged in the
Conferences of London. The principle on which
these conferences have been conducted has been that
of not interfering with the right of the people of
Belgium to regulate their internal affairs, and to
establish their government according to their own
views of what may be most conducive to their future
welfare and independence, under the sole condition,
sanctioned by the practice of nations, and founded
on the principles of public law, that in the exercise
of that undoubted right the security of neighbouring
States should not be endangered.' *

The discussions thus declared by the King in
June 1831, to be not yet brought to a conclusion,
went on for some years afterwards, but by the firmness, perseverance, and ability of Lord Palmerston
were at length terminated, and the acknowledgment
and guarantee of all the great Powers established
the independence of Belgium.

The work of retrenchment was pursued with
vigour, and many useless places were abolished,
while the salaries of the most important and efficient
officers of the State were considerably reduced.

* Hansard's Debates, third series, vol. iv. p. 85.

Soon after Lord Grey had formed his Ministry, Lord Durham asked me to call upon him in Cleveland Row. He informed me that Lord Grey wished him to consult me with respect to the formation of a committee, to draw up the outlines of a plan of Parliamentary Reform. After some deliberation, we agreed to propose to Sir James Graham, then First Lord of the Admiralty, and Lord Duncannon, then First Commissioner of Woods and Forests, to form with us a committee for this purpose.

Lord Durham then asked me to frame, for the consideration of the committee, a sketch of the principal heads of a measure of Reform, to be submitted to Lord Grey, and if approved by him to be proposed to the Cabinet.

Thus invited to propose a plan on a great, important, and difficult subject, I felt bound to reconsider the general principles upon which a sound measure of reform should rest.

On this head I had often recurred to the reflections of Mr. Burke.

' It is this inability to wrestle with difficulty,' says that wonderful man, ' which has obliged the arbitrary assembly of France to commence their schemes of reform with abolition and total destruction. But is it in destroying and pulling down that skill is displayed ? Your mob can do this as well, at least, as your assemblies. The shallowest understanding, the rudest hand, is more than equal to the task. . . . The errors and defects of old establishments are visible and palpable. It calls for little ability to point them out ; and where absolute power is given, it requires but a word wholly to abolish the vice and the establishment together. . . . At once to preserve and to reform is quite another thing. When the useful parts of an old establishment are kept, and what is superadded is to be fitted to what is retained, a vigorous mind, steady persevering attention, various powers of comparison and combination, and the resources of an understanding fruitful in expedients, are to be exercised; they are to be exercised in a continued conflict with the combined force of opposite vices, with the obstinacy that rejects all improvement, and the levity which is disgusted with everything of which it is in possession.' *

Lord Grey, the best exponent of the principles of Mr. Fox, and now about to put into practice the advice he had often given in vain, had in his great speech of 1810 expressed these wise and memorable opinions for the consideration of the House of Lords.

' He indeed must either have been prematurely wise, or must have learnt little by experience, who, after a lapse of twenty years, can look upon a subject of this nature in all respects precisely in the same light. Still, after as serious and dispassionate a consideration as he could give to what he believed to be the most important question that could employ their Lordships' attention, it was his conscientious opinion that much good would result from the adoption of the salutary principles of Reform, gradually applied to the correction of those existing abuses to which the progress of time must unavoidably have given birth; taking especial care that the measure of Reform should be marked out by the Constitution itself, and in no case exceed its wholesome limits.'

After expressing his admiration for Mr. Fox, ' than whom there never existed one who more fully understood the principles or more affectionately appreciated the blessings of the venerable institutions under which he lived,' Lord Grey continued—' Never, my Lords, can I forget his powerful observations when, in his place in Parliament, he stated his conviction of the absolute impossibility of providing for all the variety of human events by

* Burke's ' Reflections,' &c.: Works, vol. v. pp. 303–4.

any previous speculative plans. For, said he, " I think that if a number of the wisest, ablest, and most virtuous men that ever adorned and improve l human life were collected together and seated roun l a table, to devise *à priori* a constitution for a State,— it is my persuasion that, notwithstanding all their ability and virtue, they would not succeed in adapting a system to the purposes required, but must necessarily leave it to be fitted by great alterations in the practice, and many deviations from the original design." And this opinion he was wont to illustrate by the familiar but apt example of building a house, which, notwithstanding all the study and consideration previously bestowed upon the plan, was never yet known to supply every want, or to provide all the accommodation, which in the subsequent occupation of it were found to be necessary. Nay, he used to remark that, however fine to look at a regular paper plan might be, no house was so habitable and so commodious as one which was built from time to time, piecemeal and without any regular design. To those principles of practical reform, so wisely enforced by that great statesman, I am determined to adhere,' &c.

In the same speech, Lord Grey referred to a declaration of the ' Association of the Friends of the People,' signed by the Duke of Bedford, then Lord John Russell:—

' We are convinced,' say the framers of that declaration, ' that the people bear a fixed attachment to the happy form of our government, and to the genuine principles of our constitution. These we cherish as the objects of such affection, not from any implicit reverence or habitual superstition, but as institutions best calculated to produce the happiness of men in civil society; and it is because we are convinced that abuses are undermining and corrupting them, that we have associated for the

preservation of those principles. We wish to reform
the Constitution because we wish to preserve it.' *

When, therefore, I was invited by Lord Grey and
Lord Durham to frame a plan to be proposed to
Parliament, and perhaps to become the law of the
land, it was not my duty to cut the body of our old
parent to pieces and to throw it into a Medea's
caldron with the hopes of reviving the strength
and vigour of youth. To do so would have been
to commit a folly, which I had myself reprobated so
long ago as the year 1819. On the 14th December
of that year, I had said, ' the principles of the construction of this House are pure and worthy. If
we should endeavour to change them altogether,
we should commit the folly of the servant in the
story of Aladdin, who is deceived by the cry of
" New lamps for old." Our lamp is covered with
dirt and rubbish, but it has a magical power. It
has raised up a smiling land, not bestrode with overgrown palaces, but covered with thickset dwellings,
every one of which holds a freeman enjoying equal
privileges and equal protection with the proudest
subject in the land. It has called into life all the
busy creations of commercial prosperity. Nor when
men were wanting to illustrate and defend their
country have such men been deficient. When the
fate of the nation depended upon the line of policy
they should adopt, there were orators of the highest
degree placing in the strongest light the arguments
for peace and war. When we were engaged in war,
we had warriors ready to gain us laurels on the
land, or to wield our thunders on the sea. When
again we returned to peace, the questions of internal policy, of education of the poor, and of criminal
law, found men ready to devote the most splendid
abilities to the welfare of the most indigent class

* Declaration of the Associa-   May 12, 1792. Hansard's De-
tion of the Friends of the People, bates, vol. xvii. pp. 562, 564.

of the community! And, Sir, shall we change an instrument which has produced effects so wonderful, for a burnished and tinsel article of modern manufacture? No! small as the remaining treasure of the Constitution is, I cannot consent to throw it into the wheel for the chance of obtaining a prize in the lottery of constitutions!'*

With these strong impressions on my mind, I was not likely to deviate from the track of the Constitution into the maze of fancy, or the wilderness of abstract rights.

In 1797, Mr. Grey had proposed to increase the number of county members, and to give four hundred members to districts of town and country in which every householder should have a vote. Mr. Lambton had, on the 19th of April, 1821, proposed a similar plan.†

I had myself in 1822 gone very largely into the question, and had proposed as a resolution, 'That the present state of the representation of the people in Parliament requires the serious consideration of this House.'

Mr. Canning, at the end of a long and very brilliant speech in opposition to my motion, had given me reason to expect that in some future year I might succeed. 'I cannot help,' he had said—'I cannot help conjuring the noble lord himself to pause before he again presses it upon the country. If, however, he shall persevere, and if his perseverance shall be successful, and if the results of that success shall be such as I cannot help apprehending, his be the triumph to have precipitated those results; be mine the consolation that to the utmost and the latest of my power I have opposed them.'‡

* Parliamentary Debates, vol. xli. p. 1105.

† Hansard's Parliamentary Debates, new series, vol. v. p.

369; and for Plan, see Appendix, in the same volume.

‡ Parliamentary Debates, new series, vol. vii. p. 138.

Thus encouraged and thus warned, I neglected neither the encouragement nor the warning.

There were evidently two modes in which reform might be approached. The one was to consider the right of voting as a personal privilege possessed by every man of sound mind, and of years of discretion, as an inherent inalienable right, belonging to him as a member of a free country. According to this theory, the votes of the whole male adult population form the only basis of legitimate government.

Other political writers and eminent statesmen, while of opinion that a free and full representation of the people forms a necessary condition of free government, acknowledge no personal right of voting as inalienable and essential. They consider that the purpose to be attained is good government; the freedom of the people within the State, and their security from without; and that the best mode of attaining these ends is the problem to be solved.

It seemed to me that these last reasoners were in the right. A representation which should produce bad, hasty, passionate, unjust, and ignorant decisions, could not conduce to that welfare of the people which is the supreme law. If it be said, as it may be said with truth, that no part of the property of the people ought to be levied in taxes by the Government, without the consent expressed or implied of the whole community, it may be answered that a man's life and liberty are as valuable to him as his property; yet no one contends that the judicial body and the jury in criminal trials should be selected by universal suffrage. On the contrary, the greatest care is taken to place on the judicial bench men qualified by learning and experience, and to form the list of the jury out of a portion of the community whose station in life affords some security for their average intelligence, information, and honesty. Similar care ought to be taken to entrust to a portion of the community, qualified by honesty and intelligence, the mighty power of selecting the House of Commons.

The theory of Mr. Mill, that every man ought to have a vote, but a vote weighted according to a sort of handicap, seems to me visionary in the extreme. I cannot perceive, should it be once admitted in principle that in order to form a free government it is necessary that every man should have a vote, that it is practicable, or possible, to put every man's vote into a scale; to count a merchant or a banker for more voices than a baker or a grocer, and still less, how it is possible to gauge the intellect of labourers or artisans of superior talent or knowledge, and enter them as weighing more than a fundholder or a merchant, a landholder or a great capitalist, whose mind has not been cultivated, or whose talents have never been very bright. For, besides the interminable disputes, the never-ending jealousies, the appeal of a wise baker against a foolish banker, the doubt and suspicion thrown upon the integrity of the examiners, who in fact must decide the election between the Liberal and Conservative candidate,—is there, after all, any reason to say that a man who knows the higher mathematics, who can calculate compound interest, who is wonderful in his knowledge of geography, is a better elector of a member for the county than the man who goes to market every Saturday, or is at the covert side every Monday morning? After all, were not the distinctions made by our ancestors, that a man who has a freehold of 40s. a year shall vote for the county, and a man who pays scot and lot shall vote for the borough, and that those who have not these qualifications shall not vote,—were not these distinctions much more simple, much less invidious, much more attainable by industry and thrift, and after all quite as philosophical a basis of representation as the metaphysical categories of modern times ?[*]

It seemed to me at least that it would be sufficient to lay down some such conditions as the following, as necessary qualifications for the body of electors.

1. That they should be of average intelligence.

2. That they should, upon the whole, form a security for stability of property.

3. That although bribery cannot be altogether excluded, the body of electors, as a mass, should not be tainted by corruption.

4. That the electoral body should be identified with the general sense of the community—in short, with the public opinion of the time.

Such being the objects in view, there were two modes by which they were to be sought. One mode would be by the definition of the franchise; the other, by the distribution of the seats.

It appeared to me that the first mode alone would not be sufficient.

In large cities, population would outweigh property. In large counties, property would control population.

To complete the House of Commons, there were required some seats where property could support the claims of an intelligence not popular with the masses, and possibly not rich in land or funds.

In the old system, Mr. Burke, defeated at Bristol, had been returned for Malton; Mr. Fox, nearly overpowered at Westminster, had been returned for Orkney; Mr. Grey, rejected by Northumberland, had found a seat at Appleby. Such a resource, I thought, should not be entirely lost.

It was desirable, in short, as it appeared to me, while sweeping away gross abuses, to avail ourselves, as far as possible, of the existing frame and body of our institutions.

Thus, if the due weight and influence of property

* See Note J.

could be maintained by preserving the representation of a portion of the small boroughs with an improved franchise, it was desirable rather to build on the old foundations than to indulge our fancy or our conceit in choosing a new site and erecting on new soil—perhaps on sand—an edifice entirely different from all which had hitherto existed.

At the same time, I was deeply impressed with the conviction of Lord Grey, that none but a large measure would be a safe measure; that to nibble at disfranchisement, and to cramp reform by pedantic adherence to exisiting rights, would be to deceive expectation, to whet appetite, and to bring on that revolution which it was our object to avert.

I endeavoured, therefore, to cut away what was rotten, to preserve what was worth preserving, and to introduce what would strengthen and improve.

I have now before me the plan which I framed in accordance with Lord Durham's desire. It is indorsed on the back in Lord Durham's handwriting—

    No. I.

      Lord John Russell's Plan. *

And in my handwriting—

Submitted to Lord Durham, Lord Duncannon, and Sir James Graham.

Dec. 1830.   J. R.

The plan itself, which is written on a sheet of writing-paper, is in the inside. It contains the following heads, with some alterations and erasures in pencil:—

Fifty boroughs of the smallest population, according to the census of 1821, to be disfranchised. *This would disfranchise all Boroughs of 1,400 inhabitants.*

* What is here in italics is in the MS. in the handwriting of Lord Durham.

II. Fifty more of the least considerable to send in future only
one member to Parliament.

This would apply to Boroughs of 3,000 inhabitants.

III. In all cities and boroughs
which preserve the right of sending members to Parliament, persons qualified to serve on juries
to have the right of voting.

IV. In cities and boroughs
which preserve the right of sending members to Parliament, no
person to vote except in *the City
of London, Westminster,* and
Southwark, unless he is a householder rated at £10 a year, has
paid his parochial taxes for three
years within three months after
they became due, and has resided
in the city or borough for six
months previous to the election.

V. Eighteen large towns to
send members to Parliament.
The unrepresented parts of London to send four or six additional
members. Twenty counties to
send two additional members
each.

VI. The right of voting in the
new towns to be, in householders
rated at £10 a year, or in persons
qualified to serve on juries.

VII. Copyholders and lease-
holders having an interest of more
than twenty-one years to vote in
counties.

VIII. The poll to be taken in
hundreds of divisions of counties,
but not more than fifteen with
the consent of the candidates.

IX. In cities and boroughs the
poll to finish on the second day.
X. No new right of voting to
be acquired in counties by any
property of less value than £10
a year.

The first two proposals were agreed to, Lord
Durham having first ascertained from the population
returns that the first list of fifty would comprehend
boroughs under 2,000 and not 1,400 inhabitants, and
the second list of fifty, boroughs under 4,000 and not
3,000 inhabitants.

These two lists, with some modifications of the
data of disfranchisement, formed Schedules A and
B of the Reform Bill.

A discussion then took place on the right of
voting for boroughs. We agreed that it should be
uniform, our opinion being that the freemen and the
scot-and-lot voters had, in process of time, become
generally either dependent or corrupt.

We endeavoured to fix a qualification which should
give the right of voting to the greatest number of
independent men, and, as far as we could roughly
guess, be an equivalent for the old householder
right of voting of the seventeenth century. We
fixed the right of suffrage by filling up the blank
with ten pounds.

This was the same qualification which I had proposed for Leeds, when I introduced, in 1820, a Bill
for granting to that town the franchises forfeited by
the corrupt and convicted borough of Grampound.
We agreed in subsequent meetings to introduce this
right of voting in every town sending members to
Parliament; thus giving to ' the community ' (according to the old term of our charters) the power
which had been long enjoyed by close corporations.
This decision opened Bath, Portsmouth, Scarbo-

rough, Cambridge, and many other towns, to the inhabitants. We also settled a list of towns to be enfranchised, and of counties to receive additional representatives. Having the assistance of Lord Duncannon for Ireland, of Mr. Cockburn, then the Scotch Solicitor-General, for Scotland, and of Mr. Stanley, now Lord Stanley of Alderley, for the additions to the Welsh boroughs, we attempted to adapt our reform to the state of Ireland, Scotland, and Wales, no less than of England. The task was an arduous one, and in more than one particular we fell into errors of detail. The statistical data, especially, upon which we had relied for the preparation of our list of boroughs to be condemned, were not a sufficient basis for the superstructure we raised upon them. The population tables gave parishes and not towns as their units; and thus while, in some instances, the parish stretched beyond the borough, in others the borough comprised several parishes.

But, with the exception of difficulties thus arising from our inexperience, the plan itself had a marvellous success.

When the proposals were completed, Lord Durham wrote an admirable report upon the plan, which was presented, in the name of the committee, to Lord Grey. The plan, approved by him, was unanimously adopted by the Cabinet, and Lord Grey, carrying it himself to Brighton, explained it fully to the King, by whom it was readily and cheerfully sanctioned. It should be mentioned that, in one of the last days of our sittings, vote by ballot was, against my earnest advice, adopted by the committee. It was, on the recommendation of Lord Grey, omitted by the Cabinet. In talking over the whole matter with Lord Grey, I stated my impression that, if the plan were kept secret till the moment of its being announced to Parliament, its popularity would ensure its success; but that, if prematurely divulged, an adverse vote might stifle the infant in its cradle.

In this opinion Lord Grey fully concurred, and so strongly impressed upon his colleagues the necessity of secrecy, that, of more than thirty persons who knew the plan, not one was found indiscreet.

After the Cabinet had adopted the plan of Reform, and the King had sanctioned the measure, it became necessary to communicate it to Mr. Wynn, the Secretary at War, and Lord Stanley, the Secretary of the Lord-Lieutenant of Ireland. I undertook to open the plan to Mr. Wynn, while Lord Althorp engaged to explain it to Lord Stanley upon his arrival from Ireland to attend Parliament. Unfortunately I did not succeed in overcoming the scruples of Mr. Charles Wynn, and he finally determined to resign his office. Lord Althorp, having invited Lord Stanley to come to his house on his arrival from Ireland, and having explained to him the plan of Reform, sent for me to assist him in that task. When we had fully stated our views, I was happy to hear Lord Stanley declare his full concurrence in them, and in the subsequent debates his talents shone with the greatest lustre, especially in replying to Mr. Croker, whose speeches were able and eloquent, though declamatory and exaggerated. However, no one, however able, could stem the tide of public opinion, when allowed to flow in and overflow the opposing barriers.

The scene in the House of Commons on the 1st of March was unexampled. The plan went so far beyond all expectation, that the Whigs wondered whether it could possibly be carried; the Tories concluded that it certainly could not; and the Radicals, with justifiable exultation, felt sure that no temporary defeat could destroy a plan to which the Whig leaders, the friends of Mr. Canning, and the reformers throughout the country, would thereafter be irrevocably pledged. Sir Henry Hardinge, speaking to Sir James Graham in the Lobby, said, ' Well, you are honest fellows ; you have acted up to your

principles; but I suppose you all go out to-morrow
morning!'

The cheers of exultation from some members on
the Opposition side were quite as loud as from any
supporters of the Ministers.

Sir Robert Peel had convened some of his chief
supporters a few days before, to consider the course
to be taken.   They acquiesced generally in his
opinion that the introduction of the Bill should not
be resisted; indeed, Sir Robert Inglis was the only
person present who gave a contrary opinion.   As
this decision of Sir Robert Peel was in itself a great
mistake in policy, and in fact rendered all subsequent
opposition hopeless, such a course, on the part of so
eminent a party leader, may excite surprise.   But
it may be thus accounted for.   Two years before,
Sir R. Peel, wishing to save his country from the
risk of civil war, had sacrificed all his prejudices, all
his pride, and the confidence of his party, to be that
'daring pilot in extremity' who should place the
vessel of the State in harbour, at any loss of power or
fame for himself.   But the immolation had been painful in the extreme.   Some time afterwards, meeting
Sir Thomas Frankland Lewis at an inn in Wales, Sir
Frankland started the subject of the Reform Bill,
and said that he wondered that such a statesman as
his companion had not saved the country from the
wild revolutionary measure of the Ministers, and introduced a safe and moderate Reform Bill of his own.
Sir Robert answered, in substance, that nothing
would induce him to do again what he had done on
the Catholic question.*   He had himself quoted, in
those debates, the lines of Dryden—

> ' 'Tis quickly said, but, oh! how hardly tried
> By haughty souls to human honour tied,
> The sharp convulsive pangs of agonising pride!'

To this excited feeling of disappointment and disgust

* His phrase as reported to me by Sir Frankland Lewis,
was, 'I would sooner lie dead upon that floor.'

is, I think, to be attributed the unwillingness of the
great leader of the Tory party to incur the responsi-
bilities of office, and undertake the conduct of a
Reform Bill. In the meantime, the seven days of
debate on the introduction of the Bill gave time for
the flame of enthusiasm to rise, and not time for it
to abate. A second blunder of the Tory party enabled them to obtain a majority, and gave Lord Grey
an opportunity. of which he instantly availed himself, of advising the King to dissolve Parliament.
The triumph of the Reformers, so long a defeated
minority, was signal and general ; for, of eighty-two
members for the forty counties of England, seventy-
six were returned pledged to support the Reform
Bill of Lord Grey.

It would take too much space to relate the vicis-
situdes of the Reform Bill. It was carried in the
House of Commons mainly by the entire confidence
felt in the integrity and sound judgment of Lord
Althorp. ' Sir,' he said, replying to a very acute
and ingenious speech, ' the hon. and learned gentleman's arguments are very plausible. I do not re-
collect the reasons which prove his objections to be
groundless, but I know that those reasons were perfectly satisfactory to my own mind.' And the House
voted, by a great majority, against the plausible arguments, and in favour of the unknown replies. Lord
Althorp, as leader of the House, determined that
the Reform Bill should not be brought forward for
discussion unless either he or I were present. He
took for his special task the frame and wording of
the clauses, which he prepared with the assistance
of the law officers and the Reform lawyers in the
House of Commons, while I took the division of
counties, and the boundaries of boroughs, with the
aid of Lord Hatherton and Admiral Beaufort, acting as commissioners, appointed for the purpose.

Many were the difficulties of ascertaining the
true boundaries of existing boroughs, and of fixing

the new limits of the boroughs to be preserved or created.

Happily, with the aid of the two persons I have named, and with reports from assistant-commissioners, these difficulties were fairly and impartially surmounted, and the Bill passed the House of Commons.

In the House of Lords the obstinate resistance of the majority, marshalled under the authority of the Duke of Wellington, and guided by the powerful ability of Lord Lyndhurst, was at length overcome by the perspicuous wisdom and consistent integrity of Lord Grey, supported by the wonderful eloquence and vigour of Lord Brougham, and borne along to triumph by the invincible energy and enthusiasm of the people. The recollection of the struggle of May 1832 will never pass from the memory of those who bore a part in that great but bloodless Revolution.

The Reform Bill thus became an Act of Parliament. For upwards of thirty years it has been part and parcel of the Constitution of these realms—for thirty years the Constitution has been more loved and respected than it ever was before—for thirty years the success of measures approved after free and general discussion has been no longer obstructed by the nominees of individuals, or by representatives who purchased seats for corrupt boroughs in order to protect monopoly, maintain colonial slavery, and reject the claims of civil and religious freedom.

Having had such an experience of the reformed Parliament, we can tell how far it has in its working answered the expectations and fulfilled the purposes of its authors. Lord Grey had expressed these purposes in the clear and constitutional language which was habitual to him when he advised the King, in June 1831, to use these terms in his speech on the opening of Parliament :—

'I have availed myself of the earliest opportunity of resorting to your advice and assistance after the

dissolution of the late Parliament. Having had recourse to that measure for the purpose of ascertaining the sense of my people on the expediency of a
reform in the representation, I have now to recommend that important question to your earliest and
most attentive consideration, confident that in any
measures which you may prepare for its adjustment,
you will carefully adhere to the acknowledged principles of the Constitution, by which the prerogatives
of the Crown, the authority of both Houses of Parliament, and the rights and liberties of the people
are equally secured.'*

It cannot be denied that under the operation of
the Reform Act, the prerogatives of the Crown, in
spite of many sinister prophecies to the contrary,
have been secure.

As little can it be affirmed that the authority of
the House of Lords has been infringed or menaced.
Notwithstanding Mr. Canning's alarming predictions,
supported by his quotation from Mr. Fox, implying
that if the House of Lords did not please the House
of Commons, they would be overthrown by that democratic body, in its reformed shape, the authority
of the House of Lords has been ' cherished and protected ' by the House of Commons.

But the functions of the House of Commons have,
since the days of Walpole, been far more important
than those of the House of Lords.

It is theirs to guard the liberties of the people.
It is theirs to protect every subject of the realm
in the enjoyment of his property and his legal
rights.   It is theirs to point out to the Crown, by
extending their confidence to one party and refusing
it to another, by giving it to certain men and refusing it to certain other men, which is the party,
and who are the statesmen qualified to govern this
mighty empire, to administer its laws, to preserve

* Hansard's Debates, third series, vol. iv.

its honour in the face of other nations, to advise the Crown in matters of peace and war, to maintain the character of the nation unsullied, and its station neither impaired by timidity, nor imperilled by rashness.

It is obvious that a House of Commons, fully competent to guard the liberties of the people, and to secure them against any unlawful or unjust invasion of property, may be unfit to fulfil the third function which the Constitution has assigned to them.

It is manifest that the reformed House of Commons have adequately performed the first and second of these duties; have they been competent to the third?

To this I might answer in general terms, that it must be admitted that, whether of the Liberal or of the Conservative party, men fitted for the task have been at the disposal of the Crown and of the nation, in the various departments of Government.

But may there not still be improvements? Each of the last four Ministries have been willing to add, as it were, a supplement to the Reform Act. For my part, I should be glad to see the sound morals and clear intelligence of the best of the working classes more fully represented. They are kept out of the franchise which Ministers of the Crown have repeatedly asked for them, partly by the jealousy of the present holders of the suffrage, and partly by a vague fear that by their greater numbers they will swallow up all other classes. Both those obstacles may be removed by a judicious distribution of the proposed suffrage, and by a happy sense on the part of the public that an addition of the votes of the most intelligent of the working classes to the constituent body will form a security, and not a danger.

The ten-pound householders are, it is generally admitted, unwilling to share with others the privilege of voting for a member of Parliament. This reluctance, I imagine, would be felt, though in a less

degree, were the extension lateral instead of vertical
—in other terms, if it were proposed to build a wing
to the house instead of another story.

Be the reluctance, however, what it may, we may
presume that the body of ten-pound householders
are at the least as pervious to public opinion as the
old close corporations of Bath, Scarborough, Portsmouth, &c. If so, they will yield to any clear
demonstration of the national will, as expressed by
elections, public meetings, the press, and other
channels of public opinion.

It must be added, that the opponents of any
plan for lowering the franchise have placed their
resistance on the most odious as well as the most
untenable ground. The small shopkeepers do not
differ much in position, and are not at all superior
in intelligence to the workmen receiving twenty,
thirty, or forty shillings a week in wages, residing
in the same town. The declared exclusion of working men, as intemperate and ignorant, is so invidious,
that their immediate superiors, who live in ten-pound
houses, will not like to remain long in the position
of barring the door at once against the best of
their customers and the most enlightened of their
neighbours.

The other and more formidable objection is, that
the new-comers will swamp the old voters. This
objection, though not very carefully distinguished
or analysed by those who make it, rests on one of
two grounds. The first is, that the voters who live
in houses below the value of ten pounds are unfit to
have a vote; the second is, that this class is so
numerous, that if admitted, all other classes will
virtually be disfranchised.

With respect to the first objection, the answer must
be—That, in fact, the working men of England are
not as a body either ignorant or dishonest. They
largely avail themselves of those facilities to acquire
political and historical knowledge, which, by the

cheapness of books and of newspapers, have of late
years so much increased. Their daily employments,
depending as they do upon their industry, skill, and
steadiness, are a guarantee for the character of the
majority among them.

The addition of such men to the number of electors
is, therefore, a security, and not a danger. It will
tend to improve the quality of the elected body, and
to render Parliament more sound in its general
views, and more attentive to the national interests.
In fact, those who have declared the working men
of England unfit to exercise the franchise, erect a
barrier where none ought to exist.

For the working men do not form a caste apart,
separate in their feelings and their interests from
the rest of the community; they are not likely to
disregard those connections and ties which bind
them, like the upper and middle classes, to their political party or religious communion; nor are they
likely to feel less for the honour and welfare of
England than any other class in the nation.

All the endeavours made in this direction by
the Conservative party are, I conceive, mistaken in
judgment and unwise in policy. They tend to make
a democracy where it does not exist; to enclose
our political Constitution within a pale of privilege;
and to brand with degradation men who ought to be
honoured for their honesty and intelligence.

Thus, instead of giving to our Constitution new
security, the efforts of those who maintain that the
franchise must never be lowered, or that, if extended, it should be only in a lateral direction, are
tending to create a new danger. The working class
are not very eager to have the franchise. It is a
privilege which must be accompanied with increased
risk of differences and jars between employers and
employed. But when the working class are told
that they are an ignorant class, an intemperate class,
and a dishonest class, those who might have borne

the injury very patiently will hardly put up with the insult. It is an imprudent as well as an untrue imputation. It tends to make that very hostility of classes which it pretends to deprecate.

The extension of the franchise, therefore, should be vertical as well as lateral. Numbers have proved their fitness; let numbers be admitted.

What should be the precise amount of rent or of rate which should entitle the inhabitant of a borough to vote, or whether the old householder right of voting with three years' occupation might not usefully be the test, I will not here pretend to determine. A lodger suffrage of £10 rent might, perhaps, be added.

The objection, that by such an increase of borough votes the whole representation would be given to one class, is an objection to which I should allow the greatest weight, were there any foundation for it. I should allow it weight, not because I think that a House of Commons exclusively representing working men would instal anarchy, destroy property, or uproot the monarchy. They would, I am persuaded, do none of these things. But I should attach weight to the objection, because I think a representation of one class would not give an image of the property, the experience, the knowledge, the wisdom of England, so well as one of the character of our present House of Commons.

For what is that character? It is a character of extreme diversity of representation. Elections by great bodies, agricultural, commercial, or manufacturing, in our counties and great cities, are balanced by the right of election in boroughs of small or moderate population, which are thus admitted to fill up the defects and complete the fulness of our representation.

For instance, Mr. Thomas Baring, from his commercial eminence, from his high character, from his world-wide position, ought to be a member of the

House of Commons. His political opinions, and
nothing but his political opinions, prevent his being
the fittest person to be a member for the City of
London. But the borough of Huntingdon, with
2,654 inhabitants and 393 registered voters, elects
him willingly.

Let us take another instance. Sir George Grey,
from his sound judgment and experience in political
affairs, ought to be a member of any deliberative
assembly pretending to represent England. But,
in Northumberland, the territorial influence of the
Duke of Northumberland must work his perpetual
exclusion from the representation of the county.
Morpeth, with 13,796 inhabitants, but only 446
electors, returns him to Parliament.

Sir Roundell Palmer is *omnium consensu* well
qualified to enlighten the House of Commons on any
question of municipal or international law, and to ex-
pound the true theory and practice of law reform. He
finds a seat at Richmond, a borough with 5,134
inhabitants and only 306 registered voters.

Dr. Temple says, in a letter to the 'Daily News,'*
—'I know that when Emerson was in England, he
regretted to me that all the more cultivated classes
in America abstained from politics, because they
felt themselves hopelessly swamped.'

It is very rare to find a man of literary taste and
cultivated understanding expose himself to the rough
reception of the electors of a large city. The small
boroughs restore the balance which Marylebone
and Manchester, if left, even with the ten-pound
franchise, undisputed masters of the field, would
radically disturb. But, besides this advantage,
they act with the counties in giving that due
influence to property, without which our House of
Commons would very inadequately represent the
nation, and thus make it feasible to admit the

* May 19, 1865.

householders of our large towns to an extent which would otherwise be inequitable, and possibly lead to injurious results.

These are the reasons why, in my opinion, after abolishing 141 seats by the Reform Act, it is not expedient that the smaller boroughs should be entirely extinguished.

The £12 rated franchise, which is now the law in Ireland, might well be adopted for English and Irish counties. But these matters require time, thought, and concert.

There must be a country prepared to ask for a Reform Bill, and a House of Commons ready to entertain it. Parliament should then treat the Constitution as a skilful physician treats an honoured patient, not as a prison surgeon cuts into the body of a criminal delivered over to him for dissection.

In that way will be preserved in its spirit and integrity that assembly which Sir James Graham rightly called the ' noblest assembly of freemen in the world!' It is by such a body that the Crown is advised, but never insulted; that the House of Lords is impelled, but always respected. It is thus that a Government is maintained which the Liberals of the world love for its freedom, and the Conservatives of the world envy for its stability!

When the question can be fairly entertained, I trust the suffrage will be extended on good old English principles, and in conformity with good old English notions of representation.

I should be sorry to see the dangers of universal suffrage and of unlimited democracy averted, or sought to be averted, by such invidious schemes as granting to the rich a plurality of votes, or by contrivances altogether unknown to our habits, such as the plan of Mr. Hare, though sanctioned by the high authority of so profound a thinker as Mr. Mill.

If there were to be any deviation from our customary habits and rooted ideas on the subject of representation, I should like to see such a change as I once proposed, in order to obtain representatives of the minority in large and populous counties and towns. If, when three members are to be chosen, an elector were allowed to give two votes to one candidate, we might have a Liberal country gentleman sitting for Buckinghamshire, and a Conservative manufacturer for Manchester. The local majority would have two to one in the House of Commons, and the minority would not feel itself disfranchised and degraded.

Yet even this change would be difficult to introduce, and would perhaps be unpalatable in its first working.

We are a people who love our free institutions, not only because they are good, but also because they are old. When our ancestors banished James II. and changed the whole practice of the Constitution, they took care to assert that he had abdicated the throne, and to display the precedent of Richard II. as a justification of their conduct.

Institutions, it is true, do not grow like a tree; they are the work of man's hands, and are not fit subjects of our idolatry. Yet there is something venerable in old privileges. Mechanical inventions and physical discoveries have no assignable limits, but it is difficult to believe in this age of the world that there are models of government, still untried, promising a cup of felicity and of freedom which England has not yet tasted.

The limit appears to me to have been rightly laid down by Lord Grey. That which tends to increase the security of the prerogatives of the Crown, the authority of both Houses of Parliament, and the rights and liberties of the people, may well be accepted; the plan which has other objects, and looks to a different form of government, ought at once to be rejected.

Let it not be forgotten, that the intolerance of a despotism and the insolence of a democracy are alike unknown in the temperate zone of our ancient form of government; that the liberty to think as we please, and speak as we think, which was a rare felicity in the time of the Roman Empire, is the common, vulgar, and general happiness enjoyed under a British Sovereign; that the freedom of thought, of invention, of discovery, of writing and of publishing, which is a pledge for the progress of our people in science, in religion, and in morals, is also the best security for our political liberties.

This general diffusion of opinion fills up many a void in the form of our institutions.

But I am not without apprehension on a different score. There appears to me a danger more pressing and more insidious than that of universal suffrage and democracy.

This danger is, that with a view of satisfying the demands of those who require an extension of the suffrage some apparent concession may be made, accompanied by drawbacks, or securities, as they will be called, inserted with a view to please the large Conservative party in the two Houses of Parliament. This is no imaginary danger: Lord Althorp in vain warned the members of his own party against granting to £50 tenants at will the same right of voting in counties as had been hitherto enjoyed by independent forty-shilling freeholders. The sound of extension of franchise tickled the ears of the Reformers; the Chandos clause was carried, and, as Lord Althorp predicted, the county representation has been weighed down by the influence of the great landowners.

At the very moment of carrying the Reform.

R

Bill, Lord Grey was beset by the section called the Waverers, who endeavoured to induce him still further to degrade the county electoral body, by transferring to the boroughs the votes of the forty-shilling freeholders in towns and boroughs.

By a similar provision, coupled with a power of sending votes by the post, the last Conservative Reform Bill would have created thirty or forty nomination boroughs, and this perhaps in a way unperceived by the professed authors of the Bill.

In fact, the subject is full of unknown pitfalls, and it is far better for the great Liberal party in the country to place no weights in the scale against democracy, to trust to no nice tricks of statesmanship, no subtle inventions of ingenious theorists, than to be parties to a plausible scheme which, under the guise of an improvement of the Reform Act of Lord Grey, might sweep away its fruits, and give worthless husks in exchange.

The fund of popularity with which the Reform Act enriched the Ministry, made it incumbent on them to risk that popularity in striking down abuses which were strong in interests and pre-scription.

Among these there was no perversion of law so injurious to the welfare, or so threatening to the future peace of the community, as the abusive administration of the Poor Law. During the most critical period of the French war, a practice had arisen in the South of England of paying out of the poor-rates a portion of the wages of labour,—that portion to be measured by the number of the labourer's family. Hence the parents became the stipendiaries of the parish, and their income was measured, not by their industry as labourers, but by the number of their children. In this way, the sons became the useless and superfluous members of a community which had increased, not according to natural laws, but according to artificial contrivance.

In 1830, the evils arising from these mistakes of ignorance and want of foresight had gathered to the most alarming height. For some winters, young men of eighteen and twenty had been put to nominal work as an excuse for giving them a scanty and eleemosynary pay. Their days were spent in idleness; their nights in poaching, thieving, drinking, and excess. Their disorder grew to outrage and riot; the sky was reddened by nocturnal fires; the fields were the scenes of combat, and the farmers came forth as yeomanry cavalry to suppress the insurrections of their labourers.

It was the determination of Lord Althorp, the Duke of Richmond, and the other members of Lord Grey's Cabinet, to grapple with this frightful evil. Mr. Senior, Archbishop Whately, and others, had, on the grounds of science and political economy, proved the destructive nature of the abuses which prevailed. A Commission was named, a remedy was recommended, a Bill was framed, considered and approved by the committee of the Cabinet, of which Lord Melbourne, Lord Althorp, the Duke of Richmond, Lord Ripon, and I were members.

Thus was framed the Poor Law Amendment Act. It was introduced into the House of Commons by Lord Althorp; and such was the difficulty of the task, that nothing but his perseverance, patience, and thorough knowledge of the subject would ever have carried it against the interests, the ignorance, and the deeply-seated prejudices with which he had to contend.

Another task of equal urgency was to restore tranquillity to Ireland, and suppress the agrarian disturbers of that part of the kingdom. In the year 1833, a severe but temporary measure was passed for that purpose. At the same time, the

R 2

Irish Church was reformed, the number of bishops reduced, and the Establishment rendered more efficient.

In the same year, slavery in our colonies was abolished, twenty millions being voted as compensation to the proprietors of slaves,—a sum generous as a gift, but inadequate as an indemnity. Still, the erasure of such a blot on our civil policy, and the grant of freedom to 800,000 human beings, was an act of which the Reformed Parliament might justly be proud. The present Lord Derby was the mover on the part of the Government in these measures, and raised his fame as a legislator and an orator by surpassing energy in action, and eloquence in debate.

In 1835, the municipal corporations of England, Scotland, and Ireland were reformed, and those bodies, often the seats of monopoly and the hotbeds of corruption, were subjected to vigilant popular control.

A year or two afterwards, Sir Robert Peel declared that this reform had proved, as he expected, a conservative measure. Indeed, it may be said that every measure which effaces a blot in our institutions, which removes a topic of just complaint, and affords a remedy for an obvious and offensive grievance, tends to confirm the attachment of the people to their government, and is thus a conservative measure.

'There are,' said Lord Palmerston, in his great speech of 1850, 'revolutionists of two kinds in the world. In the first place, there are those violent, hot-headed, and unthinking men, who fly to arms, who overthrow established governments, and who recklessly, without regard to consequences, and without measuring difficulties and comparing strength, deluge their country with blood, and draw down the greatest calamities on their fellow-countrymen.

These are the revolutionists of one class. But there are revolutionists of another kind,—blind-minded men who, animated by antiquated prejudices, and daunted by ignorant apprehensions, dam up the current of human improvement, until the irresistible pressure of accumulated discontent breaks down the opposing barriers, and overthrows and levels to the earth those very institutions which a timely application of renovating means would have rendered strong and lasting.'* Of such a nature were the renovating means which, applied between 1830 and 1850, have restored to our institutions a strength which was about to decay.

In the same year, 1835, the commutation of tithes for a fixed rent-charge—a measure which Mr. Pitt had meditated in vain—was successfully carried. At first, the country gentlemen in the House of Commons were inclined to think the Bill proposed too favourable to the Church; but, with some modifications, restricting the amount of charge, the commutation was accepted by all parties. In the course of twenty years, the whole arrangement was carried into effect; and, from that time, the clergyman has no longer been exposed to harassing conflicts with his parishioners, and the farmer has no longer been compelled to share with the tithe-owner the profits of improvements, of which he and the landowner bear all the expense. Thus, works of drainage, and the cultivation of waste lands, which, under the former state of things, were not undertaken because unremunerative, became practicable, and have, to the great advantage of the country, been carried into effect.

Similar changes have since been commenced on the subject of church leases, thus giving a security

* Debate on Foreign Policy, June 25, 1850. Hansard, vol. cxii. p. 132.

to capital and industry, while the Church receives
an equitable compensation.

During the period when Lord Brougham held
the Great Seal, law reforms of considerable importance were made.   Not only did he abolish
many offices, but he reduced many others, and absolutely surrendered a sinecure of £10,000 a year,
which had provided for the family of one of his predecessors for nearly half a century.

But the economical reforms of Lord Brougham, his
absolute relinquishment of advantages which legally
belonged to his high office, and his sacrifice of the
means of ample provision for his family, were only
parts of a great public career.   The extraordinary
speech on Law Reform which he delivered in 1826;
the comprehensive principles which he enunciated,
and the prodigious details which flowed easily and
smoothly from his capacious mind, astonished and
delighted the world.   His suggestions in 1826 were
his plans in 1831; and whether we look to the
Court of Chancery or to the Common Law Courts;
to the organisation of the Judicial Committee, in
place of the general irregular body of the Privy
Council and the unwieldy Court of Delegates; or to
the institution of County Local Courts, obstructed,
delayed, but finally enacted; we shall see in all
these instances a great intellect flashing through
the fogs of law, throwing its light on the defects
of a venerated fabric, and sweeping away the cob-
webs which had so long concealed what was un-
sightly or unsound.

Lord Brougham also shared in another work of
improvement, begun by Sir Samuel Romilly and Sir
James Mackintosh, and promoted, in some measure,
by Sir Robert Peel.   I allude to the reform of the
Criminal Law.   When Sir Samuel Romilly first
raised the voice of enlightened humanity on this
subject, it was declared by the great sages of the

law, that unless a man were subject to be hanged
for stealing to the amount of 40s. in a dwelling-
house, no person would be safe in his home.

On the 21st of May, 1823, Sir James Mackintosh proposed by resolutions a great reform of the
Criminal Law.

He proposed that the punishment of death should
be taken away in the cases of larceny from dwelling-
houses, from shops, and on navigable rivers; for
the greater part of the offences made capital by the
Black Act, and all the offences made capital by the
Marriage Act; for horse-stealing, sheep-stealing,
and cattle-stealing : for forgery and uttering
forged instruments; sending threatening letters,
and various other offences.

He was opposed by Sir Robert Peel, who, while
he agreed to abolish the punishment of death for
several offences for which it was scarcely ever put
in force, could not agree to part with the security
that punishment afforded in cases of larceny to the
amount of 40s. in a dwelling-house.

On a division, the previous question was carried
by 86 to 76. Sir Robert Peel, however, introduced several valuable amendments in the Criminal
Law.

In the year 1832, under Lord Grey's administration, capital punishment was abolished for horse-
stealing, sheep-stealing, larceny to the value of £5
in a dwelling-house, coining, and forgery, except of
wills and powers of attorney to transfer stock.

In the year 1833, for house-breaking.

In 1834, for returning from transportation.

In 1835, for sacrilege and letter-stealing by servants of the Post Office.

In 1837, upon the Queen's accession, the offences
subject to capital punishment were virtually reduced
to the following :—

Murder and attempts to murder: burglary with

violence to person ; robbery with cutting or wounding ; arson of dwelling-houses, persons being therein ;
rape, with some few offences of rare occurrence.

In 1841, capital punishment was further abolished
for rape, embezzlement, and riot.

In 1861, for all offences except murder and high
treason. The practical effect of these changes has
been the following diminution in the number of
persons sentenced to death, and of those actually
executed :—

				Sentenced to Death.				Executed.
1823	.	.	.	968	.	.	.	54
1824	.	.	.	1066	.	.	.	49
1825	.	.	.	1035	.	.	.	50
1833	.	.	.	931	.	.	.	33
1834	.	.	.	480	.	.	.	34
1835	.	.	.	523	.	.	.	34
1837	.	.	.	438	.	.	.	8
1838	.	.	.	116	.	.	.	6
1839	.	.	.	66	.	.	.	11
1843	.	.	.	97	.	.	.	18
1844	.	.	.	57	.	.	.	16
1845	.	.	.	49	.	.	.	12
1853	.	.	.	55	.	.	.	8
1854	.	.	.	49	.	.	.	5
1855	.	.	.	56	.	.	.	7
1860	.	.	.	48	.	.	.	12
1861	.	.	.	50	.	.	.	15
1862	.	.	.	29	.	.	.	15

In taking the average of decennial periods, we
find—

				Sentenced to Death.				Executed.
1823 to 1832	.	.	.	1279·5	.	.	.	56·3
1833 „ 1842	.	.	.	325·2	.	.	.	17·1
1843 „ 1852	.	.	.	61·6	.	.	.	10·7
1852 „ 1862	.	.	.	50·9	.	.	.	11·1

Taking the proportions to the population, the
diminution is still more striking.

	Sentenced to Death. One in	Executed. One in
1823 to 1832	10·123	229·177
1833 „ 1842	45·634	813·185
1843 „ 1852	274·692	1,581·390
1853 „ 1862	373·220	1,711·434

The first set of numbers in these tables, shows the great changes which have taken place in the law; the number of capital sentences has diminished from 1279 to 51, or from 1 in 10,123 in the population to 1 in 373,220. The second set of numbers shows the changes in the application of the law to be from 56 to 11, or from 1 in 229,000 of the population to 1 in 1,711,000. The great diminution in the number of executions evidently took place at the accession of the present Queen.*

But if these changes show the increased humanity of our people, under our very imperfect system of secondary punishment, it may well bear a question whether murder is prevented by retaining the punishment of death for eight, ten, or fifteen persons in a year.

For my own part, I do not doubt for a moment either the right of a community to inflict the punishment of death, or the expediency of exercising that right in certain states of society.

But when I turn from that abstract right, and that abstract expediency, to our own state of society, —when I consider how difficult it is for any judge to separate the case which requires inflexible justice, from that which admits the force of mitigating circumstances,—how invidious the task of the Secretary of State in dispensing the mercy of the Crown,—how critical the comments made by the public,—how soon the object of general horror becomes the theme of sympathy and pity,—how narrow and how limited the example given by this condign and awful punishment,—how brutal the scene of the execution,—

* See Note K.

I come to the conclusion that nothing would be lost to justice, nothing lost in the preservation of innocent life, if the punishment of death were altogether abolished.

In that case, a sentence of a long term of separate confinement, followed by another long term of hard labour and hard fare, would cease to be considered as an extension of mercy.

If the sentence of the judge, in cases of murder, were imprisonment for life, there would scarcely ever be a petition for remission of punishment sent to the Home Office. The guilty, unpitied, would have time and opportunity to turn repentant to the Throne of Mercy.

In the year, 1837 a mighty question in regard to the government of Canada was brought before Parliament.

In 1791, Mr. Pitt and Lord Grenville had given to that province an impracticable Constitution. The province was inhabited by Frenchmen, whose manners were those of the age of Louis XIV., with no taint of the Revolution, and no mark of improvement. It should have been the task of the English Government to infuse into the province English freedom, English industry, and English loyalty.

Instead of that sensible course, it was the object of Mr. Pitt and Lord Grenville to separate English energy from French inertness; to shut up the industry of the English in the upper part of the colony, and to preserve the Lower Province as a sort of museum, where a French *noblesse*, with feudal titles and orders of knighthood, and tithes and seignorial rights, might be crystallised for ever as a memorial of the happiness of France before her jacobin Revolution.

But ' fancy's fairy frostwork ' melted away before the light of human progress. The titles and orders projected never were created; all fell into confu-

sion ; a legislative Council, formed of enlightened
men, attached to British connection, monopolised
all the patronage of the Crown, and became odious
to the French popular party. The representative
assembly of Lower Canada refused supplies.

Lord Bathurst, Colonial Secretary, having in his
possession a clock that would not go, took its regu-
lation into his own hands. He voted by his own
authority the supplies to the Crown, which the Assembly refused to grant.

But this policy could not last many years. Parliament, on the advice of ministers, rejected the
proposals of the French Canadians for a Legislative
Council of their own nomination. The consequences
quickly followed. Lower Canada, pent up in feud-
alism, rebelled for privileges and tithes; Upper
Canada, nursed in democracy, rebelled for a republic.

Lord Durham was sent out by Lord Melbourne's
Government to solve this mysterious problem. He
examined it with the eye of a statesman; penetrated
the views of the various discordant parties, and pronounced for Union. The moment was a critical
one. Some said, 'Let the French Canadians have
their way, or you will have a repetition of the
American war.' Others said, 'The grant of what
is called "responsible government" is a grant of
independence : it must be resisted.'

Between these two extreme courses the British
Government took their stand. They came to an
understanding with the representatives of the Ca-
nadian Liberals, that under the term 'responsible
government' should be included all questions of internal but none of external policy. Responsible
government, thus defined, was granted.

Mr. Powlett Thomson, sent out as Governor to
effect the Union, put to himself the question, 'Am
I the sovereign, or am I the minister?' and he
answered it by determining that he was the minister.

Doubtless the machinery of Colonial Government, with the internal affairs left to the guidance of the Colonial Ministry, and the external affairs, with the naval and military departments, placed under the control of the Queen's Government, became exceedingly complicated—more complicated even than the British Constitution itself. But with good will and good sense nothing is impossible: revolt and disaffection were the results of the Act of 1791; obedience and loyalty have been the results of the Act of 1837.

There was, indeed, one inevitable but not irremediable defect in the Act of Union. Lord Sydenham could not have obtained a majority in its favour unless he had agreed that the number of representatives of the Lower Province should be equal to that of the Upper. But it was obvious that if the population of the Upper Province should, by the breaking down of the barrier between it and England, and by its natural fertility and richness, greatly increase beyond that of the Lower, justice and policy would alike require some change of the equality built upon a shifting soil. This is what has now happened. It will task the wisdom of Parliament to fix the foundations of the new building, but the omens are favourable.

Many subjects of great importance occupied at this time the attention of Parliament.

Ireland had been treated in 1829 as Mr. Pitt had proposed she should be treated in 1800. But this long denial of justice had produced discontent and disaffection; had caused rural outrages of the most atrocious character; had left the country a prey to tyranny on the part of the landlords, plots and conspiracies on the part of the priests and the peasantry. Lord Anglesey, when Lord Lieutenant, had said that the King had no party in Ireland but the King's troops.

The Governments of Lord Melbourne and his successors did much to remedy what could only be remedied by time and justice. The tithe question was settled, and the burden, removed from the peasantry, was placed upon the landlords. A poor-law, which is in fact not so much a law of charity as a law of public order, was carried. An Encumbered Estate Act, introduced in 1847, and afterwards amended by Sir John Romilly, opened the way to improved relations of landlord and tenant. The right of voting in counties, taken away from the serfs called forty-shilling freeholders in 1829, was given to occupiers rated at £12 a year. A sum of eight millions sterling was distributed by the Imperial Government during the potato famine of 1848.

The measure introduced in 1835, granting a portion of the Church Revenues of Ireland to purposes of Education, was unpopular in England, and was not carried in the House of Lords. But it is hardly possible that a Church Establishment should be preserved undiminished for about one-ninth of the population of Ireland. When England shall examine this question dispassionately, it may be expected that, although the State will not entangle itself with the support of a Roman Catholic clergy, as Mr. Pitt projected, the whole people of Ireland will be allowed to derive some benefit from so large a revenue. National Education and Public Improvements of various kinds might receive at least a portion of the revenue raised from the land for the benefit of the people.

In 1828 and 1829, Parliament had thrown open the doors of office and of the Legislature to Protestant and Roman Catholic Dissenters from the Established Church.

From 1831 to 1841, ten years had been devoted to the grant of political and municipal privileges in the three kingdoms.

In 1840, the period had arrived for reducing duties of customs, abolishing monopoly, and freeing commerce from many restrictions.

The two Humes—Mr. Joseph Hume, the Member of Parliament, and Mr. Deacon Hume, an officer of the Board of Customs—opened the road along which the free-trade army marched first in doubtful battle, but ultimately in assured triumph.

Mr. Charles Villiers, Mr. Cobden, and Mr. Bright moved the total and immediate repeal of the Corn Laws. The Whig Ministry, without going this length, proposed that the sliding scale of duties on wheat should be exchanged for eight shillings fixed duty; that the prohibition of foreign sugar should be reduced to a differential duty of twelve shillings a hundredweight, and the protective duty on timber, instead of ten shillings on colonial and fifty-five shillings on Baltic timber, should be twenty shillings on colonial and fifty shillings on Baltic timber. But the proposal for the admission of foreign sugar was rejected by a Protectionist majority of thirty-six, and, on a dissolution, a majority of ninety-one seated Sir Robert Peel as the head of a new administration.

But if the Protectionists counted on Sir Robert Peel to confirm the reign of monopoly, they were wofully deceived. It is true that, with characteristic prudence, he left for a time unassailed the corn of the landed gentry and the sugar of the West Indian colonies. But he struck down all the minor monopolies, and advancing like a great general, left the fortresses of corn and sugar held by mere garrisons in a conquered country.

Thus it happened that, in 1846, the introduction of foreign corn was sanctioned with a duty, not of eight shillings, but of one shilling, and Sir Robert Peel, amid the curses of his party, but the applause of the people, conferred an inestimable benefit on his country.

On this occasion, as on that of the Catholic Relief Bill, Sir Robert Peel was the first to give credit to those by whom he had long been opposed.

'I said before, and I said truly,' he declared, 'that in proposing our measures of commercial policy I had no wish to rob others of the credit justly due to them. I must say, with reference to honourable gentlemen opposite, as I say with reference to ourselves, that neither of us is the party which is justly entitled to the credit of them. There has been a combination of parties generally opposed to each other, and that combination and the influence of Government have led to their ultimate success; but the name which ought to be associated with the success of these measures is not the name of the noble Lord, the organ of the party of which he is the leader, nor is it mine. The name which ought to be, and will be associated with the success of those measures, is the name of one who, acting, I believe, from pure and disinterested motives, has, with untiring energy, made appeals to our reason, and has enforced those appeals with an eloquence the more to be admired because it was unaffected and unadorned; the name which ought to be chiefly associated with the success of these measures is the name of RICHARD COBDEN.'[*]

This just tribute did the highest honour to the fairness and magnanimous candour of the statesman who uttered it.

In the same year, 1846, the Ministry which succeeded him swept away the differential duties on sugar, and reduced those duties in a manner which will be presently explained.

In 1848, the Navigation Laws were repealed; and on that occasion Sir James Graham, in a memorable speech, recorded the benefits of the repeal of the corn laws, and celebrated the triumphs of free trade.

[*] Parliamentary Debates, third series, vol. lxxxvii. p. 1054.

Some of the fruits of this signal change of policy, partly sanctioned by the very Parliament which had been elected to defend the Corn Laws and to guarantee the gains of protection, and partly carried into effect by the succeeding Parliament, remain to be recorded.

But other beneficial reforms must be added to the glorious catalogue.

In 1861, a Treaty of Commerce with France broke the fetters which restrained our intercourse with a country abounding in wine, in oil, in silk, in beautiful fabrics, but deficient in coal, in iron, and in cheap manufactures.

In this task, the Emperor of the French proposed, and the British Cabinet accepted, the plan of the Treaty; but Richard Cobden was the chief worker in carrying the design into effect.

Nor was the measure merely one of free trade. Two nations, the foremost in the world for triumphs in peace, and for triumphs in war, were thereby connected by a thousand links which may, it is to be hoped, convert a relation of ancient hostility into one of friendly and peaceful rivalry.

The results of these free-trade and financial measures remain to be noticed.

Let us first take the official value of the imports and exports of British, Colonial, and Foreign goods in 1842, 1853, and 1863—in short, the whole extent of our commerce :—

Imports—1842	.	.	.	.	. £ 65,253,266
,, 1853	.	.	.	.	. 123,099,313
,, 1863	.	.	.	.	. 171,913,852
Exports—1842	.	.	.	.	. £113,841,802
,, 1853	.	.	.	.	. 242,072,224
,, 1863	.	.	.	.	. 313,113,188

Next, the real value of Exports of British and Irish manufacture :—

1842	.	.	.	.	. £47,361,023
1853	.	.	.	.	. 98,933,781
1863	.	.	.	.	. 146,489,768

The real value of some few of the more important articles of British manufacture may next be recorded:—

	1842	1853	1863
	£	£	£
Cotton Goods . . .	13,907,884	25,817,249	39,424,010
Earthenware and Porcelain	555,430	1,338,370	1,334,275
Hardware and Cutlery	1,398,487	3,665,051	3,826,784
Linen Manufactures .	2,346,749	4,758,432	6,509,970
Machinery	554,653	1,985,536	4,365,023
Iron and Steel . . .	2,457,717	10,845,422	13,111,477
Woollen Yarn . . .	637,305	1,456,786	5,065,432
Woollen Manufactures	5,185,045	10,172,162	15,818,842
Silk, thrown and manufactured	590,189	2,044,361	2,229,591

It will be recollected that, in 1823, Mr. Huskisson contended, amid a storm of obloquy, that silk manufacturers could, after due time for preparation, withstand a competition protected by a duty of only 30 per cent.; that, in 1845, Sir Robert Peel reduced the protection to 10 per cent.; and that, in 1861, Mr. Gladstone took it away altogether.

Yet, in 1823, the declared value of the total of British silk goods exported amounted only to £351,409; and, in 1863, the thrown and manufactured silk exported amounted in value to £2,229,000.

Let us take two further articles, sugar and ships. In 1841, I had proposed to reduce the duties on colonial and foreign sugar to 24s. and 36s. respectively, thus giving colonial sugar a protection of 12s. a cwt. This was rejected as insufficient. In 1846 I proposed a duty of 14s. a cwt. on Muscovado sugar of the British colonies, and, instead of the prohibitory

s

duty of 63s. on foreign sugars, a duty on foreign
Muscovado sugar of 21s.; and that, from July 1851,
a duty of 14s. should be applied alike to all Muscovado sugars, taking away protection altogether. This
was approved. The consumption of raw sugar has
been, in spite of a subsequent increase of duty during
the Russian war, which lasted till 1863,—

Cwt.	Cwt.	Cwt.
1842	1853	1863
3,866,437	7,272,833	9,202,524

In 1841, the consumption of sugar was 17 lb. a
head; in 1853, it was 26¾ lb. a head; in 1863, it
was 35¾ lb. a head. Such were the blessings conferred by a relief from taxation, which enabled the
people to consume an article of wholesome food, free
from high and prohibitive duties.[*]
In 1848, Mr. Labouchere, as the organ of the
Government, carried the repeal of the Navigation
Laws—a measure at which the shipowners stood
aghast, and at which even Adam Smith had hesitated. The consequence has been, in regard to
the increase of tonnage,—

	1842	1853	1863
British .	5,415,821	9,064,705	15,263,047
Foreign .	1,930,983	6,316,456	7,762,116

In regard to the coasting trade, which was thrown

* Hansard's Debates, vol. lxxxvii. p. 1319.   See also vol. xxxviii.
pp. 260, 261.

open to foreign shipping in 1854, the increase has been—

	1842.	1853.	1863.
British	. 10,785,450	12,820,745	17,465,635
Foreign	. —	—	61,897

So much do the strengthening breezes of freedom prove better nurses of hardy offspring than the confined atmosphere of monopoly and restriction.

Let us now turn for a few moments to our financial changes.

More than a century ago, after the Seven Years War, historians and philosophers pointed out that we had heavy taxes on salt, on candles, on leather, and on soap; on coals carried by sea; on every article of manufacture which was not prohibited; on malt, beer, glass, paper, newspapers. The land-tax amounted to 3s. in the pound. They inferred that the debt would break our backs.[*]

Yet, after more costly and more burthensome wars than we had ever before sustained, the taxes on necessaries have been taken off; the taxes on glass and paper, and most of the taxes of excise, have been abolished; and the land-tax remaining fixed, while the rent of land has greatly increased, has been much lightened.

In the meantime, the wealth of the country has so much augmented, that the income-tax of 2s. in the pound, which only produced 15 millions in 1815, would have produced 26 millions in 1864.

If it be said that Ireland is now subject to the tax, it must be reckoned, on the other hand, that the currency of 1815 was depreciated 25 per cent., while that of 1865 is equal in value to gold.

There are two ways, however, in which it is usual

---

[*] See especially Sinclair's History of the Revenue, with the Appendix.

s 2

to give an exaggerated view of our expenditure and of our taxation:—of our expenditure, by lumping, as a proof of our yearly extravagance, the taxes applied to pay the interest of our national debt; the expense of paying the judicial and police establishments of the country; the civil list; and the half-pay and pensions due to the officers, soldiers, and sailors of our army and navy.

No one proposes to diminish the vast sums payable under these heads by a single shilling, but they are made to figure among the totals of our expenditure, and pass muster as proofs of our national waste, extravagance, and profusion.

The other way is that of exaggerating the burthen of taxes by taking, not the rate of the tax, but the sum paid. Thus, if 24*s.* a cwt. is charged on sugar, and that rate is reduced to 12*s.*, it is clear that the burthen on the people is greatly reduced. But if the quantity consumed under the high duty is under four millions of hundredweights, and under the low duty is above nine millions, it is clear the sum paid from this source will be increased, and a pretence is obtained for saying the burthens of the subject are augmented.

Thus, if a shilling income-tax produced 7½ millions of revenue in 1815, and a sixpence income-tax, in 1865, were to produce 8 millions, it would be said that the burthen on the people had been increased.

What is really to be ascertained is: how much a man is taxed in proportion to his means; a tax of a million in a poor country may be more oppressive than a tax of five millions on a population of equal numbers in a kingdom,

Ingeniis opibusque et festâ pace virentem.

On the subject of foreign politics much obscurity prevails in the minds of men as to the principles by

which British policy has been guided in the past,
and will be guided in the future. Much of this obscurity arises from the double sense which is attached
to the term intervention. The usual and more proper meaning of the term intervention is, interference
in the internal affairs of other nations. The new and
less accurate application of the term is to all interference in the disputes of independent nations. The
correct use of the term is when it is applied to the intervention which took place by Austria, Prussia, and
Russia in the internal affairs of Piedmont and of
Naples in the year 1821, and by France and the
Northern Powers, in the internal affairs of Spain,
in the year 1823. The incorrect use of the term
is, when it is applied to the interference prompted
by Mr. Canning, in the year 1826, when England
interposed, as she was bound by treaty to do, in defence of the independence of Portugal.

It is obvious that great confusion would arise from
using the same term and applying the same argument to the two kinds of interference.

All public writers have declared that a nation has
the right to settle its own form of government, provided it does not injure other nations in its mode of
doing so; just as every householder may regulate
his own house, provided he does not cause a nuisance to the neighbourhood.

But if one nation attacks another, all nations are
at liberty to judge whether their interests, and the
general independence, are affected thereby.

Thus, the first kind of intervention should, as a
rule, be forbidden and avoided. Of late years, we
have seen the kind of intervention in the internal
affairs of other nations, against which Lord Castlereagh protested in the case of Naples in 1821, and
Mr. Canning in the case of Spain in 1823, entirely
renounced, in the case of Italy, both by Austria and
by France.

It is true that France has interfered in the inter-

nal affairs of Rome and of Mexico, and that England
has interfered in the internal affairs of China; but
in these instances it has been declared that such intervention was exceptional and temporary, and was
contrary to the general principles upon which the
foreign policy of England and France is founded.

But the case would be quite different if, when a
great Power attacks a small independent State with a
view to conquest, other Powers were as a rule to remain quiescent. In that case we may be sure that two
consequences would follow :—first, that there would
soon remain none but great Powers; and, secondly,
that all those great Powers would have a despotic
form of government, no other being endurable in the
eyes of mighty sovereigns in the command of numerous and formidable armies. Such was in fact the
danger which threatened Europe both before and
after the great catastrophe of 1814.

Against such dangers free and independent nations are bound to make provision. This provision
in favour of the weaker States is in fact the system
called the balance of power, which all European
nations conceive themselves bound to regard in their
treaties and acquisitions.

It does not follow, however, that in every case of
invasion with a view to interference in the internal
concerns of a State, neutral Powers are bound to
resist the invader.

Thus, when, in 1823, France, under the protection
of Austria, Prussia, and Russia, designed to invade
Spain, and suppress its free Constitution, a very
difficult question arose for the Government and
Parliament of Great Britain. The Ministers of
England, while protesting against this interference
with the internal government of an independent
State, doubted whether Spain might not wisely and
prudently so modify her Constitution as to disarm
the hostility of France. The Duke of Wellington,
the saviour of Spanish independence, advised such

modifications. The Spanish Government rejected all such advice, and stood, as she was entitled to do, on her right.

But was England bound to assist Spain in arms, whatever might be the consequences? Lord Liverpool and Mr. Canning declined to give such assistance, and placed their refusal on the following, among other reasons. After relating the course of the recent negotiations, Lord Liverpool thus continued:—

It may now be expected by your Lordships, that I should state the reasons why His Majesty's Government consider neutrality to be the policy of this country, and I have no wish to abstain from that statement. In considering the duty of this Government, as to the alternative of neutrality or war, I am bound, in the first instance, to advert to our own domestic situation and policy. Now, my Lords, I have no hesitation or difficulty in again declaring what I stated on the first day of the session, that if either the honour or the essential interests of this country should require us to engage in war, we have the means of carrying on war with effect.

' But, my Lords, when I say this, I must add, that after the unexampled contest which we waged for two-and-twenty years, from which we are just now recovering,—a contest as unexampled in magnitude and extent as in its duration,—after all the hardships and sufferings which, in consequence of our unparalleled exertions, the country has undergone,—it cannot be consistent with true wisdom or sound policy to re-plunge the country into all the evils and inconveniences of a new war, without a clear and obvious necessity, more particularly at a time when we find our commerce and manufactures not only recovering from the depression which they more sensibly experienced on the conclusion of peace than while hostilities were raging, but advancing to a degree of prosperity which they never before enjoyed; and when we find our agriculture—the last interest to recover, because the last to suffer—beginning to revive from the difficulties and distress under which it has been labouring. I ask, if there is any rational man, my Lords, who does not feel that, at such a moment, it is most desirable that this country should continue at peace, if peace can be preserved consistently with our honour, and consistently with our essential interests; and that we should not throw a great proportion of the advantages which we now enjoy into the hands of other countries,—a result which must inevitably happen, if war, no matter under what circumstances, should unfortunately occur? I do not wish to state these advantages, my Lords, for more than they are worth; but they are worth much, and ought to have their due weight upon your Lordships' minds.'

Mr. Canning, to the same purport and the same end, said—

' Neither will I discuss over again that other proposition, already sufficiently exhausted in other debates, of the applicability of a purely maritime war to a struggle in aid of Spain, in the campaign in which her fate is to be decided. I will not pause to consider what consolation it would have been to the Spanish nation—what source of animation, what encouragement to perseverance in resisting their invader—to learn, that though we could not, as in the last war, march to their aid, and mingle our banners with theirs in battle, we were, nevertheless, scouring their coasts for prizes, and securing to ourselves an indemnification for our own expenses, in the capture of Martinico. To go to war, therefore, directly, unsparingly, vigorously, against France, in behalf of Spain, in the way in which alone Spain could derive any essential benefit from war co-operation—to join her with heart and hand—or, to wrap ourselves up in a real and *bonâ fide* neutrality,—that was the true alternative.

'Now, before I quit the Peninsula, a single word more to the honourable Member for Westminster and his constituents. Have they estimated the burthens of a Peninsular war? God forbid that, if honour, or good faith, or national interest required it, we should decline the path of duty because it is encompassed with difficulties! But at least we ought to keep some consideration of the difficulties in our minds. We have experience to teach us, with something like accuracy, what are the pecuniary demands of the contest for which we must be prepared, if we enter into a war in the Peninsula. To take only two years and a half of the last Peninsular war, of which I happen to have the accounts at hand, from the beginning of 1812 to the glorious conclusion of the campaign of 1814, the expense incurred in Spain and Portugal was about £33,000,000.'

Again, in speaking of the prospects of the war, if undertaken, he said—

'Let no man flatter himself that a war now entered upon would be a short one. Have we so soon forgotten the course and progress of the last war? For my part, I remember well the anticipations with which it began. I remember hearing a man, who will be allowed to have been distinguished by as great sagacity as ever belonged to the most consummate statesman,—I remember hearing Mr. Pitt, not in his place in Parliament (where it might have been his object and his duty to animate zeal and to encourage hope), but in the privacy of his domestic circle, among the friends in whom he confided,—I remember well hearing him say, in 1793, that he expected the war to be of very short duration. That duration ran out to a period beyond the life of him who made the prediction. It outlived his successor, and the successors of that successor, and at length came suddenly and unexpectedly to an end through a combination of miraculous events, such as the most sanguine imagination could not have anticipated. With that example full in my recollection, I could not act upon the presumption that a new war once begun would be speedily ended. Let no such expectation induce us to enter a path which, however plain and clear it may appear at the outset of the journey, we should presently see branching into intricacies, and becoming encumbered with obstructions, until we were involved in a labyrinth, from which not we ourselves only, but the generation to come, might in vain endeavour to find the means of extrication.' *

Many, especially of the Whig party, blamed Lord Liverpool and Mr. Canning for the course which they pursued on this occasion. But I think it would now be generally acknowledged that they did all that they were called upon to do, and that to have gone to war for Spain at that time would have been an unnecessary, and probably a fruitless sacrifice of blood and treasure.

Two causes have of late years excited to a very high degree the public sympathy. Nor can it be denied that public sympathy was rightly bestowed.

The cause of Poland, so cruelly conquered, and so treacherously used in the first partition, must always commend itself to the heart of a generous nation.

The cause of Denmark, when attacked by Powers who had bound themselves by treaty to respect that integrity which they were the first to violate, naturally excited pity and indignation.

But when it became a question whether England should take up arms in either case, it was necessary to look narrowly into the cause for which these arms were to be used.

* Hansard's Debates, new series, vol. viii.

Was the cause of the Polish Insurgents the same as the cause of the observance of the Treaty of Vienna?

But the Polish insurgents repudiated and renounced that Treaty, and, had the war been successful, would never have consented to be bound by it.

In the case of Denmark, Great Britain proposed, in September 1862, terms of agreement which would have preserved the integrity of Denmark, have fulfilled the promises made in 1851 by Denmark to Austria and Prussia, and have prevented for all time the interference of Germany in the internal affairs of the kingdom of Denmark.

By whom were these terms accepted, and by whom were they rejected?

They were accepted by Austria and Prussia, and rejected by Denmark.

When, therefore, the Poles wished to create a great kingdom of Poland, comprising, besides the territory known by that name, Lithuania, Podolia, and Volhynia, was England bound to go to war on their behalf?—or when the Danes, in violation of their promises, attempted to incorporate Schleswig with the kingdom of Denmark, was Great Britain bound to abet them in such a pretension?

In all such cases, if what is rigidly just cannot be obtained, no right course remains but a recommendation to both sides to agree to reasonable terms of accommodation; nor does it follow, because such terms are rejected with haughty disdain at the . moment, that they will not serve to temper the violence even of those who in their hour of pride and passion so rejected them. A further reflection occurs on the provisions of the Treaty of Vienna regarding Poland, and on the Treaty of London regarding Denmark. The Great Powers undertook that Russia should maintain the Constitution of Poland, what-

ever it might be.   But they did not and could not
engage that the Poles should maintain their union
with Russia, even if Russia gave them the most
liberal Constitution, and observed it with the most
scrupulous fidelity.   So also regarding Denmark.
The Great Powers engaged themselves to respect
the integrity of Denmark.   But they did not and
could not engage that the Danish Government
should treat their German subjects with justice or
good faith.

All such Treaties, therefore, which mix external
with internal relations, and which are held to bind
one side and not to bind the other, are almost impossible of execution, and the best way in future
is to avoid all such impracticable compacts.

Nor does it follow, because a State is weak, that
it must always be in the right; nor, because it is
powerful, that it must always be in the wrong.   A
fair examination of the question in dispute, and a
fair adjustment of opposite claims and complaints,
is often a long and troublesome process to which
nations will scarcely submit.   It is far easier to
act from sympathy, or anger, or pride.   And yet, if
impartial reason had been listened to, how many
fruitless wars might have been spared, how much
blood and treasure might have been saved to the
nations of the world!

When I come to sum up, even in an imperfect
catalogue, the many improvements which have
taken place in the United Kingdom, her Colonies,
and Foreign Relations since 1824, I find Parliament reformed, Slavery abolished, Test and Corporation Acts repealed, Roman Catholic disabilities repealed, Jewish disabilities partially repealed,
Tithes commuted in England and Ireland; Municipal Corporations reformed in England, Scotland,
and Ireland; Poor Law reformed in England, enacted in Scotland and Ireland, Bishops' revenues

equalised in England; large sums made applicable to spiritual destitution and small livings; Education of the poor promoted; Customs duties reduced from many hundred to twelve; differential duties abolished; protective duties repealed or reduced; Corn Laws repealed; Taxes on glass, soap, coals, candles, paper, newspaper stamps, and many other articles, repealed, Independence of Belgium and Greece established, Unity of Italy recognised.

Turning in my mind these mighty changes which had been accomplished by the regular working of Parliamentary Government, and seeing in 1863 so very different a state of public feeling from that which prevailed in 1817, in 1819, and in 1830, I remarked, in a speech in Scotland, that the people seemed to have adopted a motto inscribed on a stone, at the side of the road at the top of one of their Scotch mountains, ' Rest, and be thankful.' I added, that for my part I was not disposed to quarrel with the feeling of the people at that time; although, doubtless, there were other hills to be climbed, and other roads to be made. It was sufficiently obvious, I thought, without my pointing it out, that neither the road-maker nor the traveller, when he has got to the top of the hill, though he may rest his weary limbs, and contemplate for a time with gratitude and admiration the space he has traversed, and the prospect around him, thinks of making a perpetual bivouac on the summit he has reached. He may hope, indeed, that his future course may be less arduous, the rocks less steep, the torrents less difficult to traverse, the marsh less unsafe to the tread; but he will still move on after his period of repose, and pursue his journey, all the more confident in his path from the success he has already achieved.

But, to drop metaphor, it seems no violent assumption to suppose, after overcoming the strength of resistance armed with legislative power in the boroughs disfranchised by the Reform Act,—the force of religious prejudices entrenched in the Acts which excluded Roman Catholics, Protestant Dissenters, and Jews from the privileges of the Constitution— the powerful combination of interests which guarded the Corn Laws and all other monopolies,—that after the victorious issue of all these contests, the remaining struggles with fear, selfishness, and ignorance will not offer the same difficulties, nor be achieved at the same hazards. I speak, of course, in the expectation that no great organic changes are to be attempted by any considerable party in the State.

The following anecdote is told in Lord Sidmouth's Life:—' In September 1791, after Burke's breach with Fox, Pitt invited him for the first time to dine with him: Lord Grenville, Burke, Addington, and Pitt constituted the party. After dinner, Burke was earnestly representing the danger which threatened this country from the contagion of French principles, when Pitt said, "Never fear, Mr. Burke, depend on it, we shall go on as we are till the Day of Judgment." "Very likely, sir," replied Mr. Burke; "it is the day of *no judgment* that I am afraid of." ' *

In considering whether the people of these islands would increase their political freedom and social happiness by deliberately adopting or unconsciously gliding into a more democratic form of government, we should take care not to be misled by the notion that we should thereby be placing ourselves under the sway of pure reason. In North America, after the separation from England, monarchy, aristocracy, and church establishments were impossible; but the wisest of the founders of the great Republic, such men as Washington and Hamilton, beheld with

* Life of Lord Sidmouth, vol. i. p. 72.

anxiety the absence of those barriers by which the
stream of democracy might be somewhat restrained.
They knew well that the hope of forming a government on pure reason was a pure delusion. Man
may be rendered more humane by civilisation,
better informed by education; but to extirpate his
passions, to prevent the aberrations of his will, is
impossible.

The man of railways and iron-clads; the man
of the electric telegraph and the steam-press; the
man who can weigh the attraction of the planets
to each other, and divide an inch into 10,000
parts; the man whose telescope can bring the
moon within a few hundred miles of the earth, and
whose power of analysis can ascertain the compound metals of the sun,—this man, in capacity so
like a God, is, in his appetites and his passions, in
his love and his hatred, in his rapacity and his ambition, different only in degree from the Achilles
and Agamemnon of Homer.

Was it pure reason which induced the men of
1864 to rush in arms against each other, and to
meet in mortal combat, both in Europe and in
America?

It is because man is a creature of passion and of
imagination, as well as of reason, that in the constitution of a government by which he is to be ruled
and directed, it is the concern of wise and far-
seeing men to avail themselves of all the influences
which may give moderation, force, and sanctity to
the supreme authority. Such may be, in a monarchy, the reverence paid to Royalty, the awe inspired by religion, the respect which grows around
an ancient aristocracy, the attachment to long-
established laws, the refinement of polished manners, and the social kindness which adorns and
animates the domestic relations of a cultivated
people. Let no one imagine that without such

influences, or some of them at least, a political constitution can reach its highest perfection.

In like manner also, it is clear that, in a Republic, by wise provisions, by giving reasonable duration to a well-constituted Senate, and by placing in the hands of learned and upright judges the administration of fixed and impartial laws, the chief ends of government may be obtained. For what are the chief ends of government?

There was a time (not yet forgotten) when it was supposed to be the duty of government to inculcate religious truth, and to punish the teachers of religious error.

There was a time when it was supposed to be the duty of a government to provide for the wealth of the community; when the Inquisitors of State of Venice sent assassins to put to death those who carried the mechanical skill of a Venetian workman to foreign parts; a time when Colbert put in the pillory the French weavers who did not make the warp and the woof of the length and breadth which he in his wisdom prescribed; a time when the same Minister punished with great severity the men guilty of having exchanged the manufactures of Holland for the wines of France.

There was a time, also, when it was thought the duty of a government to fix the price of bread and meat, and the minimum of wages; when men who refused to part with corn for less than its value, or to give for labour more than it was worth, were considered the proper objects of the criminal law.

But these errors, and many like them, are fast passing away. It is now known that the proper objects of government are to secure freedom and order within, and independence from any enemy without. These are tasks heavy enough, noble enough, to require the energies of the highest political minds for their fulfilment. At the same time, the utmost liberty of thought and expression, the utmost latitude of domestic industry and foreign trade, should be protected as the fairest fruits of a free constitution. The task of English legislation for half a century has been to break the chains which fettered civil, commercial, and religious freedom.

Thus far I have spoken of the measures that have been proposed and carried during these forty memorable years. But some tribute is due to the departed leaders by whose large discourse, looking before and after, these measures have been devised, and by whose followers, still living, they have been upheld and defended.

First of these stands Earl Grey, to whom when living this work was first dedicated. Endowed with the noblest spirit, the truest wisdom, he contended throughout for the grant of all the privileges of the Constitution to the Roman Catholics of Ireland, and for an enlarged and reformed representation of the people. He stood by the side of Mr. Fox during his great struggle against the French war. His private letters, published by his son, show an abhorrence of all that is mean and narrow, which, if it deprived him of power under George III. and George IV., was worthy of his illustrious career, and must commend him to the veneration of posterity.

George Canning belonged during the war to the school of Pitt. He was their animating genius during the Spanish liberating war,—at a time when, according to an expression of Madame de Staël, 'the Tories of England were the Whigs of Europe;' and if, by a happy inspiration, he had accepted the Foreign Office, when offered to him towards the close of that war, he would surely have infused into the Treaty of Vienna

T

of 1815, some of that respect for the independence
of nations, some of that grateful regard for the
rights and liberties of the German, the Spanish,
the Italian, and the Polish people, which he felt,
and in which that Treaty is so mournfully deficient.
For when Mr. Canning in 1823 succeeded Lord
Castlereagh, when little could be done to repair
former errors, he yet by the high tone of his speeches,
and by one or two acts of vigour, greatly raised the
spirit of the nation, and gave hopes to those friends of
liberty on the Continent, who, after shedding their
blood to overthrow a foreign military despotism, had
been deserted when Europe had been delivered,
and imprisoned or banished for their exertions in
behalf of freedom.

Mr. Canning had not the force of argument
of Plunkett or of Brougham, but his taste was
classical, his diction beautiful, and his wit of the
most polished as well as of the most pointed kind.
' They who oppose improvement because it is innovation,' said Mr. Canning, ' may one day have
to submit to innovation which is not improvement.'
Such was his wise spirit, and in that spirit he
supported warmly the free-trade measures of Mr.
Huskisson.

Sir Robert Peel was the third among the leaders,
now no more, who contributed by his influence, by
his abilities, by the mastery which he obtained over
the minds of young statesmen of the Conservative
party, to guide the struggling bark of his country
into the haven of safety. I do not need to speak
of his powerful understanding, of his ready memory
for all which could illustrate or enforce the con-
clusions to which he desired to lead the sovereign
assembly of the empire; of his eloquence when
eloquence was required; of his still more prevailing
power of marshalling facts, of giving life to statistical details; of the ability he showed in improving

the currency, in restoring the finances, in maintaining the dignity of Government. For this bright luminary has not so far sunk into the twilight of past years but that its radiance still cheers and warms the horizon it has left.

But there is a singularity in the career of Sir Robert Peel which will long startle and perplex the readers of the history of these times. His father, on a solemn occasion, declared that he had devoted him, as a successor of Pitt, to the service of his country. Twice he was the undisputed head of the Tory party,—a Minister in possession of the confidence of the Crown, the leader of a compact majority of the House of Commons. Twice he risked, twice he lost the eminence of power, and the adhesion of a party majority.

The first time he did so to give peace to Ireland, and avoid a dangerous conflict. He said, at the conclusion of a speech to which I have already alluded,—' I am well aware that the fate of this measure cannot now be altered: if it succeed, the credit will belong to others; if it fail, the responsibility will devolve upon me and those with whom I have acted. These chances, with the loss of private friendship, and the alienation of public confidence, I must have foreseen and calculated upon before I ventured to recommend these measures. I assure the House that, in conducting them, I have met with the severest blow which it has ever been my lot to experience; but I am convinced that the time will come, though I may not live to see it, when full justice will be done by men of all parties to the motives upon which I have acted,—when this question will be fully settled, and when others will see that I had no alternative but to act as I have acted. They will then admit that the course which I have followed, and which I am still prepared to follow, whatever imputation it may

expose me to, is the only course which is now necessary for the diminution of the undue, illegiti-
mate, and dangerous power of the Roman Catholics,
and for the maintenance and permanent security
of Protestant interests.' *

On his last surrender of power, having lost the
confidence of his party in that year upon the Corn
question, as he had lost it in 1829 upon the Catholic
question, he said, at the conclusion of his speech on
the 29th June 1846—' Within a few hours, probably, that power which I have held for a period
of five years will be surrendered into the hands of
another,—without repining, without complaint on
my part, with a more lively recollection of the
support and confidence I have received during
several years, than of the opposition which, during a
recent period, I have encountered. In relinquish-
ing power, I shall leave a name severely censured, I
fear, by many who, on public grounds, deeply regret
the severance of party ties, — deeply regret that
severance, not from interested or personal motives,
but from a firm conviction that fidelity to party
engagements, the existence and maintenance of a
great party, constitutes a powerful instrument of
government. I shall surrender power, severely censured also by others who, from no interested motives, adhere to the principle of Protection, considering the maintenance of it to be essential to the
welfare and interests of the country. I shall leave
a name execrated by every monopolist, who, from
less honourable motives, clamours for Protection because it conduces to his own immediate benefit;
but it may be that I shall leave a name sometimes
remembered with expressions of goodwill in the
abodes of those whose lot it is to labour, and to
earn their daily bread by the sweat of their brow,
when they shall recruit their exhausted strength

* Parliamentary Debates, new series, vol. xx. p. 1290.

with abundant and untaxed food, the sweeter because it is no longer leavened by a sense of injustice.'*

No one, I think, can doubt that on the first occasion, the justice and expediency of removing Roman Catholic disabilities—on the second, the justice and expediency of repealing the Corn Laws, had fully penetrated his clear and sagacious mind. To give effect to his convictions, he forfeited the confidence of that party which had nurtured his talents, and adopted him as its chosen child and champion.   In this sense—

> 'Fuit in parentem
> Splendide mendax.'

But he had another parent, of stronger affinity and paramount claims: his country, her welfare, her safety, had a right to his filial duty, and for her sake he twice made a sacrifice for which he deserves her perpetual and grateful commemoration.

But, having made the sacrifice of opinions deeply rooted, and party ties warmly cherished, no one can doubt, I think, that he did right when, on the first occasion on which the want of confidence displayed itself, he surrendered office.   To have relied on old opponents to support him in measures which, in 1831, must have been measures of Parliamentary reform, and, in 1846, measures for the abolition of the differential sugar duties and the repeal of the Navigation Laws, would have been a weak and unworthy course.   A resignation of power was the only fit consummation of a career which could not otherwise have been unquestioned in its motives, or, indeed, have borne peace to his own bosom.†

But Sir Robert Peel was to me only a public man.   There are others among the departed who

---

* Parliamentary Debates, vol. lxxxix. p. 1054.
† See Note L.

by me must be ever loved, ever honoured, ever mourned:—Lord Holland, the inheritor of Mr. Fox's principles, the attached friend of Lord Grey; Lord Lansdowne, the temperate and wise promoter of every liberal reform; Lord Althorp, the honestest, the most disinterested of statesmen. Holland, Lansdowne, Althorp, Melbourne, Carlisle, have been friends by the side of whom I have contended on some of the gravest affairs involving the fate of a nation, with whom I have lived and conversed in hours of the most familiar society, and on all occasions, public or private, grave or gay, with entire confidence, with mutual trust, without a drop of the gall of envy or of jealousy. To their eminent, to their happy and amiable qualities, I should like to have given a full and grateful testimony.

But I must refrain: it is the object of this Chapter to point out that Earl Grey, with the generation of statesmen who have guided the nation since the close of the great war,—whose task it has been to heal its wounds, and bring plenty to be the companion of peace,—have not deserved ill of their country.

NOTES.

NOTE (A). PAGE 23.

'FOR their images, some of them were brought to
London, and were there at St. Paul's Cross, in the sight
of all the people, broken; that they might be fully convinced of the juggling impostures of the monks. And
in particular, the crucifix of Boxley, in Kent, commonly
called the *Rood of Grace*, to which many pilgrimages
had been made; because it was observed sometimes to
bow, and to lift itself up, to shake and to stir head, hands,
and feet, to roll the eyes, move the lips, and bend the
brows; all which were looked on by the abused multitude, as the effects of a divine power. These were now
publicly discovered to have been cheats. For the springs
were showed by which all these motions were made.
Upon which, John Hilsey, then Bishop of Rochester,
made a sermon, and broke the rood in pieces. There
was also another famous imposture discovered at Hailes,
in Gloucestershire; where the blood of Christ was
showed in a vial of crystal, which the people sometimes
saw, but sometimes they could not see it: so they were
made believe, that they were not capable of so signal a
favour as long as they were in mortal sin; and so they
continued to make presents, till they bribed Heaven to
give them the sight of so blessed a relic. This was now
discovered to have been the blood of a duck, which they
renewed every week: and the one side of the vial was
so very thick, that there was no seeing through it, but
the other was clear and transparent: and it was so
placed near the altar, that one in a secret place behind
could turn either side of it outward. So when they had
drained the pilgrims that came thither of all they had
brought with them, then they afforded them the favour
of turning the clear side outward: who upon that went

home very well satisfied with their journey, and the expense they had been at. There was brought out of Wales a huge image of wood, called *Darrel Gatheren*, of which one Ellis Price, visitor of the diocese of St. Asaph, gave this account: On the 6th of April 1537, "That the people of the country had a great superstition for it, and many pilgrimages were made to it: so that, the day before he wrote, there were reckoned to be above five or six hundred pilgrims there: some brought oxen and cattle, and some brought money; and it was generally believed, that if any offered to that image, he had power to deliver his soul from hell." So it was ordered to be brought to London, where it served for fuel to burn Friar Forrest. There was an huge image of Our Lady at Worcester, that was had in great reverence; which, when it was stripped of some veils that covered it, was found to be the statue of a bishop.'— *Burnet's History of the Reformation*, vol. i. p. 242.

'But the richest shrine in England was that of Thomas Beckett, called St. Thomas of Canterbury the Martyr. For three hundred years he was accounted one of the greatest saints in heaven, as may appear from the accounts in the Ledger-books, of the offerings made to the three greatest altars in Christ's Church, Canterbury. The one was to Christ, the other to the Virgin, and the third to St. Thomas. In one year there was offered at Christ's altar £3. 2s. 6d.; to the Virgin's altar, £63. 5s. 6d.; but to St. Thomas's altars, £832. 12s. 3d. But the next year the odds grew greater: for there was not a penny offered at Christ's altar, and at the Virgin's only £4. 1s. 8d.; but at St. Thomas's, £954. 6s. 3d. By such offerings, it came that his shrine was of inestimable value. There was one stone offered there by Louis VII. of France, who came over to visit it in a pilgrimage, that was believed the richest in Europe.'—*Burnet's History of the Reformation*, vol. i. p. 244.

NOTE (B). PAGE 28.

The following speech of Secretary Cecil, on monopolies, is altogether characteristic of the reign of Elizabeth :—

Mr. Secretary Cecil stood up, and said, 'There needs

no supply of the memory of the Speaker; but, because it pleased him to desire some that be about him to aid his delivery, and because the rest of my fellows be silent, I will take upon me to deliver something which I both then heard and since know. I was present with the rest of my fellow-councillors, and the message was the same that hath been told you; and the cause hath not succeeded from any particular course thought upon, but from private informations of some particular persons. I have been very inquisitive of them, and of the cause why more importunity was now used than afore; which, I am afraid, comes by being acquainted with some course of proceeding in this House. There are no patents now of force which shall not presently be revoked; for what patent soever is granted, there shall be left to the overthrow of that patent a liberty agreeable to the law. There is no patent if it be *malum in se*, but the Queen was ill apprised in her grant. But all to the generality be unacceptable, I take it, there is no patent whereof the execution has not been injurious. Would that they had never been granted! I hope there shall never be more. (All the House said, Amen.) In particular, most of these patents have been supported by letters of assistance from Her Majesty's Privy Council: but whosoever looks upon them shall find, that they carry no other style than with relation to the patent. I dare assure you, from henceforth there shall be no more granted. They shall all be revoked. But to whom do they repair with these letters? To some out-house, to some desolate widow, to some simple cottage, or poor ignorant people, who rather than they would be troubled, and undo themselves by coming up hither, will give anything in reason for those caterpillars' satisfaction. The notice of this is now public, and you will perhaps judge this to be a tale to serve the time. But I would have all men to know thus much, that it is no jesting with a court of Parliament, neither dares any man (for my own part I dare not) so mock and abuse all the states of this kingdom, in a matter of this consequence and importance. I say, therefore, there shall be a proclamation general throughout the realm, to notify Her Majesty's resolution in this behalf. And because you may eat your meat more savoury than you

have done, every man shall have salt as good and cheap
as he can buy it or make it, freely, without danger of
that patent, which shall be presently revoked. The
same benefit shall they have which have cold stomachs,
both for *aqua vitæ* and *aqua composita*, and the like.
And they that have weak stomachs, for their satisfaction shall have vinegar and elegar, and the like, set at
liberty. Train-oil shall go the same way; oil of blubber
shall march in equal rank; brushes and bottles endure
the like judgment. The patent for pouldavy, if it be
not called in, it shall be. Woad, which, as I take it, is
not restrained either by law or statute, but only by proclamation, (I mean from the former sowing,) though for
the saving thereof it might receive good disputation,
yet, for your satisfaction, the Queen's pleasure is to
revoke that proclamation; only she prayeth thus much,
that when she cometh on progress to see you in your
counties, she be not driven out of your towns by suffering it to infect the air too near them. Those that desire
to go sprucely in their ruffs may, at less charge than
accustomed, obtain their wish; the patent for starch,
which hath so much been prosecuted, shall now be
repealed. But, not to make any further performance of
the well-uttered and gravely and truly delivered speech
of the Speaker, I must crave your favours a little longer
to make an apology for myself. I have held the favour
of this House as dear as my life, and I have been told
that I deserved to be taxed yesterday of the House. I
protest my zeal to have the business go forward in a
right and hopeful course; and my fear to displease Her
Majesty by a harsh and rash proceeding made me so
much to lay aside my discretion, that I said, it might
rather be termed a school than a council, or to that
effect. But by this speech, if any think I called him
schoolboy, he both wrongs me and mistakes me.

'Shall I tell you what Demosthenes said to the clamours
which the Athenians made? That they were *pueriles et
dignos pueris*. And yet that was to a popular State. And
I wish that whatsoever is here spoken may be buried
within these walls. Let us take example of the Jewish
synagogue, who would always *sepelire senatum cum
honore*, and not blast their own follies and imperfections.
If any man in this House speak wisely, we do him great

wrong to interrupt him; if foolishly, let us hear him
out,—we shall have the more cause to tax him. And I
do heartily pray that no member of this House may *plus
verbis offendere quam consilio juvare.'—New Parliamentary
History*, vol. i. p. 934; 1601.

Note (C). Page 29.

Speaking of the imprisonment of Mr. Wentworth,
who was committed, by order of the House, to the Tower,
for a speech in which he said the Queen had committed
dangerous faults, Mr. Hume says, 'The issue of the affair
was, that after a month's confinement, the Queen sent to
the Commons, informing them, that, from her special
grace and favour, she had restored him to his liberty,
and to his place in the House. By this seeming lenity,
she indirectly retained the power which she had assumed
of imprisoning the members, and obliging them to
answer before her for their conduct in Parliament. And
Sir Walter Mildmay endeavoured to make the House
sensible of Her Majesty's goodness, in so gently remitting
the indignation which she might justly conceive at the
temerity of their member. But he informed them, that
they had not the liberty of speaking what and of whom
they pleased; and that indiscreet freedoms, used in that
House, had, both in the present and foregoing ages, met
with a proper punishment. He warned them, therefore,
not to abuse further the Queen's clemency, lest she be
constrained, contrary to her inclination, to turn an
unsuccessful lenity into a necessary severity.' *

This account is somewhat incorrect. Upon referring
to the Journal of Sir Simon D'Ewes, which Mr. Hume
has quoted, we find that the Queen did not inform the
House by her message, that she had restored Mr. Wentworth to his liberty and his place in the House; but
that 'whereas a member of the same, on the first day of
this session, February 8th, in a set speech, uttered divers
offensive matters against Her Majesty, and for the same
had been committed prisoner to the Tower *by that House*,
yet Her Majesty was graciously pleased to remit her
justly-occasioned displeasure for the said offence, and to

* Hume, vol. v. 4to, p. 240.

refer the enlargement of the party *to the House.*'   So
that she by no means 'indirectly retained the power·
which she had assumed of imprisoning the member,' by
her proceedings in this case, whatever they may have
been on other occasions.   This explanation, too, takes
away the edge from Sir Walter Mildmay's speech, the
important part of which I here subjoin.   It will be seen,
that it consists of generalities, and that Mr. Hume has
culled out those parts only which suited his theory.   It
must never be forgotten in reading Mr. Hume, that he
found an opinion established in England, that the Stuarts
had governed like tyrants, and Elizabeth like a good
patriot. He attacked this, as he did all other established
opinions, from a love of argument and of paradox.   He
is to the Whig writers and historians what Bayle is to
the ancient and modern philosophers.   Sometimes he
goes so far as to doubt the benefit of liberty altogether.
But it is time to pass to Sir Walter Mildmay.—'That
for so gracious a dealing it was our bounden duties to
yield unto Her Majesty our most humble and hearty
thanks, and to beseech Almighty God to enlarge her
days as the only stay of our felicity ; and not only so,
but to learn also, by this example, how to behave ourselves hereafter ; and not, under the pretence of liberty,
to forget our bounden duty to so gracious a Queen.
True it is, that nothing can be well concluded in a
council, where there is not allowed, in debating of causes
brought in, deliberation, liberty, and freedom of speech ;
otherwise, if in consultation men be either interrupted
or terrified, so as they cannot, nor dare not, speak their
opinions freely, like as that council cannot but be reputed
for a servile council ; even so all the proceedings therein
shall be rather to satisfy the wills of a few, than to determine that which shall be just and reasonable.   But
herein we may not forget to put a difference between
liberty of speech and licentious speech ; for by the one
men deliver their opinions freely, and with this caution,
that all be spoken pertinently, modestly, reverently, and
discreetly ; the other contrariwise uttereth all imper-
tinently, rashly, arrogantly, and irreverently, without
respect of person, time, or place ; and though freedom of
speech hath always been used in this great council of
Parliament, and is a thing most necessary to be preserved

amongst us, yet the same was never, nor ought to be, extended so far, as though a man in this House may speak what and of whom he list. The contrary whereof, both in our own days and in the days of our predecessors, by the punishment of such inconsiderate and disorderly speakers, hath appeared. And so to return, let this serve us for an example, to beware that we offend not in the like hereafter, lest that, in forgetting our duties so far, we may give just cause to our gracious Sovereign to think that this her clemency hath given occasion of further boldness, and thereby so much grieve and provoke her, as, contrary to her most gracious and mild consideration, she be constrained to change her natural clemency into necessary and just severity; a thing that I trust shall never happen amongst wise and dutiful men, such as the members of this House are thought always to be.'

This speech, with a very few alterations in language, would make a fair official speech in our own day.

Note (D). Page 54.

The same cause may have operated with Napoleon against the life of the Duc d'Enghien. It is singular also, that in the rest of the chapter, Machiavel seems to have given directions to persons in the situation of Cromwell and Bonaparte. He tells us, that those who have become '*tiranni*' of their country ought to examine what the people wish for, and that they will always find they wish for two things: the one, revenge upon those who have been the cause of their servitude; and the other, the restoration of their liberty. In the first of these, the new prince may satisfy them completely. In the second, he may satisfy them in part. For if he analyses the wish of the people for liberty, he will find that a small part only desire it for the sake of power, and that the great majority only desire liberty that they may live in security. The few he may either remove, or raise to such posts and dignities as will satisfy them; the many will be contented by the enactment of just laws, and a strict observance of them on the part of the sovereign. Thus, he says, the kings of France disposed of the arms and money of the State; but in other things, obeyed the laws. Napoleon, who was a great reader of Machiavel, seems to have taken the advice which is here given by the most profound of political writers.

NOTE (E). PAGE 76.

It may not be uninteresting to the reader, to read an account of two cases in which the poor man, with the law on his side, triumphed over the pretensions of the highest persons in the kingdom. The first is the more curious, as a relation of it is contained in a letter of Lord Thurlow to a nephew of Mr. Justice Foster. It was a prosecution against the Princess Amelia for stopping up a footpath in Richmond Park.

'DEAR SIR,

'I write, at the hazard of your thinking me impertinent, to give you the pleasure of hearing that of your uncle, which, in all probability, you will not hear from him,—I mean the great honour and general esteem which he has gained, or rather accumulated, by his inflexible and spirited manner of trying the Richmond cause, which has been so long depending, and so differently treated by other judges. You have heard what a deficiency there was of the special jury, which was imputed to their backwardness to serve a prosecution against the Princess. He has fined all the absentees £20 apiece. They made him wait two hours, and, at last, resort to a *tales*. When the prosecutors had gone through part of their evidence, Sir Richard Lloyd, who went down on the part of the Crown, said, that it was needless for them to go on upon the right, as the Crown was not prepared to try that, this being an indictment which could not possibly determine it, because the obstruction was charged to be in the parish of Wimbledon, whereas it was, in truth, in Mortlake, which was a distinct parish from Wimbledon. They maintained their own poor, upheld their own church, and paid tithes to their own parson; and Domesday Book mentions Mortlake. On the other side, it was said that Domesday Book mentions it as a baron's fee, and not as a parish; and that the Survey in the time of Henry VIII. mentions Wimbledon *cum capellis suis annexis*, and, also, that a

grant of it in the time of Edward VI. makes a provision
of tithes for the vicar, to officiate in the chapel of Mortlake. The judge turned to the jury, and said, he thought
they were come there to try a right which the subject
claimed to a way through Richmond Park, and not to
cavil about little law objections which have no relation
to that right. He said, it is proved to be in Wimbledon
parish ; but it would have been enough, if the place in
which the obstruction was charged had been only reputed to be in Wimbledon, because the defendant and
jury must have been as sensible of that reputation as
the prosecutors : but had it not been so, he should have
thought it below the honour of the Crown, after this
business had been depending three assizes, to send one
of their select council, not to try the right, but to hinge
upon so small a point as this. Upon which Sir Richard
Lloyd made a speech, setting forth the gracious disposition of the King in suffering this cause to be tried,
which he could have suppressed with a single breath, by
ordering a *nolle prosequi* to be entered. The judge said,
he was not of that opinion. The subject is interested
in such indictments as these, for continuing nuisances,
and can have no remedy but this, if their rights be
encroached upon ; wherefore he should think it a denial
of justice to stop a prosecution for a nuisance, which
his whole prerogative does not extend to pardon. After
which, the evidence was gone through ; and the judge
summed up shortly, but clearly, for the prosecutors.*

'It gave me, who am a stranger to him, great pleasure
to hear that we have one English judge, whom nothing
can tempt or frighten, ready and able to hold up the
laws of his country, as a great shield of the rights of
the people. I presume it will give you still greater, to
hear that your friend and relation is that judge : and
that is the only apology I have to make for troubling
you with this.

'I am, dear Sir,
'Your most humble Servant,
'E. THURLOW.

'*Fig-Tree Court, Inner Temple,
April 11, 1758.*'

(*Life of Sir M. Foster*, p. 85.)

* The defendant was convicted. See Burr. 908, 909.

The other case is related of the father of Mr. Horne Tooke, a poulterer, in London.

'As Mr. Horne lived in Newport Street, he was, of course, a near neighbour to His Royal Highness Frederic, Prince of Wales, father to his present Majesty, who then kept his court at Leicester House. Some of the officers of the household, imagining that an outlet towards the market would be extremely convenient to them, as well as the inferior domestics, orders were immediately issued for this purpose. Accordingly, an adjoining wall was cut through, and a door placed in the opening, without any ceremony whatsoever, notwithstanding it was a palpable encroachment on, and violation of, the property of a private individual. In the midst of this operation, Mr. Horne appeared, and calmly remonstrated against so glaring an act of injustice, as the brick partition actually appertained to him, and 'the intended thoroughfare would lead through, and consequently depreciate the value of his premises.

'It soon appeared, however, that the representations of a dealer in geese and turkeys, although backed by law and reason, had but little effect on those who acted in the name, and, in this instance, abused the authority of a prince, who was probably unacquainted with the circumstances of the transaction.

'On this, he appealed from " the insolence of office " to the justice of his country; and, to the honour of our municipal jurisprudence, the event proved different from what it would have been, perhaps, in any other kingdom of Europe ; for a tradesman of Westminster triumphed over the heir-apparent of the English crown, and orders were soon after issued for the removal of the obnoxious door.'—*Life of Horne Tooke*, vol. i. p. 11.

NOTE (F). PAGE 82.

Mr. Hume makes what I conceive to be a remark calculated to mislead, when he says, in his history of Charles I.—' Some men of the greatest parts and most extensive knowledge that the nation at this time produced, could not enjoy any peace of mind, because obliged to hear prayers offered up to the Divinity by a priest covered with a white linen vestment.'

The point is certainly ingenious, but, as I conceive, obtained by a sacrifice of candour. Both parties allowed that the surplice was in itself a matter of indifference. The objections to the orders concerning the surplice alleged on the part of the Puritans were three :—

1st. That as it was in its essence a matter of indifference, it ought not to be enjoined like an article of faith, but every one should be left to do as he pleased.

2nd. That although in itself a matter of indifference, it was not so to the common people ; for many of them thought no worship to God could be effectual, unless performed in a consecrated garment, and thus the practice kept alive a superstitious notion.

3rd. Above all, the Puritans urged that no secular person had the right to give orders on this subject. Mr. Cartwright says, ' Christ, and no other, is head of the church. No civil magistrate, in councils or assemblies for church matters, can either be chief moderator, over-ruler, judge, or determiner ; nor has he such authority as that without his consent it should not be lawful for ecclesiastical persons to make church-orders or cere-monies.' *

In the same sense Mr. Axton, when examined by his bishop, said, ' I admit Her Majesty's supremacy so far as if there be any error in the governors of the church, she has power to reform it ; but I do not admit her to be an ecclesiastical elder or church governor.'† It is true, the Puritans would call the surplice 'idolatrous gear,' and other worse names, when they had grown warm in controversy ; but they told Archbishop Parker that had the habits and a few ceremonies been left indifferent, they never would have left the church ; but 'it was the compelling these things by law made them separate.' ‡

In fine, the doctrine of the Puritans, or Presbyterians, asserted the ' word of God contained in the Old and New Testament to be a perfect rule of faith and manners.'§ They maintained that the church ought to be governed by this rule only,—that ceremonies and observances

---

* Neale, vol. i. p. 133.   † Ibid. p. 260.
‡ Neale, vol. i. p. 230.
§ Confession of Faith of Members of the Prophesyings. Neale, p. 276.

should be as few as possible, and should not be imposed
by command of any superior whatever, but left to the
free choice of the church itself. They condemned not
other churches that differed in ceremonies from theirs,
but protested against all dictation on the subject. They
held that 'no pastor ought to usurp dominion over
another;' and that 'the pastor should be chosen by the
congregation.' *

Thus we see that the question of the surplice was
connected with a great scheme of ecclesiastical reform,
—a scheme adopted and established in the native country
of Mr. Hume; and which, whatever may be thought of
its efficacy to make men better and wiser, was at least
not unworthy of 'men of the greatest parts and most
extensive knowledge.'

NOTE (G). PAGE 83.

This Act was passed in 1664. There is nothing more
remarkable in our history, or less noticed, than the noble
manner in which the Dissenters forgot, in favour of the
common cause, the severity with which they were
treated. In 1672 they urged the House of Commons to
pass the Test Act without any clause in their favour,
contenting themselves with a motion for a separate bill
of toleration, which was not likely to pass. After the
persecution of the reign of Charles II. they joined the
church during the reign of James; neither alienated by
the harsh treatment they had received, nor allured by
the indulgence offered on the part of the King. It is to
be regretted that the church have found it inconsistent
with their duty to imitate the liberality and public spirit
of their dissenting brethren.

NOTE (H). PAGE 213.

*Circular to the Austrian, Prussian, and Russian Ministers,
at Foreign Courts.—Laybach, May 21, 1821.*

(Extract.)

'Les changements utiles ou nécessaires dans la législa-

---

* Confession of Faith of the Prisoners in Newgate. Neale.

tion et dans l'administration des États ne doivent émaner
que de la volonté libre, de l'impulsion réfléchie et éclairée
de ceux que Dieu a rendus responsables du pouvoir.
Tout ce qui sort de cette ligne conduit nécessairement
au désordre, aux bouleversements, à des maux bien plus
insupportables que ceux que l'on prétend guérir.

'Pénétrés de cette vérité éternelle, les souverains
n'ont pas hésité à la proclamer avec franchise et vigueur ;
ils ont déclaré, qu'en respectant les droits et l'indépen-
dance du pouvoir légitime, ils regardaient comme légale-
ment nulle et désavouée, par les principes qui constituent
le Droit Public de l'Europe, toute prétendue réforme
opérée par la révolte et la force ouverte. Ils ont agi, en
conséquence de cette déclaration, dans les évènements
de Naples, dans ceux du Piémont, dans ceux même qui,
sous des circonstances très-différentes, mais par des
combinaisons également criminelles, viennent de livrer
la partie orientale de l'Europe à des convulsions
incalculables.'

NOTE (I). PAGE 214.

A petition presented in February 1824, signed by all,
or nearly all, the principal silk manufacturers of the City
of London, may, in these days, excite some surprise. It
was directed chiefly against Mr. Huskisson's proposed
reduction of the prohibitory duty on manufactured silks
to thirty per cent. *ad valorem.* The petitioners stated,
'that they have learnt with the utmost surprise, that it
has been proposed to adopt so important a measure as
that of a reduction from 5*s*. 6*d*. to 6*d*. per pound upon
Italian and China raw silk ; from 4*s*. to 3*d*. per lb. on
Bengal raw silk ; and from 14*s*. 8*d*. to 9*s*. 6*d*. per lb. upon
Italian thrown silk, and the admission of foreign manufactured silk goods to importation in this country without any previous communication with the important
branches of the trade, all of which are thrown into the
greatest consternation and alarm by the contemplated
measure.'—*Hansard's Debates,* new series, vol. x. p. 371.

On the 24th of February 1826, commenced the decisive debate and division which gave the victory to
the cause of free trade. It was in this debate that Mr.

Canning said—'But it is singular to remark how ready
some people are to admire in a great man the exception
rather than the rule of his conduct: such perverse worship is like the idolatry of barbarous nations, who can
see the noonday splendour of the sun without emotion,
but who when he is in eclipse come forward with hymns
and cymbals to adore him. . . . Treading with unequal
pace in his footsteps, I do not think it our duty to select
by preference those footmarks in which, from the slip-
periness of the times, he may have trodden awry.'—
Hansard's Debates, vol. xiv. p. 856.

The numbers on a division were—

For a Committee to inquire	. . .	40
Against	. . . .	222
	Majority . . .	182

NOTE (J). PAGE 224.

The following extracts from Mr. Mill's work will show
that I have not done him injustice. I quote from the
Essay on Representative Government.

[Page 172.] 'When two persons who have a joint
interest in any business differ in opinion, does justice
require that both opinions should be held of exactly equal
value? If with equal virtue, one is superior to the other
in knowledge and intelligence—or if with equal intelligence, one excels the other in virtue—the opinion, the
judgment of the higher moral or intellectual being, is
worth more than that of the inferior; and if the institutions of the country virtually assert that they are
of the same value, they assert a thing which is not. One
of the two, as the wiser or better man, has a claim to
superior weight: the difficulty is in ascertaining which of
the two it is; a thing impossible as between individuals,
but, taking men in bodies and in numbers, it can be
done with a certain approach to accuracy.

.   .   .   .

[Page 173.] 'Now, national affairs are exactly such a
joint concern, with the difference, that no one need ever
be called upon for a complete sacrifice of his own opinion.
It can always be taken into the calculation, and counted

at a certain figure, a higher figure being assigned to the suffrages of those whose opinion is entitled to greater weight. There is not, in this arrangement, anything necessarily invidious to those to whom it assigns the lower degrees of influence. Entire exclusion from a voice in the common concerns is one thing: the concession to others of a more potential voice, on the ground of greater capacity for the management of the joint interests, is another. The two things are not merely different, they are incommensurable. Every one has a right to feel insulted by being made a nobody, and stamped as of no account at all. No one but a fool, and only a fool of a peculiar description, feels offended by the acknowledgment that there are others whose opinion, and even whose wish, is entitled to a greater amount of consideration than his. To have no voice in what are partly his own concerns, is a thing which nobody willingly consents to; but when what is partly his concern is also partly another's, and he feels the other to understand the subject better than himself, that the other's opinion should be counted for more than his own, accords with his expectations, and with the course of things which in all other affairs of life he is accustomed to acquiesce in. It is only necessary that this superior influence should be assigned on grounds which he can comprehend, and of which he is able to perceive the justice.

. . . .

[Page 174.] ' The democracy, at least of this country, are not at present jealous of personal superiority; but they are naturally, and most justly so, of that which is grounded on mere pecuniary circumstances. The only thing which can justify reckoning one person's opinion as equivalent to more than one, is individual mental superiority: and what is wanted, is some approximate means of ascertaining that. If there existed such a thing as a really national education, or a trustworthy system of general examination, education might be tested directly. In the absence of these, the nature of a person's occupation is some test. An employer of labour is on the average more intelligent than a labourer; for he must labour with his head, and not solely with his hands.

A foreman is generally more intelligent than an ordinary labourer, and a labourer in the skilled trades than in the unskilled.   A banker, merchant, or manufacturer, is likely to be more intelligent than a tradesman, because he has larger and more complicated interests to manage.

.   .   .   .

[Page 176.] ' The "local" or "middle-class" examinations for the degree of associate, so laudably and public-spiritedly established by the University of Oxford, and any similar ones which may be instituted by other competent bodies (provided they are fairly open to all comers), afford a ground on which plurality of votes might with great advantage be accorded to those who have passed the test.   All these suggestions are open to much discussion in the detail, and to objections which it is of no use to anticipate.   The time is not come for giving to such plans a practical shape; nor should I wish to be bound by the particular proposals which I have made.   But it is to me evident, that in this direction lies the true ideal of representative government; and that to work towards it, by the best practical contrivances which can be found, is the path of real political improvement.

.   .   .   .

[Page 177.]   ' Let me add, that I consider it an absolutely necessary part of the plurality scheme, that it be open to the poorest individual in the community to claim its privileges, if he can prove that, in spite of all difficulties and obstacles, he is, in point of intelligence, entitled to them.   There ought to be voluntary examinations, at which any person whatever might present himself, might prove that he came up to the standard of knowledge and ability laid down as sufficient, and be admitted, in consequence, to the plurality of votes.   A privilege which is not refused to anyone who can show that he has realised the conditions on which in theory and principle it is dependent, would not necessarily be repugnant to anyone's sentiment of justice; but it would certainly be so, if, while conferred on general presumptions not always infallible, it were denied to direct proof.'—*John Stuart Mill: Representative Government.*

Note (K). Page 240.

In the year 1832, capital punishment was abolished for cattle-stealing, horse-stealing, sheep-stealing, larceny to the value of £5 in a dwelling-house, coining, and forgery (except of wills and powers-of-attorney to transfer stock); and the effect is apparent in the decrease in the number of capital sentences from 1,449 in 1832, to 931 in 1833. It was further abolished—in 1833, for house-breaking; in 1834, for returning from transportation; and in 1835, for sacrilege, and letter-stealing by servants of the Post Office; and, in consequence, a further great decrease is shown in the numbers sentenced to death in 1834-35-36 and 37.

By the Acts passed in 1837 (1st Vict.), the offences subject to capital punishment were virtually reduced to the following:—murder, and attempts to murder; rape and carnally abusing girls under ten years of age; unnatural offences; burglary with violence to persons; robbery attended with cutting or wounding; arson of dwelling-houses, endangering the lives of persons being therein. It remained also for treason; piracy where murder was attempted; showing false signals to cause shipwreck; setting fire to Her Majesty's ships of war; riot, and feloniously destroying buildings; and embezzlement by servants of the Bank of England. But these latter offences are of rare occurrence.

Following the passing of these Acts, the number of capital sentences fell to 116 in 1838, and to 56 in 1839. In 1841 (4 and 5 Vict.) it was further abolished for rape &c., embezzlement &c., and riot &c. The average number of capital sentences for the following years, from 1840 up to 1861 inclusive, amounts only to 59.5.

Under the Acts passed in 1861 for the Consolidation of the Criminal Statutes, murder and treason alone remain subject to capital sentence; and the capital convictions in each of the years 1862 and 1863 have been 29 (one in 1862 having been for an attempt to murder, committed before the Acts of 1861 came into operation).

Home Office:
22nd November, 1864.

STATEMENT of the Number of Persons Sentenced to Death for Murder; of the Total Number Sentenced to Death; of the Number Executed for Murder.; and of the Total Number Executed in each Year since 1823, inclusive: with the Average of the Numbers for each Period of ten Years, 1823–32, 1833–42, 1843–52, 1853–62, and the Numbers for 1863, with the Proportion of the Average Numbers to the Population for each Period of ten Years.

YEAR.	SENTENCED TO DEATH.		EXECUTED.	
	For Murder.	Total Number.	For Murder.	Total Number.
1823 . . .	12	968	10	54
1824 . . .	17	1,066	15	49
1825 . . .	12	1,036	10	50
1826 . . .	13	1,203	10	57
1827 . . .	12	1,526	11	70
1828 . . .	20	1,165	18	59
1829 . . .	13	1,384	13	74
1830 . . .	16	1,397	14	46
1831 . . .	14	1,601	12	52
1832 . . .	20	1,449	15	54
Average of the ten Years	14·9	1,279·5	12·8	56·5
Proportion of the Average to Population . .	one in 863,234	one in 10,123	one in 996,039	one in 229,177
1833 . . .	9	931	6	30
1834 . . .	13	480	12	34
1835 . . .	24	523	21	34
1836 . . .	20	494	8	17
1837 . . .	11	436	8	8
1 838 . . .	25	116	5	6
1839 . . .	12	56	10	11
1840 . . .	18	77	9	9
1841 . . .	20	80	9	10
1 842 . . .	16	57	9	9
Average of the ten Years	16·8	325·2	9·7	17·1
Proportion of the Average to Population . .	one in 687,230	one in 45,834	one in 1,536,646	one in 813,185

STATEMENT OF PERSONS SENTENCED TO DEATH, ETC.—continued.

YEAR.	SENTENCED TO DEATH.		EXECUTED.	
	For Murder.	Total Number.	For Murder.	Total Number.
1843 . . .	22	97	13	13
1844 . . .	21	57	16	16
1845 . . .	19	49	12	12
1846 . . .	13	56	6	6
1847 . . .	19	51	8	8
1848 . . .	23	60	12	12
1849 . . .	19	66	15	15
1850 . . .	11	49	6	6
1851 . . .	16	70	9	10
1852 . . .	16	61	9	9
Average of the ten Years	17·9	61·6	10·6	10·7
Proportion of the Average to Population . .	one in 945,300	one in 274,692	one in 1,596,309	one in 1,581,390
1853 . . .	17	55	8	8
1854 . . .	11	49	5	5
1855 . . .	11	50	7	7
1856 . . .	31	69	16	16
1857 . . .	20	54	13	13
1858 . . .	16	53	11	11
1859 . . .	18	52	9	9
1860 . . .	16	48	12	12
1861 . . .	26	50	14	15
1862 . . .	28	29	16	15
Average of the ten Years	19·4	50·9	11·	11·1
Proportion of the Average to Population . .	one in 979,222	one in 373,220	one in 1,726,992	one in 1,711,434
1863 . . .	29	29	22	22

N.B.—The Proportion to Population is calculated on the mean numbers of two Censuses for each period, 1821 and 1831, 1831 and 1841, 1841 and 1851, 1851 and 1861.

In 1855, one; in 1856, four; in 1858, three; and in each of the years 1860, 1862, and 1863, one of the numbers convicted of murder were foreigners.

IRELAND.

STATEMENT of the Number of Persons Sentenced to Death for Murder; of the Total Number Sentenced to Death; of the Number Executed for Murder; of the Total Number Executed in each year since 1823, inclusive: with the Average of the Numbers for each period of ten Years, 1823–32, 1833–42, 1843–52, 1853–62, and the Numbers for 1863; with the Proportion of the Average Numbers to the Population for each period of ten Years.

YEAR.	SENTENCED TO DEATH.		EXECUTED.	
	For Murder.	Total Number.	For Murder.	Total Number.
1823 . . .	21	241	18	61
1824 . . .	49	295	41	60
1825 . . .	17	181	9	18
1826 . . .	28	281	17	34
1827 . . .	22	346	12	37
1828 . . .	33	211	16	21
1829 . . .	28	224	21	38
1830 . . .	28	262	14	39
1831 . . .	27	307	25	37
1832 . . .	19	319	17	39
Average of the ten Years	27·2	266·7	19·0	38·4
Proportion of the Average to Population . .	one in 267,816	one in 27,313	one in 383,400	one in 189,703
1833 . . .	38	237	26	39
1834 . . .	49	197	31	43
1835 . . .	31	179	19	27
1836 . . .	22	175	12	14
1837 . . .	21	154	10	10
1838 . . .	8	39	3	3
1839 . . .	30	66	15	17
1840 . . .	15	43	—	—
1841 . . .	17	40	5	5
1842 . . .	11	25	4	4
Average of the ten Years	24·2	115·5	12·5	16·2
Proportion of the Average to Population . .	one in 329,390	one in 69,015	one in 637,700	one in 492,053

STATEMENT OF PERSONS SENTENCED TO DEATH, ETC.—*continued.*

YEAR.	SENTENCED TO DEATH.		EXECUTED.	
	For Murder.	Total Number.	For Murder.	Total Number.
1843 . . .	12	16	4	5
1844 . . .	19	20	8	9
1845 . . .	9	13	3	3
1846 . . .	9	14	4	7
1847 . . .	23	25	8	18
1848 . . .	44	60	24	28
1849 . . .	—	1	—	—
1850 . . .	15	17	8	8
1851 . . .	11	17	2	2
1852 . . .	14	22	3	6
Average of the ten Years	15·6	20·5	6·4	8·6
Proportion of the Average to Population . .	one in 472,035	one in 359,207	one in 1,150,586	one in 855,250
1853 . . .	13	15	7	9
1854 . . .	4	6	3	4
1855 . . .	4	5	—	—
1856 . . .	6	8	2	3
1857 . . .	5	8	—	—
1858 . . .	5	8	4	4
1859 . . .	2	2	—	—
1860 . . .	5	7	2	2
1861 . . .	1	2	1	1
1862 . . .	6	6	4	4
Average of the ten Years	5·1	6·7	2·3	2·7
Proportion of the Average to Population . .	one in 1,210,916	one in 921,742	one in 2,686,076	one in 2,287,287
1863 . . .	3	4	3	4

N.B.—The proportion to population is calculated on the mean numbers of two Censuses for each period, 1821 and 1831, 1831 and 1841, 1841 and 1851, 1851 and 1861.

Note (L).   Page 277.

It is a satisfaction to contend in honourable rivalry
with such men as Sir Robert Peel. But in looking at
some of the libels in which he and his opponents were
maligned, even very lately, I have often thought of
the words of the Great Condé, as related by the Cardinal
de Retz, on the occasion of his looking at some of the
pamphlets and reviews in the Prince's room.   ' M. le
Prince, en voyant que j'y avais jeté les yeux, me dit:
" Ces misérables nous ont fait, vous et moi, tels qu'ils
auraient été s'ils s'étaient trouvés dans nos places." '

The Cardinal adds very justly,—' Cette parole est
d'un grand sens.' *

                    * Mém. de Retz, t. 2. p. 348.

www.ingramcontent.com/pod-product-compliance
Lightning Source LLC
Chambersburg PA
CBHW031401270326
41929CB00010BA/1277